THE DOMINION

Adarsh Ramesh

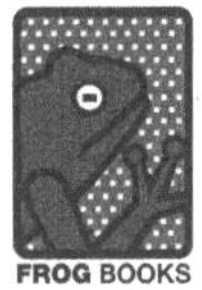

ISBN 978-93-52015-74-0

First published in India 2015 by Frog Books
An imprint of Leadstart Publishing Pvt Ltd
1 Level, Trade Centre
Bandra Kurla Complex
Bandra (East) Mumbai 400 051 India
Telephone: +91-22-40700804
Fax: +91-22-40700800
Email: info@leadstartcorp.com
www.leadstartcorp.com / www.frogbooks.net

Sales Office:
Unit No.25/26, Building No.A/1,
Near Wadala RTO,
Wadala (East), Mumbai – 400037 India
Phone: +91 22 24046887

US Office:
Axis Corp, 7845 E Oakbrook Circle
Madison, WI 53717 USA

Editor: Anushree Nande
Cover: Suhail Mathur
Design Credits: Pradhan Sarathy
Layouts: Logiciels Info Solutions Pvt Ltd

Typeset in Palatino Linotype
Printed at MOSS Printers

MRP : 495/-

Dedication

Sherlock Holmes, who I wish were alive and real

About the Author

Born in Bangalore, schooled and brought up in Mysore, Adarsh is an author, entrepreneur, philanthropist and an engineer who has a penchant to know a little something about everything.

He is an Electronics and Communication Engineer with avid interest in writing, criminal law, entrepreneurship, the study and practice of management, marketing, reading, world history (The World Wars in particular) and everything associated with Batman and Sherlock.

He is the CEO at Desiadda Online Services Pvt. Ltd. and the Founder & President of a non-profit called Project ReachOut (R).

To know more about him, visit https://rameshadarsh.com

ACKNOWLEDGEMENTS

In the four years that I took to write this book, there have been many who have inspired me, on whose persona and interactions characters have been created, and who have, for the better part, believed that I was kidding myself with the whole idea of writing a novel. To all these people I say – *Salud!*

To my parents who have always believed in me, given me the freedom to make any and all choices and stood by me, silently and emphatically voicing their firm stance that I would get published.

To the App on the Works of Sir Arthur Conan Doyle that took me into a locked-room to solve a case of singular interest - Chapter Six of Sir Arthur Conan Doyle's "The Sign of Four".

To Sushanth, who has edited this story as his own and has spent many an hour at my place, restaurants, classrooms and over the phone in discussing and crafting the book to a presentable form.

To the Internet, which took me around the world and made me learn about the cities and people where I had never been before or had ever met.

To Anushree Nande, the editor who probably knows about the story than I, and whose work has made the book a fine read.

To Leadstart Publishing, in particular to Mailini, an email from whom made me the happiest. The dedicated work of Uzair and team, for understanding my concern at each step and installing confidence in me. For everyone at Leadstart who added credence to all my efforts.

To Amrutha, Vishal, Gaurav, Vijay and Kshama, who have read the book in bits and pieces, but argued and guided immensely in chiseling the validity and preserving the quality of the events in the fictional world of the Dominion.

To my life as an engineer, which gave me a whole lot of free time or time that was rather well spent on researching and writing the story.

To the kid in me who once was criticized for his English.

To those friends, families and well-wishers who, irrespective of the mention in this list, will continue to stand by me and wish me well.

To better days that gave me hope and the rest that gave me strength.

CONTENTS

Prologue

'I am your friend. I am your enemy. I am a noble keeper of peace. I am a barbaric bringer of terror. I am your hope. I am your doom. I am your love. I am your reckoning. I am your devil. I am your God. I am…your Führer.'

Ding Dong Bell

CHAPTER 1

For one last time, Nahiossi Griffiths looked at Vaughn Fletcher. He stared at him, confused, and then he took his eyes off the dead senator and gawked at the knife in his hand. *What have I done!* Nahiossi whispered to the air around him, as the banging on the humongous mahogany door behind him intensified. *'I'm sorry, Julie. I'm sorry for wrecking your life all over again'.*

Distant sirens complemented Nahiossi's cry for mercy, growing more intense by the minute. Meanwhile a voice in Nahiossi's ear yelled, *'Quick! Get out!'*

Nahiossi, clutching a long white cloth that ran along the wall and touched the green zone, stood on the sill of a window that opened to a breathtaking view of the city of New York. As he gazed into the emptiness of the distant skies, he pictured his name being dragged through the mud. He could see the Phoenix, a conglomerate which he had so meticulously crafted, being torn apart and the legacy, which he hoped would live for many a decades, fading into dust.

'Nahiossi, open the goddamn door!' shouted Montego Cortez, Chairman of the Phoenix Almonte Group of Airlines.

The man in Nahiossi's ear impatiently yelled, *'Do it. Now!'*

Nahiossi turned around apprehensively and wiped all traces of blood off the Soviet NR40 Military Knife, fashioning his blue shirt red. Then, adhering to the command from the man in his ear, Nahiossi dropped the knife on the lawn and quickly abseiled down the dewy wall of stone.

The moment Nahiossi touched down, Chevrolet Impalas drew nearer to the Fletcher Manor. The inspector, donning a medallion with an eagle, shot out commands to the Emergency Service Unit, who in turn relayed the message over to the Special Weapons and Tactics (SWAT) team.

Nahiossi, his hands trembling, picked up the knife and his wet lounge coat off the damp floor. He clutched them both in his hands and made his way across the backyard, his pace slowed down only by the many puddles he jumped into. The apprehension that had always weighed him down had vanished without a trace. His trepidation had left him and all his worries had evaporated. He was a free man now. A free man who had made peace with the fact that he would lose everything he held dear.

While Inspector Tom Brian jumped out of his ride and sprinted towards the Manor, the Impalas came to a screeching halt. Meanwhile Nahiossi reached the outer envelope of the Manor and hurriedly hoisted himself up the moist wall. He then picked the NR40 off the stony surface of the compound and confidently jumped into the adjoining villa.

'Where the hell did the guards go?' The inspector thought for a brief second, when the massive gate at the entrance flung open with just a gentle nudge. He called out to his men and asked them to follow him inside, intuiting that they weren't there to prevent a crime from happening.

As Nahiossi turned his attention towards the bark of canines and officers at the Manor, an urbane and trained German shepherd swiftly sprinted from its kennel, barking and growling at the intruder. Nahiossi's short-lived sense of being tranquil was replaced with fear, and he at once leaped forward and tried to sprint out of the villa. But he wasn't fast enough for the trained canine. An unforgiving Caesar plunged his set of canines and incisors through the intruder's jeans and pierced well into his flesh. Nahiossi reflexively thrust the Soviet NR40 up Caesar's neck, while at the Manor, Inspector Brian and his men ran across the stony pathway, which led to the wide open door of the Fletcher Manor.

A series of Caesar's cartilage plates were shattered, muffling his cry for pain and sending him to his death quietly. As Caesar's clench on Nahiossi relaxed, he pushed the husky dog off him and scurried out of the villa.

'NYPD. Open the door!' shouted Tom Brian, after climbing two flights of stairs and landing in front of the door against which Cortez was helplessly leaning, his hands sore and his face timid.

The response, one similar to that of a whip against a habituated steed, provoked a team of SWAT officers to bust inside the cordoned study of Senator Fletcher.

Meanwhile, not far from the Manor, a man whose voice Nahiossi knew, but at the moment couldn't relate with a face, stealthily walked behind him and ordered him to get inside a jet-black limousine. The transport had long been waiting, on one of the cross roads that had clear visual isolation from the Manor, for the soon-to-be international fugitive. The wait had finally ended.

Nahiossi, who was now a mere puppet in the hands of a mighty syndicate, climbed into the Phoenix Group of Airlines' limousine and placed a call to LaGuardia.

'10-2, we have a problem. Looks like the suspect has escaped,' voiced a SWAT officer, who had secured the rear wall of the Manor.

'Reporting 10-33,' relayed another officer.

The second team of SWAT officials briskly prepped the battering ram and was all set to break into the room that now began to reek of blood and flesh.

As the door gave in to the ram and flung open, a pool of officers placed frantic calls to the FBI and alerted them about the gory situation at hand. An ambulance was asked to reach the Fletcher Manor without delay.

The news climbed up the chain of command, and ultimately a United States Secret Service (USSS) Agent at Number One Observatory Circle placed a call to Honorable Vice President, Jamie Edwards, and relayed the shocking news.

Vaughn Fletcher, was dead.

And so was Caesar.

At 10:00 A.M. local time, Manhattan's 17th Street was to stand witness to a con that would ensure the robbery of a Ford F-550 armored cash/valuables-in-transit (CVIT) truck that was transporting assets worth approximately nine million American dollars.

Soldatos from a confederated syndicate of the Italian-American Mafia Families boarded a Lincoln Town Car and a Chevrolet Tahoe, and boldly headed towards the 17th.

The ballistic resistant and U-shaped plastic-line tired armoured CVIT trucks were transporting banknotes, coins, bulk cash, diamonds, non-personalised smart cards, non-personalised passports and such other valuable assets from banks, companies, security firms and jewellery industries.

At exactly 10:00 AM, as planned, vapours of liquid benzodiazepine circulated through the rear air conditioner ducts of the truck and filled the cargo compartment that was separated from the driving area by means of a steel bulkhead.

'Phil! There is some sort of smoke in here!' yelled one of the three hoppers inside the hermetically-sealed compartment.

'There must be something wrong with the AC!' began the driver, Phil, as the hoppers began to feel buoyant and numb. 'Hold on, I'll get it fixed,' he added, as he brought the truck to a halt.

The loyalists of the *Padrino,* who were neatly clad in Federal Protective Service (FPS) uniforms and equipped with SIG P229s, disembarked from the Lincoln and approached the F-550. Phil immediately hit the button that unlocked the slam locks. He then scanned the faces of the innocent citizens on the road and thought, *'The Bru was right. These people don't seem to care much. Well, they don't have to when the "Department of Homeland Security" is here...Witless freaks,'* as he patiently waited for his confederates to be done with their assignment.

At the push of the button, the sealed grease fittings of the strap hinges paved way for a smooth opening of the rear door. Three of the six FPS agents jumped inside the cargo compartment of the truck with a "well this is routine" attitude, picked up the consignments and dumped it all in the FPS' Tahoe.

The door then swung shut and the slam-locks automatically locked the rear door, exactly like its goddamn engineer designed it.

Four minutes was the time elapsed for this "performance" and everything was going as per the *Padrino*'s plan.

At the strike of three minutes, CATS received a stationary GPS blip from the vehicle, triggering the protocols involved in checking the status of the vehicle and of its employees. As part of the primary protocol, a call was placed to the driver in order to assess the situation and analyse the need for secondary protocols.

'It's nothing. The heater core sprung a leak is all. It needs replacing. I've connected the heater hoses together at the firewall and bypassed it temporarily. But we can't do any more trips today. We'll deliver this consignment and get back to the garage,' said Phil over the phone and reasoned for their unscheduled stop, as the Lincoln pulled out and sped away from the scene.

'We are moving now,' said Phil and drove away casually, as if nothing had happened. The trucks were driven on the usual route, as commanded by their company-fitted GPS devices, and almost three quarters of an hour later, they reached the destination where the drivers had 'planned' to get caught.

Once there, the drivers let the sedative fill the frontal area of the truck and they knocked themselves out.

'The Manhattan Route – ' began an employee at CATS.

'It has been sorted out. Something with the AC – '

' – Wasn't the only place our truck was halted. It happened at six places. Simultaneously. Almost fifty million on the loose.'

'Then why weren't secondary protocols...because we cleared the flag. Damn!' said the inquisitive employee, as her computer screen yelled, 'Secondary protocols initiated. No response from the drivers on the following routes: Manhattan, Brooklyn, Bronx, Staten Island, Albany and Westchester. All security units, dispatch.'

Angelika Presley was the stupidest person Rupert Wallace had ever known.

On the one hand she was provocatively dull and remarkably ignorant, but on the other, she was the most beautiful woman under the Star-Spangled Banner.

The Nefertiti of the new millennium possessed dark and long straight hair, a thin streak of which splendidly brushed her pinkish white cheek. Her eyes were like that of green emerald dipped in an ocean of milk, the type of eyes that could hypnotise you the moment you saw them. A smile formed on her face, showing off her white teeth, and a pair of dimples on either side of her red lips flaunted a slight upward tilt and rounded tips. She possessed a delicate nose, charmingly molded between her caterpillar eyebrows. She was slim with slender long legs and gangly thin arms that hung from her firm shoulders. Her skin was tanned and she looked radiant. Her estrogens levels left men of all ages mesmerised. As she moved about, both men and women stared at her, the former with admiration and the latter with resentment. But interestingly ex-military strategic analyst and New York's best Private Investigator Rupert A. Wallace was an exception.

'Wow! You take my breath away,' said Thomas Baker and tenderly pecked her alluring lips.

Thomas was a top-notch lawyer and an aphrodisiac man. He was six-foot-three and exceedingly cathartic. He had classic dark blond hair with warm undertones and natural sandy highlights, which perfectly blended with his suntanned athletic body. Like an army sergeant, he always shaved his face clean and he never left his apartment without the Brooks Brothers.

'Be careful. She could literally take away your breath. Forever. You could die,' said Rupert in haste, as he stared at a painting on a wall in front of his desk.

'Thank you, bro, I'll keep that in mind.'

'I'm sure you won't. Anyway, how did the verdict pan out?'

'Tell me you won, Tom,' said Angelika, resting her hands on her boyfriend's shoulder.

'Angelika dear, would you just go over there and think about the riddle?' said Rupert in a condescending tone and motioned his hands in a way one would shoo a stray dog.

'What riddle?' asked the lawyer. 'And stop with the hand! Geez. You've known her for over three months now. It's time you start respecting her.'

'Ha! I am. If you weren't here now we'd have reached fourth base by now. Anyway, before either one of you start to blabber again, pray tell me what happened to the verdict?'

'I'll answer that once I've heard the riddle.'

Rupert ignorantly raised his eyebrow and pushed his laptop towards his little brother.

A couple was on a pleasure trip on the 15th of January at cockcrow. The two pairs of eyes in the car could see nothing but barren land till the rim. The Briggs & Stratton carburetor gave away, drifting the car to an abrupt halt in the middle of nowhere. The husband instructed his wife to stay put in the car with all the doors and windows locked, while he went in search of a mechanic. She did the same as instructed, took a dose of sleeping pills, insulated her ears with some cotton and went to sleep. The husband didn't have alternative keys to open the car and the car had a specially designed locking system that could not be opened using alternative duplicate keys. The husband arrived with the mechanic from the nearest garage that was 28 minutes away to be precise. His wife was DOA with a knife stabbed into her chest. She didn't commit suicide; this was proved by the presence of the latex fingerprints on the knife and also by the husband's affidavit stating that there was no knife inside the car. The investigation clearly suggests that the husband didn't murder his wife. The forensic report reveals that neither the glass nor the doors were broken. How then did the murderer get to her?

As Thomas was reading it, Rupert looked at Angelika staring at the legal books on his bookshelf and asked, 'Angelika dear, do you know what DOA stands for?'

'Rupert, please let her be.'

'Oh! Wait a minute, let's see if she knows what litigation means,' said Rupert hysterically, and tormented her with yet another question.

Thomas was pissed off at his brother. It was known that Angelika was dumb. Rupert didn't have to perpetually embarrass her.

'Don't be a sadist, Rupert. Come on.'

'Are you pleading or demanding?'

'The latter.'

'Yeah, sure, feel free to put in another demand. Like I haven't done enough already, scrounger,' Rupert jerked nauseously. 'God bless the women you fall in love with! First it was the ass-slinger, then the one with the giant two, then the one that came on to me – '

' – she didn't.'

' – Then the one that broke your heart and now, this dumb bitch! Fucking Christ!'

Thomas pushed back the chair and stood up angrily.

'Let's go, Pres,' said he and pulled her by the arm. 'He has gone nuts again. Guess it's his time of the week!'

'The verdict, Thomas?'

'It was a convertible.'

CHAPTER 2

Monday, October 29th 2007

The FBI Evidence Response Team and Special Agent Mason went past the crime scene barrier tapes and met with the initial responding officers. A few seconds later, Inspector Brian took over and provided various logs, initial crime scene report and such other pertinent documents to Special Agent Mason, as he walked the team through the physical aspects of the scene at his team's TOA.

'Once the SWAT team broke into this chamber, they observed that the senator's body was on this chair – ' narrated Inspector Tom, pointing at a black mesh back chair, ' – facing the door. He was stabbed in the neck and he was DOA.'

'Who reported the incident?' probed Special Agent Mason.

'Mr. Montego Cortez. He came to the Manor approximately a half hour after Mr. Griffiths showed up. He told us that he knocked on the door, at the entrance I mean, for quite some time and was set off guard when there was no response.'

Dr. Montego Cortez was Vaughn's *compadre* for over three decades. He was a bachelor by choice and despised familial relationships and responsibilities. The reason for his reluctance stemmed from the fact that he had to manage a major airline industry and a prime research institute. His work had rendered him bald and a glutton. But nevertheless, he was one the best chairmen and one of the most capable businessmen according to Forbes.

'Was he scheduled to be here?'

'He said he was here to talk something about their airline industry. He didn't want to divulge the details.'

'Okay, go on.'

'He alerted the security guards and then with their aid, broke the glass window in the kitchen and entered the Manor. He saw the butler, Jordan, beaten up on the floor, and presumed that the Senator was in danger.'

Jordan was the butler at the Fletcher Manor. He was a short, pale and corpulent French immigrant. He was proficient in his cooking skills and the living epitome of the idiom, "talk less work more".

'He then called you, I presume.'

'Yes. He called me and asked me to come immediately to the Manor.'

'Where was his daughter at the time?'

'Ms. Juliette was at the Ritz. She was nowhere near her father when he died.'

Juliette Fletcher was Vaughn's only daughter. She had lost her mother when she was five and had ever since felt insecure. She often experienced hypomanic episodes, but they didn't have any prolonged effects. After years of psychological treatments and medications, she became self-resilient, and on the onset of puberty, blossomed into a ravishing woman. Her hooded eyes, elfin crop and thin lips attracted a whole lot of attention, and consequently the insecurities slackened. She pursued the field of fashion and eventually made it to the covers of *Vogue, Elle, Cleo* and *Cosmopolitan*. Her phenomenal success in the fashion industry and her overwhelming fan-base had redeemed her mental aliment and she morphed into a stable woman. But in light of the recent happenings, the dark memories of her past were all set to invade her world of happiness and mental stability. She had lost her father, and the person whom she believed to be her soul mate was branded – "The Senator Slayer."

Response Team A had their entire inventory staged in the room adjoining the senator's study, all set to bag and tag. The photographers with the standard 35mm cameras and the videographers with their detrimental Personal Protective Equipment (PEE) were thoroughly at work and were clicking away each and every speck of dust at the senator's study.

Response Team B was conducting the same work on the outside, where spotlights, beam lights and alternative light sources were used to enhance the presence of fluids, latent prints, clothing fibers, trace evidence and transient evidence, while Response team C and a K-9 team worked the neighbouring crime scene.

'Was this room locked from the inside when you and the SWAT team arrived?' asked SA Mason, looking intently at the door, which he judged, was busted open.

Inspector Tom responded with, 'Yes. We used a battering ram to force our way in.'

'Any leads with the suspect?'

'None so far, sir. We have men looking for Mr. Griffiths.'

'Okay. Thank you, inspector, we'll take it from here.'

'You are welcome, Special Agent Mason.'

Special Agent Mason appeared older and frailer than he did a few weeks ago. He had lost a couple of extra pounds and his muscular build now ceased to exist. He aloofly donned his horn-rimmed glasses and slowly walked towards the bay window, through which Nahiossi had escaped only a few minutes ago.

Meanwhile Inspector Brian walked out of the Fletcher Manor and walked in to the adjoining villa to see if he could assist the K-9 team. Once there, the inspector heard an officer say, "Ah! This is like a scene out of our textbooks. That European is such a numbnut!"

Inspector Brain managed a faint smile and walked towards the officer. He gently tapped his shoulder and asked, 'The knife there, in that bag, is it the same knife with which the senator was stabbed?'

'I can't be sure. That is for the lab to decide.'

'Okay. Well, so, um, what else do we have?'

'We have a piece of fabric, fingerprints, shoeprints.... If I have to be honest, there is nothing much to investigate. We'll have the lab results in a week's time, but we sure as hell know that the murderer is Nahiossi Griffiths.'

The initial response documentations were collected, safety procedures were undertaken, emergency care was given, boundary conditions were established, walk-through was completed, collection, preservation, inventory and packaging was neatly done and everything that was scooped was now being transported to the laboratories and federal offices.

Tom Brian ordered two of his men to guard the scene at the Fletcher Manor and returned home a few minutes past midnight. He was a lone wolf, so it didn't matter when he went home. No one really cared. It was dark inside, but Brian didn't care to switch the lights on.

Tom straightaway walked to his room, locked the door and stood in front of a large portrait of Franklin D Roosevelt. He undressed in front of it, revealing a ghoulish tattoo of an Iron Eagle standing atop a swastika compounded inside a wreath of oak leaves, forged on his chest. The eagle was looking to its right shoulder, symbolising the *Reich*, the *Reichsadler*.

Even with the knowledge of it being illegal throughout the world, Brian flaunted it. His commitment to the founders of the Fourth Reich overweighed his worldly fears. He respected the Iron Eagle more than the Eagle medallion. He silently walked towards his bed, chanting something in German, flicked the bed lamp on and picked up a chain with a Swastika pendant off the top shelf of his bedside table. He wore it round his neck and walked towards FDR.

Inspector Brian, a minion of the Reich, stared at President Roosevelt with disgust and then he took the portrait down, revealing a ghastly portrait of Adolf Hitler. *Heil Hitler,* he whispered and smiled.

Friday, February 10th 2006.

The Continental Armoured Truck Services (CATS) learnt that the drivers on six of their companies' armoured trucks were irresponsive to the operators buzzing in on their phones for a contentious duration of time. The GPS trackers on all six vehicles were very unreasonably stationary for durations that far exceeded the thresholds for the initiation of emergency protocols.

The trucks were at areas that were geographically far apart. So it didn't take more than a fraction of a second for the authorities to figure out that the happenings weren't coincidental. Probabilistically the assertion that the act was planned and it surely was at the peril of their day's operation was beyond reasonable doubt. Those operators who were perched on the higher rungs of the hierarchical ladder flagged all six locations and alerted the Department of Transportation and the FBI.

Meanwhile the thirty *soldatos* in Lincolns and Chevrolets had deposited their loot in two of the three banks assigned to each one of them and were verging on completing the final stretch of their so-called contrivance.

Fifty-two minutes ago, as the drivers were delivering the "AC problem compendium" to their respective operators, the *soldatos* drove straight up to Nixon in order to unload their grand loot and swap it with fresh new ones that could, in no way, be traced back to any of them.

Nixon was a shell company registered with the U.S. Securities and Exchanges Commission (SEC). Its existence was supported by its name and mailing address. Period.

Like most shell companies, Nixon was a non-trading corporation. It was a legitimate business entity that was said to be holding intangible assets like patents, trademarks, copyrights, business methodologies and goodwill. Its existence could, in a word, be described virtual, though many would argue against it. The corporation, named after one of the exemplars of prodigal scams, had a savings account under the same name in ninety variegated banks of New York. The depositors, in this case the *soldatos,* under the tag of corporation employees, deposited the looted amount at the bank for day trading purposes. In simpler terms, the *soldatos* played short seller for a virtual corporation.

Of the ransacked forty-seven million dollars, thirty-eight million was in cash and the rest was jewellery, negating of course the INBS stained notes.

On reaching Nixon, the *soldatos* quickly separated the coins from the notes, and the notes were then quantified into ninety parts, making ninety units of 422,222 dollars. The *soldatos* dumped the segregated dough in three briefcases each and headed towards the banks to which they were assigned.

As the agents from the Bureau reached the scenes of the crimes, so to say, they met with the responding officers from the NYPD, surveyed the scene and then approached the trucks that were strangely parked almost at the center of the road. The traffic had to be rerouted and the truck had to be cordoned off if the intention was to pursue investigation.

At Madison Avenue, Agent Parker clutched his P229 and approached the truck with his men, constantly asking for the driver and the hoppers to step out of the truck with their hands behind their heads.

As the *soldatos* reached the third sequence of banks, Agent Parker pulled the door open and out fell the driver, Phil. The parademics immediately attended to him as Parker unlocked the rear doors and found what he had intuited when his phone had buzzed almost ten minutes ago.

Four minutes later, the final deposits were made at the banks and the *soldatos* were back on the streets, their hands rid of the loot. Meanwhile Phil was woken from his state of unconsciousness and probed by Agent Parker.

'We were on our way to one of the ATMs on Madison Avenue. All of a sudden I began to feel dizzy and I couldn't drive. I figured I might be having a head-rush. So I decided to stop for a brief second. I couldn't take any risks, you know, with all the money. Then I found it hard to breathe and before I knew what was happening, I was out. That's all I can remember, officer,' said Phil, using the exact words as that of the five other drivers.

'You didn't have time to call CATS and alert them?' asked a not-so-convinced Parker.

'No, officer. I would have if I could have. Honest to God.'

The Wolf knew every law enforcement department of the United States inside out. He knew the bosses, the handlers, the commanding officers, the recruiters, the foot soldiers, their methods of investigation, their resources, their chains of command and their lack of judgment and compromising weaknesses. He knew the field and he sure liked to play.

Agent Parker looked around with his eagle eye and found a camera located at the entrance of an apartment that was located just a few meters from where he was currently standing. He asked his men to look for evidence in and around the truck and then headed in the direction of the apartment.

As the *soldatos* deposited their cars at Giuseppe's Auto Body Paint and Repair Centre, Agent Parker met with the apartment supervisor. 'Hi, I'm Agent Parker, I'm with the FBI. I have a warrant to get the security tapes from that camera on the entrance.'

The supervisor looked at the gray-haired, suavely dressed endomorphic man and said, 'Does it have to do something with the truck up yonder?'

'Yes. It was robbed.'

'Robbed? But no one came anywhere near it,' said the supervisor, surprised.

'That is why we need the tapes. We need visual conformation.'

'Sure officer, sure. Robbed! Ha! I saw no one came near it,' blabbed the supervisor and then asked the security guard to help Parker with the tapes. The security guard reluctantly turned his eyes away from the TV, as Stefania Belmondo, a 10-time Olympic medalist in cross-country skiing, lit the Olympic Flame at Turin, Italy.

'Thank you.'

'You are welcome, officer. But I gotta say, that truck got here almost ten minutes ago and I didn't see none go near it. How could anyone possibly rob it?'

'We'll look into it, sir. I appreciate your help, thank you.'

The *modus operandi* was amusingly common in all the six cases. So a debriefing team consisting of the six agents investigating the six heists was formed and everyone had the same uncanny question, 'How could anyone rob the truck without getting near it?'

Thursday, September 27th 2007.

'Rupert, I want you to just take a look at it.'

'I don't work for vindictive idealists.'

'I'm not asking you to.'

'I appreciate that, Cole, I really do. Now, can you stop bothering me? I got work to do.'

Silence.

'Look, Rupert, you owe us – '

' – And we already decided how I was going to repay.'

Silence.

'Dad says he doesn't want that precious offer of yours. He says he doesn't mind if you aren't at his funeral.'

'Well then, you rejected my offer. He broke the deal, not my fault. It was pointless anyway, how would my presence even matter? He'd already be dead!'

'Rupert, don't play your ridiculous games with us. If you don't want to do it, then don't. We aren't asking you to help us – '

'Thank you, brother dear, for wasting my time, like always.'

'You fucking, ungrateful, sorry piece of shit, will you just listen to me for one minute! What is the matter with you? Get off your high horse and listen to us, we are...we are warning you.'

'Fuck off!' said Rupert and threw the phone at the window. The glass shattered at once, and the phone plunged all the way down the fifteen floors before it hit the hard concrete and broke into useless little pieces of scrap.

Rupert stood up and stormed out of his office at the illustrious McKinley Towers. He took the stairs, sprinted down fifteen flights and walked to his habitual street vendor, kicking at a piece of the Panasonic debris.

'Jimmy, cold coffee and bagel,' shot out Rupert and paced about like a tense soon-to-be father outside the OT, only with a slight variation in the emotional paradigm.

Rupert was a cantankerous and narcissistic individual. He was exorbitantly dexterous and New York's shrewdest sleuthhound. But apart from these he was just another quintessential citizen of The City. His office was his edifice and his physical appearance falsely heralded the paltriness of his workplace. He graced his barber four times a year and his brother would occasionally drop off some of his hoary Brooks Brothers. He seldom worked out, but managed to look subtle and not unattractive. After all, beauty is in the eyes of the beholder.

'You look a bit groggy today, Rup. What's bothering you? The Israeli raid on Gaza Strip, the Jena Six case, Pervez Musharaf's nomination for the PPE, the Burmese anti-government protests?' asked Jim White, a black American who was Rupert's lone friend on the face on the big blue earth. He was an exact replica of Abe Lincoln, only not white.

'I didn't go through the newspaper today.'

'Well, here you go then,' said Jim White and handed over the *New York Times*.

'It's okay, Jimmy. I'm not in the mood to read newspapers.'

Jimmy put the newspaper down and sat next to Rupert. He let out a sigh and sternly asked, 'What's wrong, Rup?'

Rupert stared at the ground and said, 'Nothing new, the same old crap. Dad, Bru, Tom and his stupid miss Cupid!'

'But why are you upset?'

'I told you just now. Dad, Bru – '

'But you don't care about them. Only people whom you care about can hurt you, not the ones you don't.'

'Uh, I don't, actually. They weren't there for me when I needed them. They were in their own little nests believing they were saving the world, when in reality their own family was bleeding with pain and calling out for help! I mean, I care more about you than those fucking maniacs.'

'I must say, Rupert, I'm flattered, but let me tell this to you straight. I'm sure I would have done the same thing as Wolf. I would have been no different. He wanted to protect you. You are his favorite son. You can deny it, but I know that it is true. I can see it in him. He adores you the most, that's why he is keeping you out of his...business. Your brothers do what they are told to do. We've been through this, Rupert,' said Jim softly and patted Rupert's back. 'Come on! Help me in there, too many customers today. Come on.'

'He wants me to handle a case for him,' said Rupert, as he folded his arms and closed his eyes. 'Doesn't seem like he is trying to keep me away from danger.'

'Wait, he called you and told you that?'

'Yep.'

'Ha! That explains the Panasonic butchery. Well, I'm sure you offended him.'

Rupert smiled and opened his eyes. He took a sip of the cold coffee that Jim offered him and then asked, 'You think I should help him?'

'You don't need me to answer that. You already have decided it. In fact, I wager you knew the answer the very moment he popped the question.'

CHAPTER 3

Nahiossi was aboard a private Global Express XRS and was scheduled to reach Amsterdam before all hell broke loose.

The extradition of Nahiossi back to the United States would be a bureaucratic nightmare. The Netherlands government would never extradite their citizens. Tons of paperwork from tons of law enforcements agencies would be exchanged, the justice departments would have taxing debates, mundane news reports would be published and the Amnesty International would be fighting alongside Human Rights Commission against the death penalty.

The International Criminal Police (Interpol) would undoubtedly place him under provisional arrest in the Netherlands as per the statute. But as long as he was in his hometown, he didn't have to worry about death by execution.

The Rolls-Royce Deutschland turbofans roared as the Global Express flew over the North Atlantic Ocean. Nahiossi, the Vice President of the United States, and three business students were comfortably seated in Nahiossi's personalised exquisite cabin and were having a conversation over Dom Perignon White Gold Jeroboam. The ecstatic students had no idea of the fact that they were being held as hostages.

The Federal Aviation Administration (FAA) called the Department of Homeland security immediately after receiving the emergency notification. In response to the Deputy Secretary's first question as to when the flight took off, an FAA officer said, 'The Global Express left for Amsterdam at 2210 hours.'

The Deputy Secretary glanced down at her watch. It told her that Nahiossi was 20 minutes through his journey to his hometown. Tons of law enforcement agencies were alerted and the information was directly relayed to the Secretary of Defense (SecDef).

The Situation Room in the basement of the West Wing of the White House was momentarily filled with the Watch teams, White House Chief of Staff, the National Security Advisor, Deputy of Homeland Security and the President.

The live satellite image of the North Atlantic Ocean, the position and radars of the Global Express, the list of military agencies on stand-by, the Air Base control of various European countries and numerous other feeds were put up on the flat panel display. The Secretary of State was on a secure video-conference call from the Harry. S. Truman Building and the Secretary of Defense was conferencing from the Pentagon.

'Griffiths murdered Senator Vaughn and hijacked a Global Express XRS at LaGuardia scheduled to depart to the Netherlands. The authorities were alerted when the plane changed its course and breached the FAA regulations,' said the National Security Advisor, Lt. Gen. Colin Lake.

'We also have confirmation that Vice President Edwards, three students, two pilots and two stewardesses are aboard that plane in addition to Griffiths,' added the Deputy of Homeland Security, Nichole. S. Flynn.

'Where the hell were the USSS?' shot out President Jeremy Nolan.

'Outside the Edwardian Suite at the Plaza,' said Nichole, who was responsible for the actions of the USSS.

'How did he get on the plane?'

'We think that Nahiossi had him kidnapped and put on that plane. He needed leverage to reach his hometown.'

'It also ties the hands of the NSC (National Security Council). They won't be able to give kill authorisations or orders to shoot down the damn airplane,' said Lt. Gen. Lake.

'But we know one thing for sure, Griffiths won't blow up that plane. He needs to reach Amsterdam. He won't blow himself up for sure,' added Lt. Gen. Lake.

'That's right. We can send some aerial support and also persuade the pilots to land in a third country,' continued Flynn.

'Yes. A country with which we have amiable extradition treaty and a country willing to let our men see through this operation.'

'Get the AG on the line,' ordered the President and a call was immediately placed to Edmund Bates, the United States Attorney General.

Edmund was asked to look into the bilateral extradition treaties, search for the desired provisions, obtain legal validations, prepare the arrest warrant, affidavits, indictments, certificate of exemplification and other such procedural documents, and get in touch with the Office of International Affairs (OIA).

'What about Delta Force? Are they ready for deployment?' asked Nolan after hanging up with the Attorney General.

'I'll have them prepped in an hour,' responded the Secretary of Defense, Robert McElroy.

'Good. Get the director of CIA (Central Intelligence Agency) and DNI (Department of National Intelligence) on the line,' said McElroy as the Communication Agency established a secure encrypted line with the concerned directors.

The Defense Clandestine Service worked with the CIA and Joint Special Operations Command, of which Delta Force was a part.

The President and the Secretary of Defense briefed the CIA and DNI about the situation and asked for assistance. Numerous calls were immediately made and a Delta team was organised. They would be ready for *Operation Phoenix* in an hour.

Meanwhile a call was placed from the White House Communication Agency to the Air Traffic Control (ATC) of various air bases deemed necessary. The flight was in the "uncontrolled airspace" at the moment, meaning the ATC couldn't reach it for various practical reasons.

The Watch teams and the various analysts at the Pentagon were working on a strategy to rescue the Honorable Vice President, while Lt. Gen. Lake, Nichole and Nolan were video-conferencing with the United Nations, the de facto capital of the European Union - Brussels, International Civil Aviation Organization (ICAO) and all other organisations that were needed to be informed as per various statutes and treaties.

'We are going to have one hell of a night.'

Typical Margin Account Agreements give brokerage firms the right to borrow customer shares without notifying the customer. Hence the short sellers from Clinton Securities didn't have to give account of the actual investors to the bank authorities. The *soldatos* posing as short sellers from Clinton Securities had traded stocks worth three hundred to four hundred thousand dollars for over a month, the source of money being Wolf.

The day of the armoured truck robbery was no different. Each *soldato* deposited 422,222 dollars in three different banks under the same dummy identity. The time elapsed since robbery, fifty minutes. They then hurriedly went to each bank and bought shares worth the amount deposited a few minutes ago.

Short sellers usually borrow a large number of shares from lenders and sell the same for a certain price. When the market depreciates, the price of the same shares decreases and the short sellers buy the depreciated shares for a lower price. They pocket the difference amount and return the borrowed shares back to the lender. Here the *soldatos* played the roles of both the lender and the short seller. Nixon represented the lender and Clinton the short seller.

The agents investigating the parallel robberies notified the banks that at around 10:45 that morning, six armoured trucks were robbed and that any unknown person or people making suspicious deposits should be flagged and held for enquiry. The serial numbers of certain bank notes were issued to most of the banks in NYC. But the *soldatos* had already deposited the loot, they weren't new to the bank, the amount deposited wasn't suspicious since it was consistent for nearly a month, the depositors didn't try to hide their identity, they had made their deposit almost a half hour before the robbery and the money was now morphed into shares. The *soldatos* couldn't be pinned down. Everything was woven perfectly to blend with the fabric of reality and precision.

The debriefing team saw the footages of all the six trucks over and over and found nothing related to the robbery. No one approached the truck. CATS were the first to reach the scene, but they didn't go near the truck until the police came.

Instead of "who", "how" was the agenda. The agents' suspicion shifted towards the drivers because they alone were able to open the rear door of the truck. But they couldn't just apprehend them. No magistrate would grant an arrest warrant without any evidence against the drivers. That would be baseless and incriminating. Illegal. Unconstitutional.

The *soldatos* returned to the banks that very evening and sold all the shares they'd bought that morning. The money was transferred back to the savings account and was withdrawn. They now had new currency notes. Completely legitimate. The flagged notes were tangled somewhere in the market. It was impossible to trace the money back to the *soldatos*.

It was almost evening and the agents had no leads. They decided to visit every place the trucks had stopped that day, enquire with the onlookers and try to get footage from the surrounding buildings. The day's investigation was wrapped up and the debriefing team was dismissed.

By dusk, Wolf had thirty eight million dollars, clean and ready for disposal.

Friday, September 28th 2007.

Rupert met Thomas at Central Park and the hostility wasn't quite expunged yet. Two weeks ago, this day, Rupert and Thomas had a fall out at the McKinley Towers and they hadn't spoken to each other since. They just jogged side by side, each pissed off at the other.

'Pleasant morning, my dear brothers,' said Coleman jovially and joined them.

Dr. Derek W Coleman's physical appearance bellowed the slogan, "Under God's Power She Flourishes". His Ivy-League haircut, sublime linguistics, elegant clothing and kinship said nothing but Princeton. He had a doctoral degree in Mathematics and his recent research in the field had landed his name on the list of probable candidates for the Bocher Prize.

'The three of us meeting early in the morning at such a magnificent place. Isn't this lovely?' continued Bru and let out a profound sigh.

'Shut up,' said Rupert.

'Like it would make a difference if we met when the sun showed up,' grunted Thomas.

'Finally I got you two to agree on something.'

'We didn't agree.'

'Yeah. We didn't.'

'Well, at least you two agree to disagree.'

'No.'

'No.'

'And again,' said Bru merrily.

'Fine. What do you want me to do?' asked the youngest of the three, Thomas.

'Not just you. The two of you, together.'

Rupert didn't say anything. He just jogged silently.

'Not guilty,' said Thomas.

'Huh?' asked Rupert.

'Not guilty, like you said. Thanks.'

'I'm sure you impressed the jurors.'

'As a matter of fact, I did.'

'Pukka, it's time for you guys to move on to another case. Only this time it won't be at the courthouse,' said Bru.

'Why?' asked Thomas.

'Vindictive idealism.'

'Bullshit! It isn't vindictive idealism. It's our principles.'

'Go fuck your principles!'

Bru took a long deep breath, and then like most elder brothers, let the younger and the cranky jerk win.

'Porter Hill, one of our employee's sister's boyfriend was charged with the murder of Theodore Sebastian.'

'And you want us to prove his innocence?' asked Rupert.

'There is no point in proving it. He killed himself last night.'

'So?' asked Thomas.

'But he isn't the real murderer.'

'Says who?' questioned Rupert.

'Hill's brother, Wyatt Hill.'

'And who might he be?'

'A United States Marshal, Special Operations Group (SOG).'

'The guys at Camp Beauregard?' asked Thomas.

'Yep,' replied Bru and looked at Rupert.

'Interesting. That ought to make the suicide easier,' said Rupert.

'Unfortunately your guess is right. The marshals eased a bit on the security and the suicide prevention policy was ignored.'

They stayed quiet for a few seconds after which Rupert began, 'How do we know that Porter didn't murder Sebastian? We can't just take someone's word for it. We need evidence.'

'No, we don't. The court needs evidence. That was what I said earlier. This one is out of the courtroom.'

'All right, I'll rephrase. How does Wyatt know that his brother is innocent? They all say that. It has something to do with love and affection.'

'Not all. I would never say you are innocent,' said Bru and laughed.

'Cut the crap. Talk with relevance to the case.'

'Good to know that you are on board. Now as to your question, it has something to do with some gestures.'

'What gestures?'

'Crossing the hands and holding the ears with the index and the middle finger. As children, Wyatt and Porter were apparently wrongly accused of some wrongdoing and were punished by their headmistress. It seems that some bully set them up for having not shared their food with him. Anyway the punishment was that they had to kneel down with their hands crossed and hold their ears with the index and the middle finger.'

'So Wyatt feels that someone set his brother up…'

'For not sharing his food?' continued Rupert mockingly and smirked.

Bru and Thomas gave him a disgusted glance and Rupert said, 'C'mon, the story is so skeptical. Don't you think that the extrapolation is preposterous?'

'What about his girlfriend?' asked Thomas, completely ignoring Rupert and his annoying questions.

'What can I say, she is out of the world.'

'C'mon, Bru, she just lost her boyfriend. Give it some time.'

'I meant she is dead.'

'Oh shit!'

'You think that is shit? Take a look at this,' said Bru and passed a photograph.

'Holy shit!'

CHAPTER 4

Tuesday, October 30th 2007

Vila do Porto is the single municipality and the name of the main town on the island of Santa Maria in the Portuguese Autonomous Region of Azores. Santa Maria Airport located at around three miles from Vila do Porto was proposed by the Pentagon as the ideal destination for landing the Global Express. The airport has one runway certified as an adequate ETOPS (Extended Operations) alternative having suitable facilities to accommodate trans-Atlantic flights needing to make an emergency landing.

The United States and the Portuguese government had good extradition treaties and the diplomatic relationship was also on good terms. Jeremy Nolan personally spoke to the President of the Portuguese Republic and informed him about the chain of events. The President of the Portuguese Republic soon convened a high-level cabinet meet consisting of key parliamentary officials at his residence, Belém National Palace, at a quarter past four. The matter was deliberated and the U.S government's requests were given consent. The agents from the American Embassy obtained the written authorisations from the cabinet and mailed it to the U.S government through diplomatic channels. Delta Force was allowed to take control of the Santa Maria Airport, the 65th Air Base Wing was granted the permission to operate from the Lajes Air Base, and the provisional arrest of Nahiossi was issued.

The news was announced in the Situation Room and it received a cheering applause. However the decision from the Portugal Government wasn't just based on the treaties or bureaucratic relations. It had other strings attached. Strings which the President and his confederates agreed to tether to, the most vital of them being the strengthening of Air Base No. 4 (Lajes Air Base)

The U.S Department of Defense (DoD) has used Lajes Air Base since 1943. It has allowed Portugal to strengthen diplomatic relations with the U.S in addition to strengthening its base. The DoD, in the past, had provided two A-7P Corsair II (attack aircrafts) squadrons among various other military equipment, and co-financed the F-16 Fighting Falcon aircraft. But over the past few years, the U.S government had cancelled certain plans under the cover of budgetary constraints, causing concern over the base's future as well as the Azorean workforce. An extremely concerned Portugal government was reported to have been looking for contingencies. Now that the help of their government was sought, it tactically brought up the topic of the Lajes Air Base and secured its future through a verbal contract.

'The 65th Air Base Wing has agreed to provide en route air support. We have F-16s and B-1 Lancer ready for takeoff'

The Global Express might as well have been steered to land at Lajes Air Base. But in case Nahiossi had explosives on the plane, its detonation would be catastrophic and the Air Base had far too many assets and manpower to lose. On the other hand, Santa Maria Airport had less traffic. The few airplanes could be moved to any of the seven Airports in Azores with just a few minutes' notice.

'The PSP (Public Security Police) is evacuating Santa Maria Airport. All flights for the day have been cancelled,' said Lt. Gen. Lake.

'Excellent.' The President beamed.

'Mr. President, the 65th Air Base Wing is on standby. They are good to go.'

Nolan gave the go-ahead and two F-16s took off from the Lajes Air Base at Terceira Island. The aircrafts rocketed towards the Global Express at almost 1,500 miles/hr, nearly thrice as fast as the Global Express. The air traffic controls of various air bases sent NOTAM (Notice to Airmen) to various trans-Atlantic flights and diverted them to safer locations. Most of the airports located at crucial positions were locked down. The military forces of the respective countries took charge of the airports and cleared it off civilians.

'ATC has established contact with Global Express,' said one of the members of the Watch team.

'Great. Ask them to confirm the squawk code,' said Nolan.

The ATC communicated with the pilots of the Global Express and asked them to confirm the four-digit octal transponder code. The tension escalated in the Situation Room as they waited for the response. The pilot took his time and then after a few irascible seconds nervously squawked 7500.

The first-hand conformation of the Global Express' hijack was received at the ATC and the same was momentarily heard in the Situation Room.

The European Aviation Safety Agency (EASA) at Cologne, the de facto capital of European union at Brussels, the United Nations headquarters at New York, the International Court of Justice at the Hague, the International Civil Aviation Organization at Canada, the Portugal 1st Air Region headquarters at Lisbon, the Lajes Air base and the municipal chairman at Santa Maria were informed of the latest situation and every one of them agreed to offer unabridged support to the White House in its endeavour to apprehend the international criminal and rescue the Vice President of the United States.

The Delta operators of Operation Phoenix were picked up by the Night Stalkers from the House of Horrors and piloted swiftly and speedily to the Santa Maria Airport.

The Global Express was around three hours away from Amsterdam and around 2.25 hours away from Santa Maria Airport. The F-16s would intercept the hijacked flight in three fourths of an hour and the Delta force would have been deployed at the Santa Maria Airport in an hour.

Every news agency from around the world aired the news and numerous reporters got to the Santa Maria to capture the live footage from ground zero. The event would occupy the headlines for weeks. Phoenix Almonte Group of Airlines would be dragged into the ground. The Americans would be lauded for the daring operation and stealth. The American-Dutch relations would deteriorate. Nahiossi would be tagged as one of the most notorious criminals and Jamie Edwards would be the new Hero of the Republicans.

Saturday, February 11th 2006.

Covert Operations Division of PiCorp Security Systems, Inc. procured surveillance equipment, communication systems, vehicles, Government Issue fake identities, passports & firearm permits, safe houses and armaments worth twenty million dollars.

The loyalists like the Five Godfathers, agents of the Federal Protective Service, wardens of certain medium and high security prisons, lobbyists, lawyers, informants, directors of various archives, border security forces, U.S Customs, private hangar operators, foot soldiers and PiCorp CODs agents, mobilised in 15 countries of the world were sanctioned hefty cuts of the ten million dollars.

Meanwhile the six FBI agents studied the logs of the six armoured trucks and found it hard to believe that an hour before the reported robbery, all six trucks had stopped for over three minutes at a certain location and at almost the same time, owing to traffic. They followed protocol and obtained permits to retrieve the traffic signal surveillance tapes, CCTV tapes from the surrounding buildings, license plate records and to conduct surveillance on a select few employees and employers of CATS.

The FBI also had private eyes on the six drivers. On receiving the command from Agent Parker, the NYPD officers would arrest them and take them to the 6th, 28th, 35th, 47th, 76th and 123rd precincts.

Agent Parker obtained the co-ordinates of the truck from the GPS log and so did the other five agents assigned to investigate the other five locations. They got down to their respective zones and began their enquiries.

'I'm Agent Parker, I'm with the FBI. We are investigating an armoured truck robbery that took place yesterday morning at around eleven.'

'Would you mind if we asked you a few questions?' said his aide from NYPD.

Steve Fossett will complete the world record for the longest non-stop, unrefueled flight when the Virgin Atlantic Global Flyer lands at Bournemouth airport in southern England after a flight lasting 76 hours and 45 minutes...

'Yes. I remember seeing it. It passes by every morning. But yesterday was a bit unusual,' said a retailer from a shop that had clear line of sight with the truck's former position, as he flicked the TV off.

'Could you be more specific?'

'The Department of Homeland Security was here. They had the truck stop, and then three men, I suppose, entered the cargo area of the truck.'

'I'm sure they left the place in under three minutes.'

'You could look at the footage if you need the precise time. But bluntly, yes. They took a few bags and boxes, dumped the same in a Tahoe and sped away.'

Of course someone from the law enforcement is involved. How else could someone so flawlessly rob an armoured truck in broad daylight?

'Yes, I'd appreciate that.'

'Sure, officer.'

Agent Parker conveyed the same to the other five agents and everyone concurred. The footage was collected and statements were recorded. The team regrouped that afternoon and made an informal enquiry with the Deputy Secretary of Homeland Security. She plainly rejected the accusation and told them that she wasn't going to order an enquiry on her own "family". Women administrators can get really attached at times and Nichole was one of them. She wouldn't let anyone or anything stain the reputation of her treasured Bureau.

The footage were sent to the technicians and the thought that the people who robbed the truck could be impersonating the DHS dawned to the dull debriefing committee.

The Lincoln Town cars were serviced and neatly refurbished, while the Chevrolet Tahoe SUVs were returned to the actual agents of the Federal Protective Service.

The *soldatos* went to the 90 banks again that morning, traded shares worth four hundred thousand dollars and withdrew the money that very evening. As usual.

Rupert sat in the confines of his office and read the article, *"Ghosts rob armored trucks in broad daylight"*.

Vindictive idealism.

Wednesday, April 9, 2007.

Save yourselves before it's too late.

On an otherwise pleasant Monday morning, Theodore Sebastian, a legal consultant at the Phoenix Almonte group of Airlines and one of the most celebrated criminal lawyers in New York City, abhorred the toughest of criminals and petrified the shrewdest of lawyers.

Numerous early commuters, who happened by the corpse before the area was cordoned off, were shook to their bones and appalled by the brutality of the scene. Eventually a plethora of agitated 9-1-1 calls stormed the ESU, making the NYPD, SWAT, DHS, FPS and a myriad of other law enforcement agencies rush to the scene in record time.

Almost every news channel in New York aired the censored video LIVE from Foley Square, as the reporters blurted out a legion of speculations and theories about the crime scene.

Vaughn and Cortez received the news at the Fletcher Manor and were shaken to their very spines. The 'Almonte Brothers' were *tout de suite* choppered down to One Police Plaza Heliport in Manhattan and were thereupon rushed to take at look at their best legal advisor and esteemed friend.

'Get your best agents on the field. I don't care what it takes, but I want him at my disposal by next Monday morning. You hear me?' Vaughn yelled as he spoke to the director of the FBI. The NYPD made way for the Senator's car to go past the yellow tapes, as a stream of cameras flashed at them perpetually.

Cortez couldn't believe his eyes. He jumped out of the car even before it pulled over and started at the mutilated lawyer. Vaughn apprehensively stepped out of his car, his heart pounding and his stomach growling. He wiped the sweat off his brow, loosened his tie, and removed his coat before dropping it on the ground. He prayed for a brief moment and then walked closer to the truck, with Cortez at his side.

The truck-mounted crane was daringly parked in front of the New York County Supreme Court at 60 Centre Street. The steel arm of the crane was extended to its maximum boom length and the jib was a bit inclined. The jib led to an upper sheave, from which sturdy steel cables dangled.

As Cortez looked at the immense iron hook that was plunged inside Sebastian's rear, his stomach churned and his eyes moistened.

The sheer dragging force of the hook had torn off a significant part of Sebastian's hindquarters. A few terrifying seconds later, Cortez turned around and ran towards their car, shutting his mouth tightly with both hands. He got to the driver's window and threw up all over the seat. He hung his hands on the window for a while before his knees collapsed. He wearily crashed on the ground and wiped his mouth with his coat.

Vaughn stared at the corpse, his anger growing with the tick of the clock. Five SUVs pulled up behind the yellow tapes and a dozen agents rushed towards the senator.

Preliminary procedures were carried out and then the jib was declined and the boom was receded. Sebastian's body was lowered and now the sight became conspicuously unbearable.

The deceased had neither penis nor testicles.

Sebastian's torso was engraved with the words: *Save yourselves before it's too late.*

CHAPTER 5

Wednesday, November 21st 2007

The 23rd floor of the FBI Field Office on 26 Federal Plaza was filled with Agent Mason's team, the Assistant Director in Charge (ADIC) and two Special Agents in Charge (SACs). The lab reports and the experts' opinion were presented to the ADIC, and Agent Mason's team had an interesting theory in concurrence with the lab reports. The proceedings would be pushed up to the Department of Justice Criminal Division and National Security Division, where the concerned attorneys would contrive for prosecution and formulate criminal enforcement policies with the Attorney General's office.

'Mr. Camargo, pleasure to meet you,' said Agent Mason and shook hands with the ADIC. 'Special Agent Ottosson,' he continued, moving on to one of the SACs, 'Special Agent Marco,' he added and concluded the formalities.

Experts from the Biometric Analysis Wing, Forensic Response Wing, Scientific Analysis Wing and Forensic support team were seated around the table with numerous files stacked in front of them. Pleasantries were briefly exchanged and then Mr. Camargo asked the lead forensic expert to present the reports.

'I am proud to say that Mr. Griffiths is in a lot of trouble. Even the best defense attorney can't come up with anything to rebutt the evidence with regards to the senator's murder.'

Agent Mason's face lit up and so did the faces of many others in the room.

'Good. Go ahead, show us what you got.'

'I'll start with the weapon. This knife,' he said, pushing a bagged knife across the table, 'A Soviet NR40, was used to stab the senator.'

'Here are the lab reports,' said his assistant, placing a file in front of the ADIC. He then took a few sheets of the photocopied report and passed it around the table.

'The same knife killed Caesar,' continued Nelson, circulating the reports yet again.

'Plunged and withdrawn at exactly the same angle?' asked Marco, as he studied the report.

'Yes, Special Agent Marco. That's what my analysis suggests.'

'Okay, so we can infer that the senator was incapacitated at the time of assault,' said Ottosson, who had a thorough knowledge with regards to the physics of murder.

'Indeed. At this juncture, I would like Dr. King to walk you through the toxicology analysis.'

Every pair of eyes landed on Dr. King, the lead toxicology expert with the FBI.

Dr. King handed over the file to Camargo and passed photocopies of the same around the conference table. That was the standard procedure. *Passing the parcel.*

'We found Strychnine from the alcohol sample that was recovered from the senator's study…'

'Excuse me, Dr. King, but the manifest doesn't speak about any alcohol sample.'

'I'm aware of that, but - '

'It might have been even mixed with the food. That shifts a serious liability.'

'Yes. It does. But we are positive that Strychnine was mixed with the champagne. It doesn't speak about alcohol -'

SA Marco wasn't convinced. He read the report in haste. Then, halfway down the page, his face lit up again.

The presence of Strychnine in the sample of alcohol is verified by the analysis of the liquid sample found on Mr. Vaughn Fletcher's spectacles.

'But it certainly speaks about a certain liquid sample. Before we move on to that, allow me,' said Dr. King and picked up exhibit 33422. 'These, gentlemen, are the senator's spectacles,' he said, and held the same in his right hand. 'These were resting on his stomach and the glasses were slightly inclined. Like this,' he said, demonstrating the same.

A golden chain that was attached to the glasses' temple tips rested on his neck and suspended his spectacles. The chain allowed the specs to fall on his stomach when removed.

'Senator Fletcher found it irksome to place the glasses in a case every time he removed it. So he had it custom made and would always just let it rest on his stomach when he didn't use it. Old-fashioned, one might say, however to us it is a blessing in disguise,' said Dr. King and triggered a murmur. He paused for a few seconds and then added, 'A few drops of the champagne dropped on his spectacles while he was drinking. These drops then coalesced and got adsorbed on the surface of the glass. Soon after entering the scene, we found this sample. So we just bagged it. It's in the initial reporting officer's manifest.'

Liquid sample on 33422.

'Very nice,' said SA Marco and clapped his hands, as did a few others. 'I really appreciate your analysis.'

'Thank you, Special Agent Marco.'

'And this proves that the senator was incapacitated when he was stabbed,' cut in Nelson. The cheering died down and the discussion resumed.

'But what caused the death of the senator?' asked SA Ottosson.

'Definitely not Strychnine. Well it would have, if given more time to react.'

'Okay,' replied Ottoson, before discussing something with the ADIC. He then asked, 'Do you have anything else to say, Dr. King?'

'I'm afraid not.'

'Well in that case, thank you, Dr. King,' said Nelson.

'Always a pleasure.'

'Likewise. Now the blood spatter expert also concurs with our assertion of the murder weapon,' said Nelson and pointed at the concerned person.

'Yes, sir, we found samples of the senator's blood on the knife retrieved from the canine. The angle and the depth of impact from the knife is consistent with the spatter pattern.'

'*Rigor mortis* places the time of death at around 9:00 PM, which agrees with the time Mr. Griffiths probably murdered the senator,' said a medical examiner (ME) from the coroner's office, who was sitting beside the blood spatter expert.

'Thank you, gentlemen. So we have established the weapon used and the time of death. Does everyone concur?'

'Aye.'

'Okay, great. Now, let's move on to the Latent Prints Operation Unit (LPOU). Dr. Kelly?'

'We found finger prints on the knife, the cloth hanging along the stone wall, the compound wall, the canine and the gate in the adjoining villa. Apart from that, we found shoeprints inside the room, on the stone wall, on the pathway, on the compound wall and in the adjoining villa.'

'But why would he leave so much evidence? A man of his stature would have been more careful. Don't you think?' asked SA Marco.

'That is the precise question we asked ourselves for days.'

'And?'

'We have reasons and explanations for it all. Rest assured, Agent Mason will explain it in detail tomorrow.'

'That's good to know, Nelson,' said SA Marco and turned to his right. 'Agent Mason, I hope - for all our sakes - that your theory is good enough to convince those big shots at the Attorney General's office.'

'It sure is, SA Marco.'

'Great. Okay, where were we?'

'I was briefing you about the latent prints,' said Dr. Kelly.

'Yes. Please continue.'

'Well, that's all I had in mind, SA Marco. My team and I concur with the ME.'

The Special Agents and the ADIC studied the reports for a few minutes. Camargo then asked Nelson to present the next evidence.

'Dr. Brad, Trace Evidence Unit (TEU).'

'We found certain hair and fibre samples of Mr. Griffiths in the senator's study, and a piece of fabric in the adjoining villa. That's all usual. Nothing new. But if you could just take a look at this picture,' said Dr. Brad excitedly and projected a picture on the wall. It showed an aerial view of the Fletcher Manor.

A few copies of the pictures were also passed around and then the ADIC asked him to continue.

'Mr. Griffiths abseiled down this window and ran across the pathway. Now, here,' he continued, pointing at a location that was around three feet from the stone wall, 'we found a fibre that matches with the fabric which was recovered from the adjoining villa.

We consulted a few sources and then learnt from Mr. Griffiths' tailor that the fibre belonged to Mr. Griffiths' jacket.'

The team members looked at each other and smiled with pride, while the ADIC studied the manifest, discovery, bag and tag procedure, lab analysis and the tailor's affidavit.

'The samples are in correspondence with Mr. Griffith's path. There is a clear pattern. So I too concur with my colleagues.'

'Thank you, Dr. Brad. Your discovery will be extremely appreciated once they have heard Agent Mason's theory,' said Nelson and patted Dr. Brad.

'Anytime, Nelson and yes, I'm sure they will.'

'Now before we proceed, Mr. Camargo, allow me to just summarise what has been said so far.'

Camargo nodded.

'Mr. Griffiths murdered the senator with a Soviet NR40 after poisoning him with Strychnine. He then abseiled down the stone wall, ran across the pathway, jumped into the adjoining villa and escaped through the villa's side gate. He then hijacked a plane, kidnapped the VP and went to Portugal.'

Nelson paused for some time, waited for the information to sink in. He then continued,

'Experts in scientific analysis have probed the evidences and their reports have been promptly submitted. The ME, LPOU, TEU, toxicology expert and myself have verified the above stated facts. And for the records, I speak for the NDNAU (Nuclear DNA Unit).'

'Thank you, Dr. Nelson, we appreciate your effort.'

'It's my duty, sir. May the senator rest in peace.'

PiCorp was a private security agency headquartered in New York, USA. The Wolf founded the agency in 1963 with the goal of providing better and effective protection to common people.

Its services included a score of professional security domains, Emergency Medical Technical (EMT) units, ambassador service, conceirge service and covert operations. PiCorp had contracts with the energy sector, healthcare sector, financial establishments, leading industrialists, ports and airport authorities, transit service and also the government. The agency went public in 1969 and in 1971 it was listed on the New York Stock Exchange. The agency's Board of Directors included the sons of the five Italian-American mob bosses, an ex-FPS agent, an ex-CIA operative, two retired federal judges, two expert journalists and Bru.

As the years rolled on, the government commissioned PiCorp's workforce on various assignments. The enterprise became highly reputable for its swift and effective completion of assignments. PiCorp also developed a Research and Analysis Wing (RAW) to cater to the needs of their clients by the implementation of better and modern technologies. The IRS had a serious headache in finding out the source of income for the agency, but the confidentiality agreement kept the identity of the clients secretive and so the sources couldn't be revealed. Serious accusations were popping up in the newspapers, but then the Wolf and Bru met with the editors, news-reporters, and IRS agents and made them - by using a few methods of their own - retract, stop investigating and drop the matter. Henceforth PiCorp exposed a few scandals, nabbed a few criminals, successfully established contracts with numerous intelligence agencies who were very keen on outsourcing, obtained DoD contracts, acquired 10 security companies around the world, recruited ex-CIA operatives and made itself indispensable to the motherland. The success and profit curves inclined and PiCorp had money pouring in from the government, corporate companies, politicians, judges, business magnets and of course, civilians and criminals.

The Board was the most productive, diverse and effective organisation on the face of the United States. It had the mafia, federal agents, federal judges, CIA, investigative journalists and above all, the Wolf.

PiCorp was a government parallel to the White House. It knew almost everything the White House knew. It had a footing in 10 most important cities of the world and it also had agents in Iran and Afghanistan. The Agency was idealistic. The COD was futuristic. And the results were always fantastic.

'Your bad times are our good times.'

Tuesday, September 28th 2007.

Rupert, Thomas and Bru halted on the path off the West Dr, leading to the Ladies' Pavilion and Hernshead. The panoramic view of the Fifth Avenue and the Lake was simply breathtaking. There weren't many commuters, so it was ideal for their morning chat. Rupert and Thomas removed their gloves and windbreakers, and smoked Marlboros. Meanwhile Bru checked his phone. The Wolf had sent a message. It read: China, Samaritan, Surveillance, Deploy.

'Guys, it's Wolf, something important has come up and I have to be at PiCorp in a half hour. So let me just brief you about the investigation and the conviction of Porter Hill.'

'I'm all ears.'

'Likewise.'

'Good. 9th April at 6:45 AM, the guards at the courthouse see a crane approaching slowly towards them. As the crane inched closer, they see the corpse and alert the authorities.'

'Who was driving it?'

'That's the best part. No one. The Bureau report states that the first reporting officer found the crane to be in neutral gear. Someone shifted the gear to neutral and jumped off the crane. It slowly gained momentum down the road and then when the road became even, it gradually slowed down and came to a stop in front of the courthouse.'

'Okay. Did we get his image?'

'Yes. But as always, he was covered in black dress and ski mask. The Bureau couldn't get any latent prints or trace evidence off the crane or the road.'

'Owing to the rain.'

'Yes.'

'Lucky scumbag.'

'Not if they planned to do it when it rained.'

'That's probable.'

'Yes it is. Moving on now, a contractor by the name of Julio filed a complaint at the 7th Precinct, stating that his crane was stolen. The precinct notified the Bureau and the Bureau summoned the contractor. Julio identified the crane and also presented an alibi as a preemptive measure. The Bureau then found out from Julio that the crane was contracted to Lobo's, a café that is being constructed at Canal St. The agents went down to Lobo's and found out that both the driver and the security guarding the construction site on the 8th of April were absent from work on the 9th and on the 10th. The agents obtained their addresses and went down to the driver's apartment on Mulberry St.'

'Needless to say that no one answered the door so the FBI had to break into the house.'

'Indeed. But they weren't at the house. The next day, which is on the 11th, the agents obtained certain footage from a couple of banks and offices around Lobo's. The footage shows two men getting out of an old Ford and entering the construction site. Then one of them comes back and takes the Ford inside. 50 seconds after, the truck is driven out of the site. 5 seconds after that, the other guy locks the gate and drives away.'

'The security guard let the driver in because he knew him.'

'Once inside, they beat him up, I suppose.'

'Then the other guy takes the Ford inside and dumps the security guard in it.'

'The driver drives away in his truck and the other guy locks the gate…'

'That confirms our presumption that the security guard was incapacitated.'

'Exactly.'

'Guys, all these facts are established. Just listen to the story. I'm running late.'

'All right!'

'On the 12th, that is 3 days after the murder, the Ford was tracked down. The number plate had been identified from the footage and every patrol cop was asked to keep watch. A few hours after the search operation was ordered, the Ford was found in an alley on Duane St. The agents got down to the alley and found both of them stuffed in the Ford's trunk. They were immediately rushed to the hospital.'

'Both dead?'

'No. Neither. The car was too damn old. The car had some dents and cracks that allowed air to circulate in the trunk.'

'The driver admitted to have hit the security guard and stolen the truck, and the security guard's narration agreed with the Bureau's presumption. So the driver was taken into custody.'

'And the security guard was let go.'

'Yes. The driver admitted to the assault and robbery, but he said that he was under duress. The guy who was with him had threatened to kill him in case he denied assistance. He did what he had to do. Dying for a crane didn't seem like a decision a man with conscience would make.'

'I know I wouldn't.'

'Precisely. The driver said that he stopped the crane at an alley on Duane St., as asked by the person threatening him. You can read the driver's testimony from the file,' said Bru and again looked at his phone. 'Let's get going now. I don't want to be late for the meeting.'

'Okay. We'll come with you till PiCorp. Tell us on the way,' said Rupert.

Both Thomas and Bru looked shocked. Rupert and PiCorp. Unimaginable.

'Okay,' said Bru and smiled at his brother.

'There is nothing to be happy about it. It's truly professional. This has nothing to do with Wolf. I can never forgive him. Nor can I accept your vindictive idealism.'

CHAPTER 6

Wednesday, October 30th 2007

'We don't care even if you kill the Vice President.'

'You stooges are obviously bluffing.'

'Think what you may, but the truth is, we aren't. Jamie is a pain in the ass. We wanted to frame him in the *Rachel sex scandal.* We had teams chasing after him, spying on him and his escapades. But now that you have him, we'd really appreciate it if you kill him.'

Nahiossi's confidence depreciated. He had lost his immunity, the ticket to his homeland. But nonetheless he wouldn't give up. He had far too much to lose. To win, he had to lose.

The SecDef was in fact bluffing. President Nolan and his cabinet had authorised the Pentagon to use any form of verbal chivalry and persuade Nahiossi to land the Global Express at Santa Maria. Robert McElroy and his team consisting of the directors of CIA, DNI and the commander of JSOC had thought of a through plan to execute the same, *'Trivialise every leverage.'*

'Mr. Griffiths, we have no regards for Vice President Edwards. You can deal with him as you please. But we have certain bureaucratic obligations, which require us to shoot down your plane.'

The roar of the Global Express' engine was subdued by the boom of the F-16 and B-1 Lancer. The two fighter planes went past the Global Express, raking up Nahiossi's fear.

'You see, Mr. Griffiths, we aren't bluffing. We never do. We always get the job done.'

The Pentagon gave a few minutes for Nahiossi to contemplate the gravity of the situation.

'One thing is for sure, Mr. Griffiths, you aren't reaching the Netherlands. Either you get blown up and get scattered across the North Atlantic, or you land in Portugal. The choice is yours.'

They don't care about the Vice President. The students?

'I'm going to throw these kids out of the plane.'

'We don't care about the Vice President, Mr. Griffiths. You seriously think we are going to care about some stupid students?'

'Well-'

'We may not care about the lives of the people on that plane. But as per bureaucratic obligations, we have orders to shoot down your plane the second you open the goddamn door.'

The Vice President, the students...

The B-1 Lancer and the F-16 were scrambled to scare Nahiossi. There weren't any orders for shooting down the plane. Of course there couldn't be. There would have been an authorisation to shoot down a plane if it could be assumed that the hijackers intended to use the aircraft in a 9/11-style attack. Obviously Nahiossi didn't intend to do so. He just wanted to reach home.

'Authorise your captain to land the plane at Santa Maria and we can talk it out reasonably. We won't extradite you until the due processes are done. You won't face death penalty for whatever crimes you have committed and you'll get to see your father. I'm sure he isn't happy with what you have done. But I'm sure you have reasons and your father might agree with your reasons. Prove it to him that you aren't a bad person. Prove it to the world that you aren't a cruel person. America truly respects you and your industry. Don't tarnish your industry and don't tarnish the name of your hometown.'

The Night Stalkers flew into Santa Maria at 5:25, local time. The airport was totally isolated and the power was intentionally cut off, except for the ALS (Approach Lighting System). The Delta operators, wearing their night vision goggles, jumped off a jet that was off the DoD's official books, perfectly blending with the secretiveness of the Delta operators. The jet emptied the operators and immediately took off. The operators swiftly sprawled across the airport, picking various vantage points tactically.

Phoenix in position at ground zero.

Nahiossi stared blankly at the altimeter, airspeed indicator, turn and bank indicator, altitude indicator and the gyro, feeling a sense of defeat. His mind raced, trying to figure a way out of the whole conspiracy. The turbofans roared in his ears and made his head thump.

'Mr. Griffiths, are you with us?'

Before Nahiossi could pull himself back together and answer the Secretary General, the Vice President stabbed Nahiossi's left leg with a broken champagne bottle. Nahiossi crouched down instinctively and Jamie, gathering all his might, punched Nahiossi's skull. Before Nahiossi could retaliate, Jamie removed his belt and strapped Nahiossi's legs, while the captain removed his tie and fastened Nahiossi's hands together.

Vice President Edwards and the captain dragged Nahiossi to the cabin, as he struggled to free himself. The three students pinned him down and the Vice President, mustering every ounce of energy, kicked Nahiossi in the groin.

'This is the captain speaking. The situation is under control. Mr. Griffiths has been incapacitated. I repeat, the situation is now under control.'

The ATC sent another request for squawk code confirmation. Only this time, it wasn't confirmed. The Vice President got on the line and spoke to the Secretary General at the Pentagon. He reassured them that everything was under control. The situation was nullified without any military intervention.

Vice President Jamie Edwards had become a hero.

Deception is the cardinal aspect of a perfect crime. Think from the law enforcement point of view and formulate a crime. The law enforcement is going to formulate additional theories and reach dead ends. Always.

The footage from every closed circuit camera and the NYPD surveillance units had failed to capture the faces and any other vital information concerning the six robberies. It wasn't simply coincidence, it was a robbery well done. Wolf and his confederates had chosen places that would hide the identities of the *soladatos,* meanwhile give the FBI some apparent valuable information to go on. It would take a day or two for the technicians to study all the recordings, look for details and pull out anything that might be vital. But by then the stolen money would get washed into the vast expanse of the American economy, leaving no trails whatsoever.

'Agent Parker, bad news. My team couldn't pull out any vital information. The robbers are highly trained and they seem to know their way around the cameras.'

Agent Parker puffed at his cigarette nervously. Ten days had elapsed since the robbery and calls from the newspaper agencies poured in with every tick. Conspiracy theories were being published and the agents were being accused of being *slaves* to the politicians and being *slowpokes.*

'No offence officer, but I don't think that it's sensible to omit the DHS from the list of suspects. The elections are around the corner. The politicians need funds and the DHS hires private firms.

I don't think it's difficult for the politicians to steal some cash. It has happened before. It's not totally impossible.'

'You believe in what the newspapers have to say?' Parker whined.

'Yes, Agent Parker, I do'

'Karl, it's just a work of fiction. Those young, immature and hungry reporters who are desperately waiting to catch a break often publish alluring stories. We can't suspect the Homeland Security just because some assholes publish something. We need to honor the integrity of the law enforcement. Put that in your hat-rack,' said Parker angrily and walked closer to Karl, the technical expert with the FBI.

'Carl Bernstein and Bob Woodward. Watergate Scandal. Nixon downplayed the scandal as mere politics, calling news articles biased and misleading. You know about the CREEP (Committee for the Re-Election of the President) and the slush funds. It was two young, immature and hungry reporters and their mesmerising "stories" that brought the scandal out into the open. I'm not saying that you have to believe everything the media says. I'm just asking you to not rule out the possibilities just because they are associated with the law enforcement,' shot Dr. Karl and walked out of the debriefing room.

'And one more thing, put that in your hat-rack,' Dr. Karl added, before slamming the door on Agent Parker.

The investigating team met that very afternoon and Agent Parker presented Dr. Karl's report. Then he presented Dr. Karl's advice to include the DHS under scrutiny. There were obviously disagreements, but after a long debate the team agreed to include the DHS on the list of suspects.

'We have nothing of importance from the footage, we don't have any witnesses who could identify the robbers and we still haven't found the money,' said Agent Parker.

'But it's obvious from the footage that the robbers entered the cargo area with ease,' said the agent investigating the Brooklyn robbery.

'Also, there weren't any signs of breaking in on the rear door of the truck,' said another agent investigating the robber at Staten Island.

'One of our analysts told us that the rear doors of the armoured trucks have electronic locking systems and that only the drivers can control it,' said the investigator from Albany.

'So we can confidently assume that the drivers were involved with the robbery,' said another investigator from Bronx.

'That was obvious on the very first day. But we don't have any evidence that sticks. We can't have them arrested,' said Parker and banged his fist on the table.

'We don't have anything else to go on. We have to bring them in,' said the investigator working the Westchester robbery.

'It's 48 hours, legally.'

'What the hell are you suggesting, Dr. Karl?'

'You know exactly what I'm suggesting. Have a bunch of plainclothes do the job. You can take as much time as you want. Plus, there is an added incentive.'

'And what might that be?'

'The newspapers would report that the six drivers escaped with the money. That would shift the focus away from the FBI's inefficiency.'

'Should I consult the Director?'

'In cases of conspiracies, never contact the higher ups.'

'By a show of hands, those in favor of Dr. Karl's proposal,' said Agent Parker and raised his right hand.

Favouring the wrong to right the wrong.

February-April 2005

Ilarion Wasyl, a candidate for the Ukrainian Presidential Elections, was found dead at a cottage a few miles off Kiev, the cause of death being heroin overdose. The Ukrainian Security Services (SBU) and the U.S Drug Enforcement Agency (DEA) investigated the case together and eventually found out that Wasyl himself had bought the drugs from a trader who was transporting the consignment to Afghanistan. The dealer was arrested and the case was closed.

Anastasia, an employee at the Chief Administration in Fight with the Organized Crime (HUBOZ), wasn't convinced with Wasyl's death being attributed to heroin overdose. So she decided to dig deeper. She single-handedly investigated the case for a few weeks, and then when it turned out that she was up against the President, she decided to approach the Wolf.

Discovery and liquidation of crime schemes directed at the legalisation of income that were received as a result of criminal activities of organised groups and crime organisations was one of the many functions of HUBOZ. Anastasia found out that one of the campaign managers of Wasyl had received a hefty amount as charity for Pediatric Cardio Vascular Surgery. She traced back the source of donations and every donor turned out to be a fake. She thought of reporting the finding to her higher ups, but then she thought the better of it. She knew that they would do nothing but discourage, yell and suspend her for at least a month for conspiring against the President. So Anastasia went down to a PI and reported her findings. The PI got in touch with Thomas, who had him contact Bru, who then had him talk to the Wolf.

Anastasia eventually got in touch with the Wolf and met with PiCorp Elite Team Seven (PETS). The agents worked the case secretly in Kiev, and 16 days after they had commenced their investigation and almost two months after Lyaksandro was declared President-elect, they stumbled upon some vital evidence that linked Wasyl's death to corruption and opposition.

CHAPTER 7

Wednesday, October 30th 2007

The Global Express Bombardier touched down on the three thousand metre runway of Santa Maria Airport at five minutes to seven.

The Delta operators had gotten rid of their night-vision goggles and were geared up in military outfits, their eye concealed with goggles and faces partly concealed with ski masks.

'Global Express touching down at ground zero. Phoenix, move in.'

The snipers peered down their scopes from the control tower, apron, airside, billboards and every other vantage point. The foot operators were scattered all over the tarmac, landing pad and gates. Two helicopters of the Night Stalkers hovered above the runway, with operators ready to abseil down on the Global Express.

The F-16 and B1-Lancer circled high above the airport. They were ordered to stay in the vicinity until Nahiossi was apprehended.

On touchdown, the foot operators ran towards the Global Express and had it surrounded, while a few other operators abseiled down the choppers and took positions on the top and the wings of the Global Express.

The doors of the aircraft opened and an evacuation slide popped out, which was inflated with a non-explosive gas in under 4 seconds. The Bombardiers usually do not have escape slides. But Nahiossi had it custom-made and installed on his airplane.

The operators moved closer to the slide and took aim at the door. Nahiossi, his face reddened and his eye blackened, stood at the door. Two operators took photographs of the capital murderer and the international fugitive, and waited for him to slide down into their clutches.

Vice President Edwards stood behind Nahiossi and nudged him down the slide. Nahiossi's downfall had begun.

The operators immediately had him apprehended. They injected a certain sedative known to the R&D of the Delta Ops alone, and handcuffed him. He was escorted to a Portuguese prisoner transport airplane and immediately lifted off.

The B1-Lancer and F-16 kept up with the Learjet that was headed to the capital city of Portugal, Lisbon.

Double Eagle II Airport is a public airport located in Albuquerque, New Mexico.

The airport is primarily used as air ambulance, corporate flight, charter flight and private flight facility. The PiCorp frequently used it for transit since the traffic was less and the digital surveillance wasn't as developed. The clients, who were particularly secretive about their transportation to other countries, were driven to Albuquerque and put on a charter flight registered to PiCorp.

Two employees from PiCorp Bern, who were investigating an alleged money laundering conspiracy of an Indian politician, were asked to fly down to Albuquerque once every four days. A certain corrupt Central Bureau of Investigations (CBI) officer had implicated the Minister of Corporate Affairs in a major money laundering scam. The said minister had offered to resign should the charges against him be proved. Certain circumstantial evidence was scrambled and the Supreme Court of India found Rajiv Kashyap guilty of hiding illegal money at a certain bank in Switzerland. The Hon'ble Justice V. K. Singh then sentended Rajiv to serve ten years at Tihar Jail.

Rajiv's son, Vishal Kashyap, tried to prove his father's innocence through legal channels. But when nothing seemed to work as expected, he contacted PiCorp New Delhi and asked for their assistance in proving his father's innocence. The request reached the Wolf and he unhesitatingly agreed to help him. Since the matter deemed extreme confidentiality, the agents themselves brought the 'advancement reports' to PiCorp New York once every week. On their way back to Bern, two agents from PiCorp New York would always escort them.

This week, instead of the agents, the *soldatos* would do the escorting. Over the past three days, all six *soldatos* withdrew their accounts from the banks. They were then driven to Albuquerque and three of them were put on a charter plane with the two agents, and the remaining three were made to stay at a cottage owned by the Ruggiero Family. Four days hence, that is two weeks after the robbery, all six *soldatos* would be in Bern. All six of them would use fake passports and visas, of course. Since the trip was made twice every week, the agents were familiar with the airport security. So the *soldatos* didn't attract much attention. The *soldatos* would then be driven to Sicily, where they would spend some quality time for about a month.

In case Agent Parker and his team managed to scrape up something from one of the 90 banks (which was highly unlikely), the *soldatos* would have a legion of alibis. The CCTV footage from JFK and the records with the FAA would show that the *soldatos* boarded a plane to Italy a week before the robbery. There wouldn't be any records or footage of them flying back to the States. Also, the witnesses for their alibis would be enormous. Sicilians look up to their Godfathers with unwavering devotion. No one would dare do anything against him.

So, mischief managed.

In totality, no leads from the footage taken from the place where the trucks were found, no leads from the footage from where the money was stolen and no leads from the footage at the bank. The bank accounts of the *soldatos* were dummies, and all the accounts would lead to people who died almost a decade ago. The shell companies would lead nowhere, serving its sole purpose.

Except for the drivers, every other factor leading to PiCorp was taken care of.

Vindictive Idealism.

'The investigators picked up footage showing the assailant being dropped off by a taxi right in front of the driver's apartment. The number plate was clearly visible (or intentionally made clearly visible). The Bureau picked it up and the address of the taxi driver was obtained from the database.'

'Any discrepancies with the time?'

'No. The assailant's time of arrival matches with the driver's description of the scene.'

'Okay. Continue.'

'The driver was tracked down and the place where the assailant hired the taxicab was determined from the taxicab's GPS history.'

'Interesting. Where?'

'A grocery store on Montgomery Street near FDR Drive,' said Bru and brought his Mustang to a halt. 'God! I hate these traffic signals.'

'A blessing in disguise,' said Thomas and asked Bru to continue.

'The recordings from an ATM machine revealed that the assailant had come from the direction of the FDR drive. The agents deputed a few plainclothes and placed the FDR drive and the grocery store on surveillance. The crane driver and the security guard helped the agents with the sketches, of course.'

'Of course.'

'Three days after the surveillance had commenced, the assailant came back to the grocery store. The agents clicked a few real time pictures and videos before following him back to his abode. The FBI had the driver and the security guard confirm the assailant's identity and within minutes, a SWAT team reached the assailant's trailer and apprehended him.'

The signal went green and the Mustang roared ahead.

'The assailant's profile matched with the footage taken near Foley Square.'

The mustang took a left turn and pulled up in front of Jimmy, the street vendor.

'A few days after failed polygraphs, brain wave analysis and intense questioning, he confessed that a certain person who met him at the grocery store on Montgomery Street coerced him to do it.'

'He didn't ask for witness protection?'

'Oh yes. He did. I don't know what he is called now. That is why I'm addressing him as the assailant.'

'Here you go, gentlemen,' said Jimmy and brought them all a bagel and cold coffee.

'Hey Jimmy, thank you very much,' said Thomas and grabbed what Jim had to offer.

'I'll be right with you,' said Rupert and sent him back. Rupert then asked Bru to continue.

'They took the footage of the said date from the grocery store and had it analysed. The assailant identified the coercer.'

'Porter Hill.'

'Yes. The transactions were looked up and Hill was dumb enough to use his credit card. The FBI rhetorically contacted the credit card company and obtained Porter's address.'

'Fishy. Why would Hill use his credit card? I mean his plan was so precise and elaborate...'

'He wanted the driver and the security dead. Remember? He didn't know that they'd survive. Thanks to the wrecked old car.'

'I don't know.'

CHAPTER 8

Air Force One flew the Vice President back to the United States from Santa Maria. Immediately after arriving in D.C, VP Jamie Edwards delivered a stunning speech to his fellow Americans. His reputation was exemplified and the media portrayed him as 'The Napoleon of the United States'. He had now become a phenomenon and the word on every street of the United States.

Jamie assured the Americans that Nahiossi would be extradited and that he would be tried for the murder of Senator Vaughn Fletcher.

He said,

'The man who made the Americans proud, the man who made us reach the skies and the man who lived for the betterment of America, faced death in the most gruesome manner. I don't see Vaughn as a senator, but as a brother, a visionary and a mentor. My heart reaches out to him and his daughter, who was his only family. I assure you that Justice will be served. We will extradite Mr. Griffiths and try him for the gruesome murder of our fellow American. We aren't in the ancient times where hierarchy was deemed necessary. We live in a democratic country, a country where we represent you, the people. We need to break the diplomatic shackles and raise our voices unanimously against the problems this country is facing. We've endured too many crimes and attacks of terror over the past few years and

every time something massive happened, people poured in to express their support and grief. But eventually, as all humans do, they moved on. We don't care as long as somebody else is victimised. We don't care as long as we are safe. We don't care so long as we get what we want. That is the problem this country is facing and that is making us vulnerable. We, the government, have formulated various agencies and laws to prevent crimes, and yet there has been an increase in the crime statistics. My dear brothers and sisters, we need to understand that the politicians alone cannot help bring about a revolution. The people must raise their voices. Not only when something massive happens, but before something terrible could befall us. We cannot give back the innocent children who were most unfortunately victimised in shootouts to the parents, who'd have had various dreams regarding their child's future, we can't give happiness to the children who were orphaned, we can't give back what the victims grievously lost as a consequence of terror attacks, we can't give back the brave law enforcement agents and the defense personnel who died, fighting to save this country and neither can we give the criminals and the perpetrators the right to freedom. I can offer nothing but condolence to these victims and reassure them that they won't be forgotten, for every American is my brother. Yesterday's happenings have again alerted us that we are weak and vulnerable. We need to recuperate, we need to stand together and fight corruption, sexual harassments, abuse of power, plagiarism, drugs, homicide and terrorism. The strength of the society lies with the people, not with the politicians. You decide the fate of our motherland. You decide the future of this great country. You have the ultimate power. We need to bring a radical change in the society. We need to advance, metamorphosize and evolve. We need a new age renaissance and we owe it to America. Thank you.'

Vice President Jamie Edwards, after he had delivered his speech, met with the President, the National Security Advisor, the Deputy of Homeland Security, the Secretary of State, the Secretary of Defense, the director of CIA, the Attorney General, the commander of the Defense Clandestine Services and various other bureaucrats at the Roosevelt Room in the West Wing of the White House. Appreciations were extended, and then they got down to business.

The government had just learnt from their agents at the American Embassy in Lisbon that Nahiossi had pleaded guilty both to the murder and the hijacking. But as procedure demanded, the magistrate at Lisbon had exercised his discretion to hold Nahiossi for a period of two months, within which time the investigating team had to come up with some stipulated evidence. Once the evidence was forwarded to the OIA, Nahiossi would be again produced before the court at Lisbon and tried according to their Civil Procedure Code. The concerned court would determine his guilt and the extraditability, and then the OIA would notify the prosecutor and the U.S Customs, and arrange with the United States Marshals Service to escort him to the United States.

Thursday, February 23rd 2006.

The Puerto Rico born Lieutenant Governor of New York, Mariano Castillo, had a cousin who owned a meat storage facility in Delaware. It was here, in this factory, that the shocking case of the Lieutenant Governor's money fencing scam was exposed to the citizens of the United States.

Agent Parker's team had apprehended the drivers on the day after they decided to waylay. They employed numerous tactics – good cop, bad cop, jeopardy, food and water embargo and of course, intense fatal questioning. But nothing seemed to work the way they expected it to. This was Agent Parker's final assignment as a field agent and he wanted to retire in style. He didn't want to mask his successful career with an unsolved heist. So after numerous wake-up calls and warnings, the team unwittingly resorted to the dreadful *Guantanamo-type torture technique.*

The drivers were tied hand and foot in an arduous manner that made it impossible for them to sit. They were made to stand for twenty hours straight, urinating and defecating on themselves.

The first exposé was made in the twenty first hour. The Bronx-driver confessed to the aiding and abetting and told them that a certain guy from Delaware had hired them to commit the heist. The confirmation came from two more drivers within a five-minute buffer. Then when Parker told the other three drivers about the confession of their colleagues, they snapped and gave their confessions.

That very evening, Agent Parker arrested the three drivers "legally". The next morning, they were produced in front of a federal judge and a request for the witness protection programme was extended. In due course, the Department of Justice agreed to their request, and the US Marshals Service was asked to carry out the phasing out procedures.

Once the drivers learnt about the initiation of the programme, they gave their recollection of the Delawarean to the sketch artists. Simultaneously, a tech team worked on the Smith and Wesson's Identiti-Kit and produced the facial composite of the Delawarean, which was to a large extent consistent with the sketch artist's handiwork. The guy was cross-referenced with the Bureau database and within seconds, they had a hit. The Bureau had money transfer trails and the drivers' report on the background check of their employer to support the arrest of the Delawarean employer.

Agent Parker put together a team and flew down to Delaware. They reached a meat storage facility situated off the city limits and nabbed the employer. The agents seized the facility and began their inch-by-inch search, while the Delawarean was flown back by the Marshals to New York. Legally.

After four days of taxing scrutiny, the investigators found the "piggy bank".

The IBNS-stained currency notes, jewellery and a couple of thousand notified bank notes were found in plastic bags that were stuffed inside a dozen unfortunate pigs. The Delawarean strongly objected the discovery. He repeatedly took the stand that the said pigs stored in his facility had very recently been delivered and that neither he nor his cousin had anything to do with it. But the FBI morphed the theory and made it self-incriminating. They theorised it exuberantly and Agent Parker showed up with the Delawarean and Castillo in every American newspaper.

Now he was ready to dissociate with the FBI.

And PiCorp was ready to associate with him.

Friday, April 1st 2005

Heinrich Schüler, the *deputierte* to the *Führer* of the Fourth *Reich,* saw off the accounting, business, chemical, cost, financial, intelligence, industrial, marketing, news, public, quantitative and military analysts at the Karwendel airstrip. The leading intellectuals had just met the *Führer* and proposed the next step of infiltration. Their part of the job was done. They could go back to their families and normal life again. They wouldn't be summoned for at least one more month.

'*Sie gerade verlassen,*' said Schüler over his phone, as the United Front's Learjet took off the tarmac.

Schüler clicked off his phone and nodded at a maintenance worker, who said something to someone over a handheld transreceiver. Momentarily a Ranger Rover emerged out of the lush green forests and entered the airstrip. The Schutzstaffel (SS) guarding the exit points of the strip gave a *Seig Heil* as the Rover passed by. Three heavily-built men jumped out of it, and then the burly *Gruppenführer* Dr. Karl Norbert stepped out. He had disappointed the *Führer*. He had messed up the execution of Ilarion Wasyl and now he was called to redeem the mistake.

Dr. Norbert extended a salute to Schüler and waited for his captive. The bodyguards clad in black overalls stood behind Dr. Norbert with an upright assertive position and scanned the surroundings. The buzz of the engines was momentarily heard and the Learjet drew closer to the airstrip. The ground crew drove the stair cars to the taxiway once the plane landed. They had the stairs neatly aligned with the door and they waited for the passengers to disembark.

Soon, Anastasia walked down the stairs, ushered by Dr. Norbert's men who were assigned with the assassination mission.

'Beautiful,' said Schüler out loud the moment he saw Anastasia and took her nervous hands. 'The lady will come with me. Meet me at the Berghof,' he added, and escorted her to his transport.

Dr. Norbert and his men hastily yet not devoid of decorum, left the airstrip and climbed back into their Rovers. Schüler placed a call to one of the guards at Berghof and informed him of their arrival. He then dismissed his bodyguards and sent them over to Dr. Norbert.

The Berghof was the *Führer's* residence. It was obscured from the public and kept out of the governmental documents/records. Leading security companies had installed every other surveillance equipment around the *Führer's Helm,* and committed technicians monitored these feeds every other second of the day. No one could even get past the first of the four security posts without the *Führer's* primary security officer's approval.

This was where the *Führer* of the Fourth *Reich* propounded his elaborate and methodic plan to conquer the World and to fulfill the *Reichshanzker's* destiny.

CHAPTER 9

Thursday, November 22nd 2007

'The Vice President told us that some thugs kidnapped him from the Edwardian Suite of the Plaza at around 9:00 PM, which is almost a half hour prior to the Senator's murder. The Secret Service investigated the scene and concluded that the thugs were in the suite even before the arrival of the Vice President and that they had proper means to escape from the window at the restroom. Now we have two main questions. How did they manage to get into the suite and who hired them to do it? The former question is to be answered by the Secret Service. We are more concerned with the 'who' aspect of the question and I'm afraid that the answer is a little tricky,' said Agent Mason confidently and scanned the faces of those gathered on the 23rd floor of the Federal Plaza.

'Now I'm just going to go through our theory and correlate it with the facts and physical evidence. If you feel that something is inconsistent or I'm being incoherent, you can interrupt me. Sound good?'

The forensic experts, Special Agents Marco, Special Agent Ottosson and ADIC Camargo expressed their agreement by means of a simple, silent nod. Agent Mason took a sip of ice-cold water and waited for the projector to project the selected slide from his laptop.

A couple of seconds later, the name Nahiossi Griffiths appeared on the wall.

Agent Mason cleared his throat and began to present his theory.

'We take the stand that Mr. Griffiths, with full knowledge and sane mind, committed the murder of Mr. Fletcher. Now what made us so sure about it? Well let's see, first comes the motive. Did Mr. Griffiths have the motive to murder the senator? Yes and no. He had the motive to murder Vaughn - the father and Vaughn - the businessman. But he didn't have the motive or the intention to murder Vaughn - the senator.'

The people around the conference table grumbled and Agent Mason gave them some time to discuss. Once the noise died out and the silence was restored, he continued.

'We have from Ms. Juliette's affidavit that her father and her boyfriend weren't on good terms for a very long time. Note that I used the word 'father' instead of senator. I purposefully did so in order to emphasise the part that Mr. Griffiths (a boyfriend), murdered his girlfriend's father owing to personal relational disputes.'

Certain objections emerged from the table, but Agent Mason turned a deaf ear to them all. He slightly raised his voice and proceeded with his theory.

'Is that it? Is it all based on a simple matter of a relationship? The answer is no. It isn't completely based on this idea, but it surely is one of the factors.'

The noise gradually died down again. The reactionaries just scribbled down the objections on their jotting pads and intently tried to listen to Agent Mason.

'The major shareholder of the Phoenix Almonte Group and the CEO of the Group's European fleet had disputes over the terms of merger/acquisition. The Chairman of the Phoenix-Almonte group, Dr. Cortez stated in his affidavit that Mr. Griffiths' pestering with the company's books had become extremely intolerable. Allegedly, Mr. Griffiths didn't trust the American Board of Directors. He was under the false pretense that the board was embezzling. We had the Securities and Exchange Commission take a look at their books and they found no evidence supporting Mr. Griffiths' conspiracy. We learnt from the Board of Directors that even though the agreement clearly stated that the American shareholders were entitled to hold 51% stakes in the company and that the threshold for the European shareholders was 49%, Mr. Griffiths failed to abide by the terms and conditions. An internal investigation conducted by the SEC after Mr. Griffiths' escape tells us that Mr. Griffiths was a Black Knight. In stock market terms, a person who destroys or who is in the pursuit of destroying a company or business is called a Black Knight. I learnt from one of my contacts at the Commission that typically a Black Knight would enter a business/company as an influential person such as a major investor or a member of the board of directors. Eventually, the Black Knight would undertake dealings to enrich themselves, which normally leaves the previously profitable company in a weaker financial position. Now the financial books of the Phoenix Music Company shows us that Mr. Griffiths had his American aides buy the Group's assets at below market price and he bought certain assets of different companies at inflated prices. The Chairman of the Group, Mr. Cortez, and the American board concluded via internal investigations that Mr. Griffiths was prepping for a hostile takeover. He was to create a synergy.'

'But the statute prevents him from owning more than 7% of the company's stock,' said Special Agent Marco.

'Yes. Presently. But once he finds his White Knight, a friendly American Businessmen, they'd take over the Group together. Then the Black and White would create new rules making them and their families the emperors of the Group for eternity.'

'That's possible.'

'It is, Special Agent Marco. Now this evidently shows us that there was a professional antagonism between the majority shareholder Mr. Fletcher and the CEO, Mr. Griffiths.'

The committee appreciated this assessment. They scribbled a few key points and waited for Agent Mason to continue. But before he could do so, SA Ottosson shot a question, 'What did Mr. Cortez's board do about it? Have they filed a complaint?'

'I'm afraid not. The merger happened after a lot of critical debates and serious oppositions. Nothing of this magnitude has ever happened before. This was the inception of a new sort of business enterprise, a new way to bring the technology and resources together and a new way to bind the two major powers of the world. Mr. Cortez's Board wouldn't do anything that would jeopardise their reputation.'

'So you didn't really get into that line of questioning. You are just putting yourself in Cortez's shoes and hypothetically assuming the situation.'

'I beg to differ, SA Ottosson. I did ask the same question you asked me to Dr. Cortez and he said that they were hoping to resolve the issue verbally on the 1st of October.'

'Can we find that modicum in your files?'

'Of course, SA Ottosson.'

'Okay, we'll look into it.'

'By all means. Could I continue?'

SA Ottosson gave him the go and Agent Mason was again back on track.

'All right. Now we have two reasons to believe that Mr. Griffiths murdered Mr. Fletcher. Not Senator Fletcher, Mr. Fletcher, just another citizen of the United States'

'Logically, I'd agree with you. But the law is going to see it as the murder of a high-level government servant.'

'By all means. I'm just stating my views. That's all.'

'We appreciate it, Agent Mason. Please do proceed.'

'On the day of the murder, the Senator called Mr. Griffiths and Mr. Cortez to discuss the inhospitable situation prior the Board meet. Fletcher had also called upon the Vice President, but as always his schedule was jam-packed.'

'Yes. We already know that Agent Mason.'

'My apologies, Mr. Camargo,' said Agent Mason and added, 'Moving on now, Mr. Griffiths was under a shitload of pressure and he couldn't handle it any longer. He had two options, one, leave the company and go into hiding in disgrace. Two, kill both the majority share holders - '

' - In which case the share prices would go down, the Board of Directors would freak out, the employee's pay would be cut down and there would be chaos,' said one of the experts.

'Precisely. Then Mr. Griffiths would have his comrade takeover the Group. Simple,' said Mason and waited for the information to settle.

He then said, 'But fortunately Dr. Cortez had to meet with a scientist from CERN at the Almonte Research Lab. So he showed up almost a half hour past the time of appointment - '

' - By which time Mr. Griffiths had already murdered the senator,' said SA Marco.

'I'm afraid not. It should have been "By which time Mr. Griffiths had already poisoned Mr. Fletcher". He murdered him only after he saw Dr. Cortez.'

'As per your theory - '

' - Forensic reports and affidavits,' added Agent Mason and gave a slight smirk, which Marco didn't notice.

'I'd now like to answer SA Marco's question as to why Mr. Griffiths would leave so much evidence. Now that I've told you that the murder was premeditated, the question gains more weight.'

'Yes it does,' said SA Marco, feeling elated.

Agent Mason ignored the comment. He changed the slide and it now displayed two columns. One of them said, 'intentional', the other one said 'incidental'.

'I hope that the thought as to why Mr. Griffiths had to stab Mr. Fletcher after he had already poisoned him, occurred to everyone,' he said, and looked around. Poker faces.

'We presume that the poisoning was the 'intentional' part and the stabbing the 'incidental'. Now let us quickly and briefly walk through the days' events. The Senator met with the Vice President at the Plaza that morning at around 8 AM. The two had breakfast at the Edwardian Suite and at 10:30, they went down to the New York State Capitol. They stayed there till sundown and then went back to the Plaza. At around 7:00, the Vice President headed off to a charity ball and the Senator headed back to the Manor. Mr. Fletcher reached the Manor by 7:45 and confined himself to his study.'

The time appeared on the screen - 7:45, and below it, came the names of the concerned people and their locations/alibis at the said time.

7:45 PM.

Vaughn Fletcher – Fletcher Manor.

'The Vice President finished his contributions and left the Rockefeller Centre at around 8:30. He reached the Plaza by 8:45 and confined himself to his suite.'

Jamie Edwards – The Plaza.

'Mr. Griffiths and Ms. Juliette were on a date in Central Park. Ms. Juliette told us that it was their first anniversary as a couple and that was the place where they had gone on their first date.'

Nahiossi Griffiths – Central Park.

Juliette Fletcher – Central Park.

'Mr. Cortez, as I said earlier, was meeting up with a scientist from CERN at the Almonte Research Lab.'

Montego Cortez – Almonte Research Lab.

'And the butler, Jordan, was in the kitchen, cooking.'

Jordan – Kitchen.

'These are all the people who were at the Manor that day around the time of Mr. Fletcher's murder.'

'What about the maid servants?'

'Their shift ends at 6:00 PM.'

'The security?'

'They were at their posts. We have closed circuit footages to support the fact.'

Agent Ottosson gazed at the screen for a couple of minutes and then asked Agent Mason to proceed.

'Now the plan. Mr. Griffiths would finish his date with Ms. Juliette and head back to the Manor, alone. Ms. Juliette was to stay at the Ritz-Carlton.'

'Because?' asked SA Ottosson.

'Because it was their anniversary and they wanted to spend the night together at the Ritz.'

'Obviously,' said SA Marco.

'Mr. Griffiths needed Jordan to stay in the manor. So he didn't think of any plan to shake him off.'

'Why did he need him?'

'We'll know that soon enough, SA Marco. Now as per Mr. Griffiths' original plan, after reaching the manor, he'd go over to Mr. Fletcher's study, accompanied by Mr. Cortez. He'd sit through the discussion patiently, and then during the fag end of the meeting, open up the champagne bottle that had Strychnine mixed into it. He'd play the bartender and subsequently play his 'anniversary card' to get away from the Manor. Obviously Jordan would see Mr. Fletcher and Mr. Cortez walking down the stairs with

Mr. Griffiths. The composition and dosage of Strychnine was such that the reaction would start only an hour after Mr. Griffiths' egression. But by then Mr. Griffiths would have Ms. Juliette call Jordan and ask him to get down to the Ritz with a certain file or something. Anyway the point is that no one would be at the Manor when the two Almonteyers would start experiencing the effects of Strychnine poisoning - spasms, convolutions, lactic acidosis, hyperthermia, rhabdomyolysis and postictal depressions. These would eventually paralyse the neural system and lead to asphyxiation, implying death,' said Mason, and turned towards SA Marco and asked, 'Does that fit under "A man of his stature would have been more careful"?' asked Nelson to SA Marco.

'I think so.'

'Let me make it more intricate. The next time I ask you that question you'd swear on your mother's grave that Mr. Griffiths had a very intelligent plan.'

'My mother is still alive, Agent.'

'I didn't say dead mother's grave. Anyway Mr. Griffiths needed Jordan to, one, help him with the 'saw them alive while he left the house' situation. Two, Mr. Griffiths would ask Juliette to call Jordan only a half hour after he left. So for a full thirty minutes Jordan would have seen the two men alive. That testimony of his could be of great help to Mr. Griffiths and three, the investigators would assume the possibility that after Mr. Griffiths left, Jordan poisoned them. The investigation would be set off course for a few days, by which time he could easily fly down to the Netherlands without any pandemonium.'

'That sounds just fine,' said SA Ottosson. A new slide popped up and a timeline appeared.

'It sure does, SA Ottosson. Now Dr. Kelly found the fingerprints on the knife, cloth hanging along the stone wall, the compound wall, the canine and the gate in the adjoining villa. As to the shoeprints, they were found inside the room, on the stone wall, on the pathway, on the compound wall and in the adjoining villa. Observe that none of these figure in the 'intentional' part. Well except for the shoeprints inside the room. Agreed?'

The response was good. ADIC Camargo was really happy.

'So the aftermath of the 'intentional' part of the plan would reveal that Mr. Fletcher and Mr. Cortez died due to poisoning. But the investigators would never find the source. Mr. Griffiths would have brought the champagne with him in his briefcase and would have taken it back in the same briefcase. He would have cleaned the glasses and had them reinstalled on the bar-rack. And of course the brand of champagne would be one of those brands that were usually available at Mr. Fletcher's bar.'

A new slide rolled down and under the heading 'Aftermath of the intentional plan', came the line *No evidence of the source.*

'Then the investigating team would work on the timeline. Jordan's account of Mr. Griffiths' 'activity around the time of death' and Juliette's alibi would shift a major portion of the liability off Mr. Griffiths. He would still be in the list of suspects, no doubt. But it would certainly not zero in on him.'

Witness statement.

Alibi.

'Then Mr. Griffiths would have made Jordan disappear and made it look like Jordan was fleeing from the FBI. I want you to remember that it wasn't difficult for Mr. Griffiths to do so. He had a few thugs in his pockets. Thugs who had the balls to kidnap the Vice President. Nabbing Jordan would hardly qualify as difficult, relatively.'

Frame Jordan.

Derail investigation.

'Jordan would eventually be found at a hotel or something. Dead, of course. He'd have a suicide note confessing to the crime. Then we'd wrap up the case, come with some bizarre theory and greatly mourn the Senator's death. Maybe declare a state-wide holiday for a day or two.'

The team laughed at his sarcasm and the ADIC appeared to be content with the theory.

'I'd certainly ask you look into Mr. Griffiths more seriously. He had the motive,' said SA Marco.

'We figured out the motives by connecting the dots backwards. It just blends with the theory, adds more credit to it. Assuming that everything panned out as per Mr. Griffiths' original idea, we wouldn't be talking about the relationship part of the motive since Ms. Juliette wouldn't have talked about it. Mr. Fletcher and Mr. Cortez were the only two people she cared about, apart from Mr. Griffiths that is. With both of them dead, she wouldn't rat out the only other person she cared about and she definitely wouldn't think that Mr. Griffiths was behind the murder. She'd say, "It was our anniversary. He was with me when my dad died. He has nothing to do with it. Yes, there were misunderstandings, but that doesn't mean that they didn't care for each other. Every family has misunderstandings. That is the essence of a familial relationship. It helps us bond furthermore".'

'He is right,' said SA Ottosson.

'Thank you, Special Agent. And as to the business part, it is entirely based on Mr. Cortez's affidavit and a few unsolicited internal investigation reports. Obviously we wouldn't have Cortez's affidavit and we most certainly wouldn't use the unsolicited reports. And as to the SEC reports, it wouldn't serve the purpose of pinning down Mr. Griffiths for Mr. Fletcher's murder. He would probably be tried for some illegal trading. But apart from that, we wouldn't have much on him.'

'There is also the possibility that he might have shredded all the incriminating documents and reports the very next day.'

'SA Marco, if you had asked him to unnecesssarily look into Mr. Griffiths, then I would have said, "When you have a man who confessed to the crime and when that man had a motive or the man who coerced him to do so had the motive, and when there was enough physical evidence to pin that man, why the hell would you want to go gallivanting on an alternate path wherein the alleged perp has a clean background, enough alibis and no association with the physical evidence found at the crime scene?" Uncle Sam has plenty of wealth in his pockets. Doesn't mean we can keep draining it unnecessarily.'

'Thank you, Mr. Camargo. Assuming the worst-case condition, Mr. Griffiths could have easily flown back to the Netherlands. We wouldn't have been able to just hold him here, and once there things would have gotten simpler for him.'

'And extremely difficult for us.'

'And his aide would be running the industry.'

'I swear on my mother's grave that Mr. Griffiths had a very intelligent plan.'

Friday, March 3rd 2006.

'Mariano Castillo hired six distraught taxicab drivers who were formerly working in Georgia and a bunch of corrupt police officers from Puerto Rico to commit the heist. We cannot disclose the names of the drivers since they are being processed for witness protection,' said Agent Parker to his superiors at 26 Federal Plaza. His team had solved 'the armored truck robbery case' and were now laying out the specifics of the investigation to the Federal attorneys handling the case, *People State of New York v. Mariano Castillo.*

'The Lieutenant Governor needed some money to help his friends in Puerto Rico with their drug trade. In particular a dealer named Emilio. Well-known by the title *Patrón.* According to the DEA (Drug Enforcement Administration) report, a large portion of Emilio's network was recently torn down. An anonymous post had been delivered to their agency, which contained a list of 15 locations where methamphetamine and heroin were being cooked. The

DEA called upon the FBI SWAT, and together they took down all 15 of them. They recovered drugs worth six million dollars, ready for disposal. They shut down the hot spots and had twenty-three dealers arrested. It was reported that Emilio fled from Puerto Rico soon after he got the news. So we think that Castillo was trying to help him out. That is the motive.'

Motive: Helping to keep afloat an illegal drug trade.

'Now, the case.'

'Mr. Castillo had CATS recruit the Georgians two months before the heist. The Georgian drivers provided original IDs of non-existing people. Of course Mr. Castillo's name isn't on any papers, but the drivers told us that a certain man had them join CATS in January. We'll learn about that man shortly.'

'Are the drivers going to confess to the same in court?'

'Yes, Special Agent Kramer. But provided their witness protection programme is approved by the DOJ.'

Special Agent Kramer shot a glance at Judge J. B. Walberg and smiled.

'Please do continue,' said Walberg, trying not to answer the question. Committing six felons to witness protection who were a part of a colossal heist was extremely cumbersome. Judge Walberg didn't want to publicly disclose the DOJ's mélange. So he simply chose to dodge any question that might come his way until the DOJ had a final answer.

'Um, okay. The Georgians blended with the agency for about two months before the commission of the crime. Then on D-day they were asked to stop the truck at a certain location for a few brief minutes, during which time the police officers from Puerto Rico, dressed in DHS uniforms, would show up and transfer all the contents in the truck to their cars. Since it was the Department of Homeland Security, people wouldn't panic and call 911 to report a crime. So the getaway part was pretty easy.'

'Very thoughtful.'

'The drivers drove for another half hour or so and then stopped the trucks. The CATS' control unit learnt that the GPS on their company's armoured truck was stationary for a contentious duration of time. So they went down to the six locations after alerting the police. Our FBI team eventually got down to the six locations and began the investigations. We traced numerous leads for days, but everything lead to dead ends. Then on the 14th the drivers came to the 1st Precinct and surrendered. They told us that they'd confess to the crimes and point us to the handler if we assured them witness protection. We forwarded the request to the DOJ and assured them that the application would be duly processed.'

'Do we have the names and identities of the Puerto Ricans?'

'Yes, Mr. Walberg, we have it and two of them might testify against Mr. Castillo.'

'Excellent. Okay, go on.'

'We had the drivers assess the DOJ report and then made them tell us about their hirer. The drivers didn't know their hirer's name or identity. But they had seen his face. So we had them help us with the sketch, and then we traced the money to Mr. Castillo's cousin in Delaware.'

'Okay, so after the heist the police officers posing as DHS agents transported the money to Delaware and had them stashed at the meat storage factory.'

'That is correct, SA Kramer. We found certain fingerprints embedded into the IBNS stained notes and the prints led us to Mr. Castillo. We took him under custody and had the Financial Crime Section check his bank transactions. They FCS stumbled upon a certain slush fund. They joined hands with the FEC (Federal Election Commission) and put Mr. Castillo's Campaign Secretaries on the radar. A few days later they found out that the money was transferred from a certain company named Nixon. We then had the SEC look into Nixon and found out that it was an illegal shell company. So we arrived at the conclusion that Mr. Castillo had the money robbed and then transferred to his account through an illegal shell company.'

'That's a nice theory. But how does Mr. Castillo or his cousin plead?'

'Not guilty.'

'Of course. What about the police officers?'

'Some plead guilty, some plead not guilty.'

'Cliché.'

'I'm afraid so.'

'Agent Parker, is that it?' asked Justice Walberg curiously.

'Yes, Mr. Walberg. But allow me to recapitulate.'

'Go on. Make it real quick.'

'Six drivers and two of the twelve police officers plead guilty to the crime and testify against Mr. Castillo. We have a few stained banknotes, bank notes whose serial numbers match with the flagged notes and a few jewels found at Mr. Castillo's cousin's meat storage factory as physical evidences. Also we have Mr. Castillo's fingerprint on one such note. The FCS report shows us that slush funds was transferred to Mr. Castillo's bank, the FEC reports tells us about the involvement of Nixon and the SEC report gives an account of the money laundering. These and the motive clearly tells us that the Lieutenant Governor Mr. Castillo was involved with the robbery.'

'Even if he pleads otherwise.'

Friday, September 28th 2007.

Rupert and Thomas sat on a couch at the lobby of McKinley Towers and waited for the elevators to be totally isolated. It was around 8:30 am and the employees of nine enterprises occupying the twenty floors of the McKinley Towers were pouring in.

'Rup, what the hell are we doing here? We are supposed to investigate a case, not sit in the lobby and stare at people.'

Rupert didn't respond. He just sat and stared at the elevators.

'Forget it. I'm calling Angelika.'

'No you won't. So long as you want us to work together, you won't call her.'

'I already hit the call button.'

Rupert leaned forwards and snatched away his brother's phone. He cut the call and switched the phone off.

'What the hell...'

'Come, let's go. That elevator is empty,' said Rupert and sprinted towards an elevator situated at the far right corner of the lobby.

'Rupert, give me back my phone.'

'Will you just shut the fuck up and come with me? Don't make me have you thrown out of this place,' groaned Rupert and pressed Thomas's arm.

Thomas was anguished. But he didn't want to fight with his brother. So he stopped retaliating and decided to just do whatever Rupert asked him to.

As they walked towards the elevator, Rupert called the maintenance officer of the building and said, 'June, the Burrow.' He then clicked off the phone and stepped into the elevator, with only his brother by his side. The CCTV cameras inside the particular elevator were turned off and once the doors closed, the elevator began to descend.

'There is a floor below minus two?' asked Thomas quizzically.

'Yes. This is where I work complicated cases. It is my clandestine workspace. I call it the Burrow. No one can go down there without my permission. It's impossible,' said Rupert as the doors opened to a darkened corridor.

Rupert pressed the button marked 'G' on the elevator keypad and stepped out of the car. The doors of the elevators closed and then it lifted off.

'Does this place have lights? I can't see anything,' freaked Thomas.

'Don't talk. Just stay here,' said Rupert and shushed his brother. He took a few steps ahead, leaving behind Thomas and walked inside the pitch-black corridor. He reached a heavy steel door and hit a button at the top right corner. A camera on the door shot an infrared image of Rupert and pushed it to Jimmy's phone.

Jim White saw the photograph, and having confirmed it as Rupert, entered the access code to turn on the lights that lined the corridor. The lights turned the corridor alive and revealed a huge steel door.

The entrance to the Burrow was through a bulletproof steel door, capable of stopping even Magnum 57 bullets. The door offered anti-fire protection, reluctance to cutting/welding equipment and the use of explosives. It had two inboard engines and locks in ten places with .75-inch pins on all sides of the door.

Rupert entered a 10-digit passcode and had his retina scanned. Immediately certain clicks and clanks were heard as the engines moved some gears and unlocked the .75-inch pins. Half a minute later, Rupert and Thomas entered the Burrow and the door automatically locked behind them. The lights and the IR cameras in the corridor were turned off and a steel door reeled from two slits, locking the elevator chamber below basement number two.

'I didn't know that you were so paranoid.'

'Of course you think I'm paranoid. You are totally ignorant of what this place houses.'

'Doesn't make you any less paranoid.'

'Now you most certainly won't get access to the inner depths of this place. You have once again exuberantly proved that you are unreliable and remarkably useless,' said Rupert and angrily guided him through the Burrow.

The Burrow had two levels. The upper lever had a magnanimous library, filled with various court transcripts, investigation reports, census repots, newspapers, databases and archives of various important files and documents ranging from the details of John. F. Kennedy to Adolf Hitler to Joseph Stalin to Martin Luther to Osama Bin Laden. The lower level had a huge empty wall, with a movable ladder standing at a corner. There were three wide screen computers with Internet access via cable. There was a mini-bar and a kitchen at one of the corners on the side opposite to that of the wide empty wall and next to it was a restroom. There was a couch a few feet off the computers and a huge mahogany table adorned the center of the hall. There were no clocks, no mobile phone access, no television and no photographs. Both the floors were centrally air-conditioned and the oxygen levels were suitably maintained.

'This place is amazing Rupert. I've never been here before.'

'I'm sure you haven't.'

'I bet that Wolf helped you with this.'

'Yes, indeed. He set this up when I was working for him. Before I got to know that he was my father.'

'And you are still using it. Never mind. I'm going to go make us some coffee. Let's get started with the investigation.'

'Okay. Suit yourself,' said Rupert and walked towards the wall. He simply stood in front of it and searched for answers.

A few minutes later, Thomas and Rupert drank a cup of coffee and ate some hot dogs. They chatted about some old cases and had a few laughs. It had been ages since they talked to each other jovially. They had many painstaking responsibilities and jam-packed schedules. They hardly met and when they did, they seldom spoke about anything but work. Today they kept their minds light for some time and discussed each other's lives. They downed a few cups of coffee and then involuntarily fell asleep.

Who said sleep is a symptom of coffee deprivation?

CHAPTER 10

Monday, October 29th 2007

An Unknown Man with a grim voice, who drove Nahiossi to LaGuardia after the senator's murder, handed over a letter to him from a centimetre wide gap on the upper portion of the tinted window. His identity was completely obscured because of the window, and he asked Nahiossi to go over the frame up story. Nahiossi hesitantly climbed into the car and after placing the call to LaGuardia, began reading the bizarre letter. The letter was written from Nahiossi's point of view and it read,

"I came home from the Ritz-Carlton and headed to Vaughn's study, just as planned. But when I got there, I found out that Montego wouldn't be joining us until after 9:30. I didn't know what to do. I had everything planned out elaborately and I didn't want to push it to another day because I was afraid that Vaughn would use his power to produce evidence against me to the board and have me thrown out of my own company. So I decided to wait. We spoke for some time and then I opened my briefcase to retrieve some files regarding the shares that I'd sold to my friends at the Phoenix Music Company. While I was at it, my dad called me. So I left the briefcase open and excused myself. In the meantime, Vaughn took the bottle of champagne from my briefcase and poured himself a drink. He figured that I would anyway give it to him later. When I hung up the call with my dad and returned to Vaughn's study, I didn't really notice the champagne bottle missing from my briefcase. The briefcase was already shut and the files were out on the table. So I just kept my briefcase aside and began to discuss the case. Also, I didn't really think much about the champagne bottle on the table. There were already quite a few bottles of the same brand on the table.

We discussed the SEC reports and the share prices for some time and then, all of a sudden, he began vomiting and before I could contemplate this as an effect of poisoning, he called out for Jordan. Jordan immediately ran upstairs only to find Vaughn vomiting blood on the floor and having serious spasms. He ran downstairs to the kitchen to call for help. But it hit me that if Vaughn was taken to the hospital in time and if the doctors would save his life, then I would be facing charges for conspiracy to murder because Vaughn knew that whatever happened to him was an effect of the champagne which he took from my briefcase. I obviously didn't want to be caught. So I ran downstairs and beat Jordan up. I stopped him from calling for help. I dragged him to the kitchen and left him there and as I was returning to Vaughn's study, I saw Montego getting out of his car. Now I was really in trouble. I couldn't just run away. If I did, Vaughn would be saved and I'd go to prison. I couldn't even stay there and pretend that I didn't do anything because eventually they'd find out through Vaughn that I poisoned him. Again, I'd end up in prison. So at the nick of the moment, I ran upstairs and locked myself inside Vaughn's study. I wasn't sure whether I was going to stay or flee. But at that moment I thought that getting rid of the champagne bottle was a good idea. Even if Vaughn blamed me for poisoning him, the police wouldn't have any evidence to prove the same. So instead of putting it in my briefcase, I wrapped it up in my blazer and threw it out of the window. Then Jordan came to my mind. I'd just beaten him up and he had also seen me with Vaughn. I just stood there and thought of just running away and flying off to the Netherlands. But

I knew that I wouldn't be able to reach Netherlands unless I had leverage. So I called one of my contacts and told him to kidnap Jamie from the Plaza.

As I ended the call, Vaughn took my briefcase off the table and hit me with it. I impulsively picked up the knife that was kept on the table right next to me and stabbed him. I had murdered him and it didn't go as I had planned. I really didn't have much to do. I knew that I had made a huge mistake. I knew that my life was over. But I didn't want to die. So I took a few tablecloths from Vaughn's cupboard and thought of escaping through the window. Just then the banging on the door became intense and I knew that I couldn't stay there any longer. So I just abseiled down the wall. Then I noticed that my coat had landed just a few feet off the wall. So I took it with me and escaped from the Manor. You know the rest."

Thunderbird was the code name of PiCorp's Elite Team Seven (PETS). Six of the seven agents were a part of Special Activities Division (SAD) of the CIA. In 1985, they were deployed to El Salvador during Duarte's presidency and this unfortunately turned out to be their last deployment as CIA agents.

A United States-backed strategy, reported in 1985, created 12 free-fire zones in the northern Chalatenango province. The U.S Reconnaissance flights backed the El Salvador Air Force, and together they bombarded rebel-held zones and caused the deaths of hundreds of civilians. Serious allegations were thrown around and the U.S Defense Secretary sent six CIA agents to investigate the matter and to resolve it. But little did he know about the secret torture camps that a certain military personnel independently ran with the Salvadorians. The agents probed the issue and acquired intelligence regarding the routine use of twenty-nine different types of torture techniques applied to political prisoners, and that U.S. military advisers often supervised and sometimes participated in the said barbaric interrogations. The advisors feared that they would be charged with war crimes. So they tricked the agents to a certain village and conducted another aerial bombardment while they were wedged in the zone. The attack claimed the lives of 40 civilians. But certain soldiers of the Farabundo Martí National Liberation Front (FMLN) snatched them away in time and put them in an underground bunker. Once the bombardments had stopped, the FMLN soldiers told them that the bombardments were particularly conducted to kill them. The agents were enraged and they unhesitatingly committed treason by divulging some confidential information with the FMLN soldiers. But the FMLN didn't want to release them. They were transferred to a local prison and were held captive. The agents eventually came up with an escape plan and after a lot of struggle, came back to the U.S and joined Wolf. PiCorp gave them an arena to take up any case without the intervention of a procedural chain of command, it gave them an opportunity to help people around the globe without any fear of diplomacy, it gave them complete and uninhibited jurisdiction, it gave them an opportunity to exploit their skills and use it to save the lives of innocent people and to fight for the betterment of the society.

These memories never faded from their minds. They kept coming back time and again. Agent C recollected all these memories on the way to Puerto Rico. Two and a half months before the armoured truck robbery, the agents were sent to Puerto Rico to investigate a certain drug trade, which had allegedly claimed the lives of five police officers and three civilians. The media dubbed it as a raid gone wrong. The police officers were praised for their bravery and the civilians and their families were unfortunately victimised. But one of the relatives of the dead civilian, who happened to be a teacher, had a local newspaper publish an article giving an account of his son-in-law's innocence. PiCorp got the news and they decided to look into it.

The agents stayed at Puerto Rico for ten days and found out a lot about the drug trade. They then sent an anonymous post to the DEA, listing 15 locations where methamphetamine and heroin were being cooked. Also in the process, they tracked down one of *Patrón's* whores, and discovered from her bank account that the Lieutenant Governor, using a false identity, had been funding the *Patrón*. So they decided to use this as a cover-up story to account for their robbery.

Bru set up two police officers with the whore and used her to cajole them into confessing to the charges of aiding and abetting the Lieutenant Governor in his attempt to rob an armoured truck, and the Lieutenant Governor's involvement in funding the *Patrón's* trade.

The agents wrapped up the Puerto Rico investigation and returned to New York to start their research on Mariano Castillo. They eventually found out about Castillo's cousin's meat storage facility in Delaware and they figured that the location would be ideal for the final act, the Prestige.

Agent C and C2 then went down to Delaware and spied on Castillo's cousin. They collected details regarding the clients using the facility, the suppliers, the employees, the shifts, the security and such other that were necessary to frame him. Then they got back to New York and took up jobs as truck drivers at CATS. Meanwhile Bru used his contacts and set up two shell corporations, Nixon and Clinton.

PiCorp's COD had access to the agent's mobile phones, through which a techie continuously recorded the instantaneous positions of the truck. The youngest recruit and the youngest member of the PETS had it all mapped out and printed at PiCorp. Every other evening, the agents took six specialised PiCorp cars fitted with video cameras, audio records, frequency generators, signal receivers, mobile signal interceptors and various other gadgets, and trailed the same path as they had done that morning. Only this time, they were recording panoramic video of their surroundings.

The video was analysed and the best location for the heist was chosen. It had to be a place with visual surveillance, but the cameras had to be so placed that while robbing the truck, their faces wouldn't be captured. Also, it had to be at an optimal distant from the traffic signal. Not too near, not too far. It had to be a wide road so that there wouldn't be traffic congestion for at least two minutes. After innumerable permutations and combinations, six such locations were determined, and for a period of two weeks, the agents stopped the trucks at these places for over two minutes. The CATS called a few times when the truck didn't move for a minute or so. But then, they got used to it and the new threshold was raised to two minutes. It would be raised to three before the D-day.

Meanwhile Nixon and Clinton were functioning well and the bankers were accustomed to their transactions.

Wolf contacted the suppliers and asked them to fortify the consignments.

The final stopping locations were decided on the day before the heist. That evening, the agents filled the valve leading to the air-conditioning ducts with liquid benzodiazepine, and then headed back to PiCorp. When the air-conditioner was switched on, the liquid sedative would be vaporised and circulated through the ducts, knocking out anyone who came in direct contact with it.

One of the two news reporters on PiCorp's board went down the Lieutenant Governor's office to interview Castillo and he happily agreed to it. But before the interview, she asked him sign some formal terms and conditions. He did as asked and she carefully slid the paper into a folder. Later the COD pulled his fingerprints from the paper and the forging team impersonated his signature.

Bru had the FPS vehicles stationed near the six locations where the trucks would stop for almost three minutes.

The Agents contacted a meat manufacturer in Delaware and paid him some cash in advance for a truckload of pork.

The Wolf approved the act and the Thunderbird was ready to rekindle.

Friday, April 1st 2005

Richard Wagner's *Die Walküre* (Ride of the Valkyrie) reverberated inside Schorsch Sieger's magnanimous chamber. The *Führer* of the

Fourth *Reich* sat on his plush leather chair and rested his legs on the table, as he hummed the fiery composition. The sheer ferocity of the opera kindled his mind into a complex and notorious thought process. He closed his eyes and pictured nothing but eternal victory and world dominance, his two transcendental objectives.

The intercom on his table buzzed and Sieger slowly opened his bloodshot eyes and leaned forward to pick up the receiver. Adolf Hitler stared at him from across the hall. He reminded him of the fall of the Third *Reich*, of the decline of the Nazi Supremacy and of the pulverised dream.

'Senden sie in,' said Sieger and replaced the receiver on its cradle.

The *Reichshanzker's* huge gilded bronze clock ceded the first of the ten chimes as Heinrich Schüler, Anastasia and the *deputierte's* guards stormed inside the *Führer's* chamber through a mammoth teak wood door. A few feet off the threshold, Schüler and the guards tapped the floor and poised themselves at attention. They earnestly extended their right arm to their eye level and straightened the hand so that it was parallel to the floor, and proclaimed emphatically - *Heil Sieger!*

Sieger didn't respond. His eyes remained shut and he was totally engrossed in *Die Walküre.* Schüler uncaringly put down his arm and walked towards the *Führer.*

'Haltestelle direkt dort, Goldfasan!' shouted Anastasia, fiercely.

Schüler turned and looked at his captive in bewilderment. *Goldfasan* (golden pheasant) was a derogatory term that the Germans used for high-ranking Nazi Party members. The term was derived from the brown and red uniforms with golden insignia worn at official functions and rallies by party members that resembled the brilliant colours of a male pheasant.

Anastasia, now clad in an oversized men's jumpsuit, stared at the *Führer's deputierte* and said unperturbedly, 'Yes, you heard me right. Stay right there.'

'Wie kannst du es wagen,' spit out Schüler and retrieved a Heckler and Koch VP70 from his holster. He aimed it at Anastasia and asked, 'You want me to shoot your brains out?'

'I know you wouldn't even if I happened to say yes.'

An infuriated Schüler tightened his grip and unlocked the safety.

'You are just bluffing. I know you won't shoot me, at least not in here. You people have your own ludicrous occult belief system.'

'Ludicrous!' exclaimed Dr. Norbert and said, 'Nazism is sacred and it is the most supreme religious philosophy on earth. We belong to the master race and we have been told that should anyone try to mock at us or our religion - which one day will be the religion of the world, we should see to it that that derogation is the last thing he/she will ever speak.'

'Dr. Karl, I presume,' she said and shifted her gaze from Schüler. She then took a step closer to him and said, 'I don't think that you are a true Aryan. Your mental predicament makes me think that you are a *untermenschen* (subhuman).'

Hitler's conception of the Aryan race excluded a vast majority of Slavs from being a part of the master race on the pretense that they had dangerous Jewish and Asiatic influences. Because of this the Nazis declared Slavs to be *untermenschen* (subhuman).

Dr. Norbert was enraged. He slapped Anastasia. She faced him again, undaunted, and said, '*Untermenschen*, Nazism isn't a religion, it is an ideology. It is a system of abstract thoughts applied to public matters with the goal of making the concept central to politics. People like you have misinterpreted, manipulated, distorted and patronised an absurd and ludicrous system. You fail to dig deeper into the past and analyse the factual evidence, because you are too ignorant, and such ignorant people cannot belong to the master race.'

The *Führer*, on hearing this, opened his eyes and looked at Anastasia. Her blue eyes, blond hair and tall elegant figure reminded him of Hitler's description of the Ideal German woman. He slightly bent down and whispered something to Blondi before closing his eyes yet again.

'Hitler wouldn't have recruited unfit homos with stunted mental development,' she accused, and scowled at the *Gruppenführer*.

Dr. Norbert raised his arm to slap her again, but Blondi sprang towards him and bit his right arm. Anastasia briskly pivoted, with her right leg in front and left leg at the back. She shifted her weight on to the left leg, and propelled the right leg in a sweeping, rainbow curvature. The ball of her foot struck Dr. Norbert's head before he could recover from the bite and sent him crashing on the plush carpeted floor.

Schüler was fascinated by Anastasia's agility. He had never seen a woman perform the *Dwi doleyo hulyeogi chagi* (spin hook kick) with such perfection. He figured that she was trained in *Tang Soo Do,* a form of Korean martial art. He eased his grip on the VP70 and lowered it before strapping it back inside the holster.

Dr. Norbert's bodyguards caught her by the arm and pulled her away from the *Gruppenführer.* She didn't resist nor did she fight them. She just remained calm and composed.

Sieger was now standing behind his desk and he sure as hell was impressed. The *Führer* tapped the floor and poised himself at attention. He extended his right arm and proclaimed emphatically - *Heil Anastasia!*

Chapter 11

Friday, November 2nd 2007

"Vice President Jamie Edwards, ex-Senator Vaughn Fletcher's daughter, Ms. Juliette, and the Chairman of the Phoenix Almonte Group, Mr. Cortez, paid a visit to the NYU Stern and expressed their deepest regards and apologies to the vast student body. The three students, Schell, Zenger and Hilton, were lauded for their bravery and were honoured by the Vice President. It is reported that a month ago, the three students participated in a competition organised by the Phoenix Group, which offered the winners an opportunity to meet with the CEO of the Phoenix Group, Mr. Nahiossi Griffiths, privately in the skies. But little did they know that they were chosen to be hostages. It is believed that the three students are shortlisted for the DoD Medal for Distinguished Public Service. The students humbly accepted the honours and deeply mourned the death of ex-senator Vaughn Fletcher. Catch more updates on this news with Gregory at the 9 PM news. Stay tuned," said a reporter from FOX News.

"On the evening of 29th October, at around 8:30 PM, we received a call from a certain woman, asking us if we were ready to meet with Mr. Griffiths in about an hour. We certainly had no choice but to agree. We truly admired Mr. Griffiths and we were really eager to meet with him. So we agreed. A half hour later, we were chauffeured down in a limousine

to LaGuardia. That was the first time we sat in a limo and I must confess that the experience was amazing. The airport security didn't stop us at the gates and we didn't sit through the laborious security procedures. We were straightway driven to one the hangars where we learnt that Mr. Vice President was going to join us on our flight with Mr. Griffiths..." aired the ABC News.

Meanwhile Juliette huddled in the bathtub and cried alone in the dark. The shower was running, and she was shivering. It was hard to say if it was the nippy water or the icky fear or both that made her shudder. Bizarre persecutory delusion rambled on in her mind, she blurted out incomprehensive words, she experienced frequent nightmares and Jordan feared that she might be hallucinating. Maybe she was becoming schizophrenic.

Cortez broke down the bathroom door and barged into the shower.

'Oh my God, Julie, you are shivering. Jesus,' cried Cortez and turned off the shower. He looked around, but couldn't find a towel. He laid his coat on her trembling body and sprinted out of the bathroom. He sent Jordan out, locked the door, and grabbed a towel from her cupboard. He once again rushed back to the shower and wrapped it around her.

'Come on, Julie, stand up. Julie, please, you'll do it for me, won't you? Now come on honey, let's get you dressed up. We can then go to your favorite restaurant and grab some dinner. I'll then take you to a movie, okay?' said Cortez and cried, as she listened to him and climbed out of the bathtub.

'Very good sweetie, very good,' he said, and walked her out of the bathroom. He had her sit on the couch and went to grab some clothes. 'Blue is your favourite colour, right?'

Juliette nodded wearily.

'Uncle Cortez knows best,' said Cortez and chuckled. He selected a navy blue sweater and light blue jeans, and then he heard a knock on the door.

'Who is it?' shouted Cortez.

'It's me, Megan.'

'Just a second,' said Cortez and walked towards the door. He unlocked the bolt and let his secretary in.

'Hey Julie, guess what? I have reservations for three at the Grand in about a half hour. Don't you want to go?' asked Megan.

Julie didn't say anything. She just stared at the floor.

Megan then looked at Cortez's hand and asked, 'what are you, eight? You want her to wear these to the Grand?'

'Well I-uh…'

'Save it. Get out. I'll bring her downstairs in fifteen minutes. Pull some strings and get the reservations,' she whispered

'You lied?'

'Seriously, stop being a child,' she said and forced him out of the room.

Cortez walked downstairs and placed a call to Dr. Bernard, their family physician. He asked Cortez to bring Juliette down to the hospital the next morning and assured him that there was nothing to worry about.

'Is everything all right?' asked Jordan, offering him some scotch.

'For now, yes,' he said and gulped the scotch. 'Thank you, Jordan.'

'Is there anything else I can do?'

'Yes, there is. Call the Grand and book a table for four under the name Montego.'

'Four, sir?'

'Yes. You too are coming.'

Jordan looked at him for a second and smiled. He then turned back and rushed to his room to select the best out of the few outfits he had.

Monday, April 3rd 2006

Wolf was escorted to *La vita eternal,* a heavily guarded villa located in the densest region of a privately-owned forest. The agents from PiCorp's COD, the *soldatos* from the Five Mafia Families and certain police officers from the NYPD guarded the fortress-like villa. In addition to this, a surveillance team stationed at 'The Eternal Life' continuously obtained feeds from various devices installed at different regions of the forest. No one except for the ones on the list of invitees could enter the forest.

Wolf's Hummer entered through the gates of the villa and everyone saluted as he passed by. The guards were now on high alert. Wolf's safety was of dire importance, and the price to be paid by any assailant wanting to get to the Wolf was thirty lives. No bargain.

The Hummer slowly decelerated and it came to a halt. Wolf languidly climbed out and saluted in the direction of the entrance. The guards were humbled by the honour. They bowed down in respect as the agents from PiCorp escorted the Wolf inside the villa.

The bosses of the Ruggiero, Damiano, Santorelli, Luchesco and Taccetta families stood up the moment Wolf entered the den. Each one of them came forward and devotedly kissed the Wolf's hand. The *Lupo* graciously thanked them all and led them to the cemetery on the rear of the Villa.

This day (April the third), thirty years ago, all six of them lost someone they loved. This day, thirty years ago, the Permanent Committee on Investigations (PSI), the Federal Department and the CIA committed the most cunning and notorious hits on the American citizens in order to make up for their errors. This day, thirty years ago, Alfred W Barker decided to step down as the Director of the Federal Protective Service.

Alfred W. Barker's wife, a Federal Judge presiding over the disclosures of Joe Valente, was shot in the courthouse. Vincent Luchesco's father, who was subpoenaed by the DOJ based on the allegations of Valente, was also shot in the same courthouse during forenoon. Daniel Santorelli's grandson went missing that afternoon. Anthony Ruggiero's only son was falsely implicated in the death of Alfred's wife and Vincent's father. He was later that evening killed at a certain pub. The authorities claimed that Anthony's son shot one of the officers, so they had to fire at him. That very night, Alan Taccetta's brother and Gerard Damiano's nephew were found dead at Brighton beach on Coney Island.

Early next morning, it was reported that Valente committed suicide at a state penitentiary. But no one really cared. The case was closed and the law enforcement agencies had won yet again. They had slaughtered so many lives to achieve something of apparently greater national significance. No one really questioned anything. The agents who were a part of this operation were lauded and credited. No one really seemed care for the lives of the mafia. No one, except Alfred W. Barker, a.k.a, Wolf.

'Why did he use his credit card, Thomas?'

'As Bru said earlier, Porter Hill wanted the driver and the security dead. He didn't know that they'd survive and help the police track him down.'

'Regarding that, why would he just dump them in the trunk while they were still alive? A better way would be to kill them and then dump in the truck. Don't you think?'

Thomas was silent.

'He planned everything so daringly, so methodically. I mean, he had the lawyer emasculated. He had the balls to poise him from a crane in front of the Supreme Court. Do you think he wouldn't have the courage to kill these two men and then dump them in the trunk?'

'Maybe he coerced someone else to do it. He managed to coerce two people, the driver and the driver's coercer.'

'He didn't coerce them to murder. He coerced the driver to commit assault and robbery, and he coerced the other guy to coerce the driver.'

'What's your point?'

'My point is that our mastermind - let us for now exclude Porter from the list - is intelligent enough to know that you just can't coerce someone that easily to commit murder. He was intelligent enough to choose a blind spot. He was intelligent enough to kidnap New York's best criminal lawyer and to kill him in a brutal way. He was intelligent enough to protect himself through two layers of insulation. He had them cornered at a blind spot and he had the strength, mindset and the means to get rid of them. So why would he want to coerce someone else when he could have done it himself? Why would he trust them with such an important task?'

'Maybe he didn't murder Sebastian. He had someone else do it.'

'The prosecution would have been lucky to have you on their side.'

'Strike one.'

'What?'

'I'll give you three strikes. More than three sarcastic or derogatory comments about me or my girlfriend and you are out.'

'Rather you are... Never mind. Don't strike that one. Well, where were we?'

'I was saying that the mastermind might have hired someone to murder Sebastian.'

'That's a logical presumption. But hiring is totally different from coercing. So if you are suggesting that the mastermind hired someone to kill the driver and the other guy, then I very much doubt that they'd be so damn shoddy.'

'I guess you are right.'

'You guess I'm...never mind. So I'd say that the mastermind purposefully had Porter use the card. He set up the whole thing. He knew the system.'

'Easy there buddy. Let's do this methodically. Let's take one step at a time. If we rush, we are sure to skip something in between.'

'If you say so, counsel. That wasn't derogatory.'

'I'd give you the benefit of the doubt.'

'Thank you, m'lord. Okay, now point one - why did he use the credit card? Point two – why didn't he ensure that the two coerced people were dead before he dumped them in the trunk? Point three – What was the need to dump them?'

'Point three?'

'Yes. What was the need to dump them? I know I wouldn't. It's not all that difficult to make a person disappear. Is it?'

'Depends on who is trying to make things happen.'

'Agreed. But I think that our killer is capable enough.'

'It's just a speculation.'

'For now. We'll try to dig out evidence eventually.'

'Hopefully. What next?'

'Check this out. The FBI report says that the motive for Porter to murder Sebastian was that he thought that Sebastian raped his girlfriend and in turn was responsible for her death. Is that right?'

'Yes, it is.'

'Now let me ask you a relationship question. If someone happened to rape Angelika, would she keep it from you?'

'What's the matter with you?' yelled Thomas.

'Tom, I'm not ridiculing you all right? It's just hypothetical. Don't be so hostile.'

Thomas thought for a while and then said, 'I don't think she would have. She wouldn't want to hurt me.'

'Okay,' said Rupert and opened the file containing the court transcripts. 'What if she filed a case on the person who raped her? Wouldn't you trust her?'

'Of course I would trust her.'

'So it is reasonable to assume that she has told you everything. Is that right?'

'I suppose.'

'Don't 'suppose' me. Be goddamn sure about what you speak. Would you or would you not know the truth?'

'I would know her version of the story.'

'And would believe it to be true?'

'Yes. I would.'

'Applying the same analogy to Porter's case, it is reasonable to assume that Porter knew that Sebastian was the rapist.'

'But who knows what their relationship was like? Who knows if they were faithful to each other?'

'We know he was, considering the allegation that he was ready to murder the person whom she claimed to have raped her. We are half way through.'

Thomas remained silent for some time. He gulped another cup of coffee and then said, 'I need to use the Internet. I want to find something.'

'It's right over there,' he said, and pointed at the e-joint, as he called it. 'It's all yours.'

Rupert went through the investigational procedures again and mapped it all out on the wall, while Thomas conversed with Bru through an encrypted chat messenger owned by PiCorp.

'Hey Tom, what do you think about the taxi?'

'What do you want me to think about it?'

'About the assailant hiring a taxi to the driver's house.'

'I think that it was a good idea, considering that he couldn't use his own car.'

'Brilliant, and why do you think that he couldn't use his own car?'

'Well, it's pretty obvious.'

'It's all right, please state the obvious. I want to hear it.'

'Okay, he couldn't use his car, because he knew that if he did so, he was jeopardising his plan.'

'Could you be more specific?'

'Well, someone might have recognised him and his car at the scene of the crime.'

'Excellent. Now why wouldn't that someone recognise him if he took a taxi?'

'Well...'

'Let me cut you some slack here. Now would you agree with me if I said, "Someone or something might have recognised him and his car at the scene of crime"?'

'By something you mean - '

' - NYPD surveillance units.'

'Right. I don't see why I wouldn't.'

'Excellent. So if he knew that the surveillance units could get his car, why would he think that it wouldn't get the taxi?'

'That's because there are thousands of taxis in New York.'

'Brilliant, my dear brother. But each taxi has a unique medallion number, which the NYPD surveillance units recognise oh-so-efficiently.'

One of the three computers pinged and Thomas quietly turned around to face the concerned computer.

'Tommy, what do you think?' asked Rupert, yet again.

Thomas read Bru's message on the computer and said,

'She told him.'

Chapter 12

The Phoenix, Nahiossi Griffiths, was handed over to the United States Marshals at the Lisbon Portela Airport on the 20th of December 2007.

The *Ministério da Justiça* (Ministry of Justice – Portugal) acceded to the U.S extradition request after a trenchant perlustration of copious governmental documents. The Office of International Affairs had the *Ministerie van Veiligheid en Justitie* (Minstry of Security and Justice – Netherlands) informed about the situation, and the Dutch government diplomatically agreed to cooperate with the United States Federal Government.

The marshals delegated the 'handing over' of Nahiossi and parted with the Polícia Judiciária – PJ. He was forthwith convoyed by a couple of marshals and two federal agents to a Boeing 727 owned by Justice Prisoner and Alien Transportation System (JPATS). Nahiossi slowly and timidly climbed up the stairs and lifted his feet off 'the city of seven hills'. He was now completely under the U.S jurisdiction and he sure as hell knew that the journey to New York would be everything but pleasant.

Nahiossi was tucked in an orange jumpsuit and his hands were completely immobilised with reinforced mitten. He was restrained with handcuffs as well as ankle and waist chains. The marshals didn't have to worry about the seating arrangements, as Nahiossi was the only felon on the 727.

'Let's strap you up birdie,' said SA Marco and tightened Nahiossi's seat belt.

The marshals and agents ran a few final errands, and then the Con Air perfectly lifted off and headed towards the 'land of dreams'.

After the captain's usual 'safety' announcements, the agents unstrapped Nahiossi as per the FAA regulations. The skies were clear, and there was minimum turbulence. The 727 maintained its steady pace and magnificently flew over the Atlantic.

'How is Juliette?' asked Nahiossi languidly.

Silence.

'How is my father?'

Silence.

'How is Cortez?'

Silence.

'Is Jordan all right?'

Silence.

Nahiossi looked longingly at the special agents and waited for the answers.

An infuriated SA Marco turned towards Nahiossi and said, 'I don't know how they are or what they are doing. But I sure as hell know that all of them fucking despise you.'

Nahiossi looked him in the eye for a brief second and simply smiled.

Tuesday, February 28th 2007

'Rajiv, the person who feigned your identity is still out there and he might be planning something catastrophic. I know that you are an able and a circumspective politician. But at the moment, as an adept lawyer and as an ardent friend, all I ask you to do is to just let us perpetuate,' said Mrs. Amrutha Shankar, and looked with concern at her traumatised client at the Legal Aid Centre inside Tihar.

Both remained muted for a brief interval. Mrs. Shankar gave him a few seconds to process the amiability of the plan. She then leaned over the table and clinched his hands before saying, 'You just have to trust me and my judgment, Rajiv.'

Rajiv pressed her hands and let out a gasp. He looked Mrs. Shankar in the eye and said, 'Of course I trust you, Amrutha, and I always have. I really appreciate your concern. But it is easier said than done'. He took another deep breath and continued, 'I have a family to worry about and I don't see how it is worth the risk.'

'I can understand what you are going through, Rajiv and I assure you that it is worth the risk. It is important to your family and to our country. Who knows what the real criminals have in mind? You took an oath to protect, preserve and defend this country and I hope that it wasn't just restricted to your ministerial sphere,' she said intensely and added, 'The Wolf personally told me that your opponent's work is masterly and that no one at PiCorp has been able to gather evidence that could prove your innocence...'

'Do they trust me?'

'...Sure they do. They wouldn't go through so much trouble otherwise. They have a world to look after, you know,' said Amrutha, and slowly withdrew her hands. 'Anyway PiCorp Bern procured and analysed all your alleged transactions at Lombard, Brian & Celt, and unfortunately the investigations revealed nothing credible. In fact, it endorsed the credibility of the State's case.'

Rajiv casually stood up and limped around the room, all the while evaluating his lawyer's proposition. He walked around the humid chamber for a few moments and then asked, 'Does Wolf approve of this?'

'Yes, he does. His Elite team chalked out the plan.'

Rajiv again ruminated on the plan and went back-and-forth with the decision. After a brief close-mouthed argument with himself, he gave up and said, 'I'll sleep over it. I'll have an answer by tomorrow morning.'

'All right,' said Amrutha passively and packed her briefcase. She stood up, shook hands with Rajiv, and then tapped on the door. As the guards clicked the door handle open, she turned back and said, 'I sincerely hope that you will agree with the Wolf.'

Rajiv silently nodded as the guards cuffed him and escorted him back to his cell.

Amrutha saw him off, and then walked back to the warden's office. She concisely chatted with Vijay Saxena about Rajiv's condition and about the appeal. They gradually moved on to the more personal aspects and conversed about familial quips. A half hour later, she parted with him and headed off to her office at Connaught Place (Rajiv Chowk).

She quietly listened to the news and drove peacefully for a few minutes, thinking that Rajiv would vote in favour of their decision. She drove for a few miles and when she was certain that no one was tailing her, she picked up her phone and called Sushanth.

'Sushanth, he said that he'd think it over. He'll have a decision by tomorrow.'

'Okay, where are you?' asked Sushanth, an agent at PiCorp Delhi.

'Sardar Patel Marg. I'll be at my office in twenty minutes.'

'Don't go to your office. Turn around and drive down to Jankpuri. I'll text you the address.'

'Okay. You want to tell me why?'

'No,' said Sushanth passively and hung up.

Amrutha pulled the car to a halt and waited for Sushanth's text. Once she received it, she fed it into the car's navigation system and routed her Corolla to the opposite lane. She tuned in to one of the news bulletins disseminated by the News Service Division (NSD) and drove back the way she had just come.

The 12 PM news on NDTV had just begun when Amrutha knocked on the door of the unpretentious house near Pankha Road.

'Where is your car?'

'I parked it near Janak Cinema. Thought you wanted it to be discreet.'

'Excellent. Come on in.'

Amrutha walked inside the cramped house, as Sushanth scanned the surroundings before shutting the door.

'Everyone, this is Amrutha, Rajiv's lawyer,' said Sushanth as he and Amrutha entered the only room in the house.

'Who are they?' asked the lawyer quizzically.

'They are friends who are going to help us with our ordeal,' said Sushanth as Amrutha looked around the room and saw Kalashnikovs, SIGs, tear gas canisters, bullet resistant vests and ski masks neatly organised in a corner. 'Which depends on Rajiv's decision, of course'

'Okay, who sent them?' she asked hesitantly, taken aback at the sight of the makeshift armoury.

'The Wolf.'

Wednesday, April 13th 2005

'Sorry I'm late. I was talking to Rupert about Beirut.'

'Did he agree to do it?' asked the Wolf.

'No. I suggest we leave him alone and not interfere. Clearly he doesn't want anything to do with us.'

'Thomas, he is as much a son to Wolf as you. PiCorp is founded on the depth and value of relationships. You can't be so aloof about it,' said Elle, one of the two journalists.

'Of course we can. What about the time when Sheila…' began Bru.

The Wolf cleared his throat and peered down his thick-rimmed spectacles.

'I'm sorry,' said Bru and hurried to his chair.

'We found his footage at the courthouse…'

'Excuse me, Agent W. Could you please recapitulate? I'm really sorry.'

'Wolf?'

'I've always been a good listener.'

Agent W silently nodded and restarted the slide show.

'When we got down to Kiev, we just had Anastasia's HUBOZ report and Abu al Khayr's brief testimony to proceed with the investigation,' said Agent W, and projected the testimony on the slide. It read:

'Yes, I handed over a part of the consignment to Ilarion while I was on my way to Afghanistan.'

'I work for no one.'

'Who interrogated him?'

'Officer Eugene of the Interpol.'

'Background checks?'

'He is clean and well-trained. Eugene is with the Interpol since 1986.'

'What else did he ask Abu al Khayr?'

'Who received the consignment at Afghanistan? How did he get in touch with Wasyl? Whom did he meet before getting down to Wasyl's cabin? Who worked for him? For how long had he solicited the trade? Where did he get the resources...It goes on for two more pages. Twenty eight questions in totality,' said Agent W, and passed the sheet to Bru.

Bru scanned through the interrogation transcript for a few minutes and read all the questions. He looked satisfied with the report, and so asked Agent W to proceed.

'We then sat down and analysed the sentence thoroughly, and by the end of the day, we had a solid working theory,' said Agent W proudly, and presented the next slide.

Handed over…Ilarion.

'Why did he use the words "handed over"? It could have been "delivered" or "transferred" or "passed on". "Handed over" sounds too informal, and Afghani drug dealers usually don't get informal with foreigners. Also note that he addresses Mr. Wasyl as "Ilarion". He used Mr. Wasyl's first name. Meaning, he knew Mr. Wasyl well enough.'

Elle scribbled down whatever Agent W said. She would later hand it over to Bru and it would all be deposited at the third base.

'Now observe that he says "a part of the consignment".' Meaning, there was at least one more recipient. But unfortunately there weren't any monetary trails leading to the recipient(s). So we reached our first dead end.'

'Khayr didn't get to cross the border, I suppose. Is that right?' asked Barry, an ex-CIA interrogator.

'Yes, sir. That is correct. The border patrol nabbed him and drove him down to the *viddilennya militsyii* (police station).'

'What made the border patrol nab him? Were they aware of the fact that their candidate died because of the heroin Khayr handed over to Wasyl?'

'It is reported that a PI who happened to work for Mr. Lyaksandro trailed Mr. Wasyl to the cabin and took photos of Khayr handing over an envelope to Mr. Wasyl. Even though it was illegal, the court allowed it to be used since it proved a critical fact and since the analysts found the photo to be authentic.'

'But why did he spy on him?' asked Mendez, one of the two retired federal judges.

'He thought that Mr. Wasyl might be having an affair. That sort of information is instrumental to the opposition.'

'So Abu al Khayr knew Wasyl and Wasyl himself bought the drug that killed him. These facts are indisputable, right?' asked Matt, the other federal judge.

'Our working theory was based on the presumption that Mr. Lyaksandro's party officials set him up and that Abu al Khayr's testimony was contrived - '

'I sense that there is a but at the end of that sentence,' said Bru.

' - But, we couldn't get to talk to Khayr because he died at the courthouse.'

'He consumed the same heroin that killed Wasyl,' said Beth, the ex- FPS agent.

'Yes, sir.'

'I'm sensing another but,'' interjected Bru.

Agent W smiled and said, 'But Khayr couldn't have taken it with him. The militia had checked him thoroughly before producing him at the courthouse.'

'So someone passed it over to him and this someone would, at some point of time, be captured by the closed circuit cameras installed at the courthouse,' said Barry.

'Splendid,' said Agent W and added, 'That was precisely what we did. We scrounged the footage and analysed it pixel by pixel.'

'And?' prompted Bru.

'And we found out that Alex Sedokova entered the restroom just a few minutes before Abu al Khayr ended his life.'

CHAPTER 13

Thursday, December 21st 2007

'It's good to see you again, Mr. Griffiths,' said Vice President Jamie Edwards, and imperiously welcomed Nahiossi to the United States. 'I sincerely hope that you enjoy your stay with us.'

Nahiossi remained inarticulate. Jamie savagely stared at Nahiossi for a brief moment and then had his photographer shoot some riveting snapshots. The pictures would hit the front page of every American newspaper, and with that Vice President Jamie Edwards's official campaigning for the Presidential Elections 2007 would begin.

Presidential candidate Jamie Edwards parted with Nahiossi, and the SOG chaperoned him to their transport. He was put in one of the seven Chevrolet Expresses and driven down to the Metropolitan Correctional Centre.

Reporters from various news agencies were gathered outside LaGuardia, ardently waiting to take the first pictures of the fallen Phoenix. The Secret Service and the NYPD kept a constant watch on the civilians as the Chevrolets emerged out of the hangar. Thousands of pictures were clicked staring from the moment the vehicle came into sight.

Once the convoy was out of sight, the attention was focused on the Vice President.

'Fellow Americans, this day seven weeks ago I proclaimed that we would extradite Mr. Griffiths to this country, and today we have done so in good faith. We have shown the world that no matter who the criminal is, no matter what his status is and no matter which nation he is from, we, the Americans, will always fight for justice and stand by the principles which our founding fathers so perspicaciously laid out in the constitution. God bless the citizens and God bless America. Thank you'

The Secret Service forced him to cut a long story short. The USSS had already been deluded once when a certain powerful gang of criminals managed to abduct him under their very nose. They certainly couldn't take any chances, for if something abominable happened to the Vice President, their agency would be shamed and that was the highest level of disgrace to the agents.

Jamie Edwards waved at the cameras before being whisked away by his overprotective agents.

'The pictures are being distributed as we speak,' said Jamie's chief secretary while they were on their way to the State Capitol.

'Excellent. Ensure that it hits the televisions as well.'

'It already has. In fact it's already being aired right now.'

'Perfect. Do we have any slogans yet?'

'America deserves better.'

Anirudh Bysani, an officer at the Central Bureau of Investigation, arrested Pruthvi Chopra, the chairman of the Chopra Industries, on the 26th of December 2005, on charges of perjury and corruption. The investigation led to Kevin Banerjee, to whom Mr. Chopra had offered bribe in exchange for tax deductions and land clearance. The Bureau took Chopra's statement and had the district collector, Mr. Banerjee, tried under Sections 161 and 165 of Indian Penal Code, 1860, Sections 4 and 5 of Prevention of Corruption Act, 1947,

Section 4 of Madras Prohibition Act, 1937 and Section 3 of Indian Evidence Act.

As the trail drew closer, the CBI scrapped up certain incriminating evidence and had Kevin benumbed. His lawyer, Vaibhav Shekkar, told him that Anirudh had done a tremendous job with the investigation, and that the evidence, if presented at the courthouse, would indubitably prove his guilt.

Anirudh's team had conducted a clean sweep of Kevin's residence, offices and banks, and had obtained a cell-phone from a personalised locker at the State Bank of India. They had the cell-phone retraced to the network service providers and had them furnish various logs. Next they cross-referenced the phone numbers with the CBI databases and theorised that the phone found in the locker at SBI had received frequent text messages from Lombard, Brian & Celt. So they contacted Bern and obtained the account details with reference to the Transaction Authentication Numbers (TANs) messaged to the cell-phone. The account details and the bank's electronic transfer logs clearly showed that transactions were made at the enterprise around the time the cell-phone was used. Anirudh again contacted the service providers and procured the positioning details of the phone whenever it received texts from Lombard, Brain and Celt. The officers were led to a hotel in Karol Bagh, where Kevin had used the cell-phone only a few days before getting caught. The team obtained CCTV footage, credit card statement, receipts on which Kevin had signed, and witness statements from the employees. The footage clearly gave visual conformation that Kevin was operating both his phone and his tablet at the said time. The credit card statement, witness statement, and the signature further endorsed the prosecution's case.

Shekkar, who was sure that the prosecution's case was beyond rebuttals, consulted with the prosecutor, and after heated discussions, reached a mutual agreement, according to which if Kevin happened to help the State catch the bigger fish, they'd reduce his sentence to a mere year.

Kevin liked the offer from the Department of Justice, but he also didn't want to betray the person who had helped him in his political pursuit right from inception. So he had Shekkar converse with the leader of the Janlok Party, his mentor Mr. Rohan Singhania, about the terms and conditions of the DOJ's offer. They conversed for a considerable time, and by the end of it, it was clear to Singhania that Kevin had sent for him not out of concern, but of formality. So he was sure that Kevin, however loyal, would finally break down and take the deal. He thus contacted the Chief Minister of Delhi, Mr. Varun G Sharma, and warned him that in case Kevin happened to implicate him, his party wouldn't support him in the upcoming CM elections.

The Samajwadi party was instrumental in determining the succeeding incumbent. Singhania was a benevolent politician, and his alliance with various political parties over the years had an impeccable track record of ensuring the victory of a nominee from the respective allied party. Hence Varun couldn't risk losing the Samajwadi alliance. Varun thus contacted Schüler and told him that in case he happened to forfeit his seat as a consequence of the upcoming elections, the *Führer* would incur a major setback, for the person who would most likely win in his stead was a man who breathed for transparency, anti-corrpution and social equality.

Schüler had the *Führer* informed about the Indian situation, and upon his orders had their analysts and technicians work out a plausible solution.

Führer's analysts had Anirudh's investigation reports transported to the Berghof from New Delhi, and a five member team headed by the *Gruppenführer* of India had them assiduously analysed. The case study of the report brought out a clear picture of Anirudh's investigation, and consequently the analysts were posed with the challenge of finding a foolproof method to intercept the banking security procedures and the government detection methods. They had to see to it that the cell-phone used to receive the TAN from Lombard, Brian and Celt, and the device from which the transactions had to be made, were in close proximity of the probable succeeding incumbent, Rajiv. They also had to replace Singhania's transactions at the bank with that of Rajiv's, and make sure that in no way Singhania was brought to the fore.

The first step in this intricate plan involved the task of getting acquainted to someone who was close to Rajiv, probably someone in the family. Deepika and Vishal were scratched off the list within seconds of consideration, and almost immediately, his parents' names were removed. The reason for this was obvious and the risk immaculate. So they were now left with his brother and sister. Even the sister was eliminated from the list under the pretense that it was easier for Mr. Singhania to get acquainted with Adithya, considering the fact that Adithya was desperately longing for a ticket in the upcoming elections.

Wednesday, April 13th 2005

'Alex Sedokova worked as Mr. Lyaksandro's chief secretary before springing into Mr. Wasyl's party. So when we saw the campaign manager enter the restroom just a few minutes - four minutes twenty three seconds to be precise - before Khayr killed himself, we concluded that Mr. Sedokova was responsible for both the death of Mr. Wasyl and Mr. Khayr and that Mr. Lyaksandro had him do it.'

'Do we still have the tapes?' asked Elle.

'Yes, sir, we do. Let me play it for you,' said Agent W and had the footage projected on the screen. The footage showed exactly what Agent W had narrated. The board members saw it and accredited Thunderbird's working theory.

'But the evidence wasn't enough to prove Mr. Sedokova's guilt at the courthouse. So we went down to the archives and researched everything we could about Lyaksandro, Wasyl, and Sedokova, their wives, parents, children and close acquaintances. Meanwhile Anastasia tried to find a way to legalise her findings about Mr. Sedokova's medical donations.'

'What about Mr. Sedokova's bank account? We could have investigated the bank officials with regards to the fake accounts,' said Bru.

'We did go to his bank, United Front, and we investigated the officials. But we really couldn't get anything useful. They have more than forty branches worldwide and all the money funneled into Mr. Sedokova's account was through brilliant untraceable e-transfers. So no one actually got down to the banks to see through the transfers. Those days are long gone, Bru.'

'So it is possible that some computer genius saw through the money transfer and the creation of fraudulent yet authentic accounts.'

'That's highly probable. Maybe they have someone like Agent W4 in their pockets.'

Agents W2 and W5 patted Agent W4 and the Wolf smiled at him with appreciation.

'All hail "the techie" of PiCorp,' said Azzo Taccetta.

'All hail,' repeated many of them.

'All right, let's get back to the discussion,' said Agent W and added, 'We were buried in news reports, census reports, birth certificates, death certificates, marriage certificates and decennium of other such certificates for three days. We sniffed each and every document, but nothing was of the slightest significance. Well nothing except for the fact that Mr. Wasyl had a bank account at Erwin & Fritz.'

'And how is that of significance?' asked Barry.

'Well it wasn't until Anastasia found out from Mr. Sedokova's wife that Mr. Wasyl had offered to pay a significant cut to Mr. Sedokova for switching sides.'

'How did she get that out of her?'

'What's the need for secrecy when Mr. Wasyl was dead and when her husband's ass is on the line? She probably wouldn't have said anything if Mr. Lyaksandro were dead.'

'That makes sense,' said Mendez.

'Yes, sir, it does. Anastasia also found out that Mr. Sedokova's son was suffering from Tetralogy of Fallot and that he was advised to undergo a pediatric cardio vascular surgery.'

'So the reasons pertaining to the donations aren't erroneous,' asserted Peter Damiano.

'Yes, Peter, the reason is genuine. Now as to the source, it was indeed Mr. Wasyl.'

'But how…' began Bru.

'Let me save you the trouble. Anastasia had Sedokova lured to the Hyatt Regency on the day after we found out about the bank account.'

'Wolf, we should seriously recruit Anastasia. She is one of a kind!,' said Bru avidly.

'I'm afraid that isn't possible. Her wedding is due next month,' said Agent W6.

'Princeton taught you everything but decorum,' said Wolf to Bru before asking Agent W to proceed.

'We confronted him with the facts. We told him about the HUBOZ report, the footage at the courthouse and his wife's deposition. We warned him about the repercussions he could face if we happened to pass on our investigational proceeds to the Interpol.'

'So he snapped and confessed about the source, it being Mr. Wasyl,' concluded Matt.

'Yes, sir, that's right.'

'And the computer genius?'

'He said that Mr. Wasyl arranged the funneling and that he had nothing do with the laundering.'

'I presume that the money was reaped from Mr. Wasyl's campaign funds,' said Dino Santorelli.

'Well the campaign funds were just a part of it. The rest came from Mr. Wasyl's corruption proceeds.'

'Is there any evidence to support the corruption?'

'No, sir. Mr. Sedokova told us that Mr. Wasyl was a prim and cunning player. He would never let such things leak out.'

'Sounds sensible. Okay so who planted the heroin at the courthouse restroom?'

'We think that Khayr had a stash of heroin in the sole of his shoes.'

'How can you be so sure?'

'We went to Kandahar and tracked down his house. We met his wives and had them show us his workspace in exchange for proper educational facilities to their children.'

'How many?'

'Eighteen'

'Okay. I'll ask Mustafa to take care of it,' said Wolf. 'I'm glad you made the exchange. We need to educate these young children and make them understand the importance of life over their policy of rejuvenation in the afterlife.'

'Ridiculous policy.'

'I wouldn't say that and you shouldn't either. There are always reasons for every consequence, and the validity of these reasons depends solely on perspectives.'

There was total silence in the chamber.

'Please do proceed, agent,' said Wolf after a few silent seconds.

'Certainly, *lupo*. We went to his workspace and found a locker. We drilled it open and found this,' he said, and projected a picture of a certain key.

'This key opens Mr. Wasyl's cabin in Kiev,' said Agent W emphatically and startled them all.

'Well this unassailably establishes the point that Abu al Khayr knew Ilarion Wasyl,' Beth predicted.

'And that Mr. Wasyl was a regular consumer of the heroin,' continued Matt.

'So Mr. Wasyl meeting up with Khayr at the cabin isn't actually a set-up,' deduced Barry.

'Which implies that Khayr's testimony wasn't contrived,' said Mendez.

'And the usage of "handed over" and "Ilarion" is radically justified,' continued Bru.

'Spot on. In addition to the key, we also found heroin samples being stuffed in the insoles of shoes and printer cartridges being processed for disposal.'

'This explains Abu al Khayr's death, right?' said Enzo Luchesco.

'What about his employees?' asked Dexter, Elle's professional counterpart.

'They work for us now. We have them by the balls,' said Agent W proudly.

'How many?' asked Azzo.

'Three.'

'So in a nutshell, Mr. Wasyl frequently used narcotics sold by Abu al Khayr at his cabin. A few days before the elections, the doping levels went past the threshold, and he died being solely responsible for his own death. Meanwhile Abu al Khayr killed himself at the courthouse. Is that right?' asked Luigi Ruggiero.

'It can't be more precise.'

'With regards to Mr. Sedokova, we aren't going to pursue with the illegal funds and money laundering. We are going to expunge the HUBOZ report, delete all the softcopies and shred the hardcopies. Also we are going to get rid of the surveillance tapes from the courthouse and Mrs. Sedokova's deposition. We are going to lock away Khayr's key and lockdown his workspace. Sound good?' asked Bru.

All the board members and agents concurred.

'Good job everyone. This case is closed.'

'Before we leave, you said something about Anastasia's wedding,' said Bru.

'Yes, I did,' answered agent W.

'Who is she marrying?'

'Well it isn't official yet, but she told us that it was Schorsch Sieger, chairman of the United Front.'

CHAPTER 14

Wednesday, December 26th 2007.

It was Mayday for the officers of the New York Police Department and agents of the Federal Protective Service. The mob outside the United States District Court for the Southern District of New York was whimsical, and the law enforcement agencies had a tough time in keeping the situation at bay.

The situation became exorbitantly chaotic when the Hero of the Republicans daringly showed up at the courthouse. Uniformed Division Officers of the Secret Service, clad in utility uniforms and identification vests for members of the counter sniper team, and the Emergency Response Team sprawled across Pearl Street, as Special Agents of the Secret service, cloaked in loose-fitting jackets and wearing reflective sunglasses and communication earpieces, escorted Vice President Jamie Edwards into the courthouse. Fifteen trained snipers kept a close watch on the vicinity from various high-rise buildings, and the Uniformed Division Officers kept a close watch on the frantic mob from ground zero.

'Capital punishment is the most premeditated of murders.'

'He killed our senator…He deserves to die.'

'Even God would sentence this faggot to death.'

Conservationist and Liberals were vociferous, and the news reports couldn't wish for a better field day.

'Why does he have to go to the courthouse when his guilt has already been determined? I say hand him over to the public…' roared one of the many imbecilic crackpots as the sirens blared and made its way through the barricades.

The Vice President had asked the Marshal Service to have Nahiossi enter the courthouse through the main entrance. He wanted to cajole the public, ignite the animosity, kindle their emotions, and in the end, scarf it all and make an enthralling candidacy statement.

Nahiossi, with his hands chained and face covered in a black bag of cloth, stepped out of the Chevrolet Express and stood among his many haters. The Marshals cautiously escorted the six-foot-six thickset man into the courthouse, while the Vice President stood by the entrance and watched the proceeding with delight, which he managed to not portray outwardly.

'Mr. Griffiths, hope you enjoyed your stay at the MCC,' said Jamie as he walked alongside Nahiossi. 'It's just a matter of time before we send you up the river. So until then, just cope with things.'

Nahiossi and the Vice President entered the courtroom 12A paraded by the USSS and the Federal Marshals. The clerk of court Ms. Vivian Beretta Lawrence, the district attorney Mr. Ryan Fanning, defense attorney Mr. Nicholas Freeman, inspector Martin, Cortez, Juliette, Mark, Schell, Zenger, Hilton, the court staff and a few other invitees who were asked to witness the proceedings looked at Nahiossi with melancholy.

The court marshall extended the usual buffer for the court to settle. Once everyone was instated in the designated stands, he stepped forward and said,

'All rise and give your attention. The Honorable Judge Benjamin William Patrick of the United States District Court for the Southern District of New York.'

The fifty-five-year old lion, with a Caesar cut and a Verdi styled beard, majestically entered the courtroom and moved slowly to his seat. He smiled at the Vice President and sat behind a bullet-resistant bench.

The court reporter had set-up the attorneys' laptop to connect to the court-reporting network, which electronically transmitted the real time reporting and the transcript to the laptops. The defense and the prosecution attorneys looked briefly at their laptops and verified the contents of the case, as the clerk announced,

'The people of the State of New York v. Nahiossi Griffiths.'

Judge Patrick fixed his frameless glasses and looked down at his laptop. He cleared his throat and voiced in his baritone,

'Mr. Nahiossi Henrick Griffiths, you have been charged with the first degree murder of senator Vaughn Fletcher, first degree kidnapping of Vice President Jamie Edwards, first degree kidnapping of Schell Zachary, first degree kidnapping of Zenger Eldric, first degree kidnapping of Hilton Reinmund, aircraft piracy and interfering with flight crew members, illegal border crossing, assault, destruction of public property, trespassing, intentional killing of an animal...'

The list went on to include a few more minor yet accountable charges. The audience at the gallery listened to it all in dismay as Nahiossi was being charged with almost all the criminal charges a first year law student would know.

'...How does the defendant plead to these charges?'

Mr. Freeman stood up languidly and looked at Nahiossi, eagerly hoping for a terminal change of heart. He knew that his client was guilty. But he didn't want him to plead the same for the whole scheme. He wanted to negotiate with the district attorney and try to reduce the charges and thus the sentence. But Nahiossi looked at him confidently, and passively whispered, 'Guilty.'

Freeman let out a long sigh and apprehensively said, 'Guilty, your honour.'

Judge Patrick recorded the defendant's plea and asked a few questions - have your told your attorney all the facts about your cases? Do you want more time to talk to your attorney? Do you want the court to explain about the sentencing? Are you under the influence of alcohol, drugs or narcotics? Has the District Attorney (or an assistant), your lawyer, policeman, law enforcement officer or anyone else, including the judge, made any promises, threats or coerced you or brought any pressure upon you or any member of your family, to get you to plead guilty? Do you understand that since you are not a citizen of the United States, this proceeding may have an impact on your immigration status? Is your plea of guilt freely and voluntarily made? Have you...

The district attorney made eye contact with the defense attorney and raised his eyebrows in astonishment. The Vice President stood up and traipsed over to Juliette. He sat right beside her and told her that justice had been delivered and that her father's death hadn't gone unanswered. He reassured her of his support and asked her to knock on his door whenever she needed help. He then shook hands with Jordan and with Cortez before returning to his seat beside his unimaginably attractive dark-haired and petite secretary.

Judge Patrick quizzed Nahiossi with a few more mandatory questions, after which he went through the reports that brought out the factual basis for the plea.

Nahiossi not once dared to look at Juliette, Mark or Cortez. He really couldn't afford to endanger their lives. He was perceptive enough to analyse that the people who had so cunningly framed him didn't want him dead. He had something they needed and he knew that Juliette, Cortez and Mark were their pawns to have him execute a certain stint. Implying that there was no threat to his life, unlike theirs. At least not in the near future.

'It is my duty to inform to you that the court is not required to follow the plea agreement and that the sentencing is left to the discretion of the court as per the federal sentencing guidelines,' warned Judge Patrick before giving Nahiossi an opportunity to withdraw the plea.

The defense counsel upheld their decision, and the plea was irrevocably recorded.

Judge Patrick set a date for the sentencing hearing, and then wrapped up the session by saying,

'Thank you, Counsel. We will take the matter under advisement. This hearing is adjourned.'

The marshall stepped forward and announced 'All rise' as the judge stood up and walked out of the courtroom 12A.

Nahiossi made eye contact with Juliette for a fraction of a second and he realised again just how much he loved her. He knew that he would never let her down. He knew that no matter how much his conscious self rebelled him, no matter how many predicaments he would have to go through and no matter how much of his pretentious life he would lose, he would never give up on her. He told himself that he would get the job done, whatever it was and would silently disappear, once and for all.

People in love are crazy...and so is love.

The Special Agents of the Secret Service regrouped and led Jamie Edwards out of the courthouse, as the SOG huddled Mr. Griffiths from the rear entrance and whisked him off to the MCC. Jamie waved at the cameras and once again grabbed the opportunity to address his beloved citizens.

Ronald Regan once said, "I have wondered at times what the Ten Commandments would have looked like if Moses had run them through the US Congress."

The cameras were readjusted and focused on the Vice President as the crowd cheered their charismatic leader.

'People don't trust us anymore. People think we are counter-productive and that we are just a bunch of klutzes doing dirty politics and running behind power and money. Such is the degree we've reached after all these years of preserving, protecting and defending the constitution. Certain whimsical people in power have debased our motherland's sanctity, and we are constantly being confronted with people whom we don't want to elect. We don't need a seasoned politician to run our country. We need citizens, fellow American citizens who are capable of analysing the problems this country and by far our friendly allies are facing, with a better and refined perspective, without being influenced by bureaucracies and tyrannical hierarchies. We need people who are capable of throwing out the dormant laws and bringing in renewed policies and legislations. We need people who are capable of improving our deficit and impute an end to the financial recessions. We need people who are capable of not just fighting crimes and terrorism, but being capable of reducing it. Lastly, we need people who are not just capable of speaking, but capable of getting the job done. My fellow citizens, do you agree with me?'

The crowd cheered with approval and Jamie seemed to enjoy it. He didn't mean half the things he just said. Of course he didn't want another commoner to run the States. Well, in fact it is practically absurd. He just told the people what they wanted to hear. What a hero would say. He just wanted to make a few idealistic moot points and let the people ponder over it for a few days, by which time he would have begun the baby kissing, the veteran meetings, the charity balls and various other humanitarian and chivalrous activities, which would mirage people into believing that he is the right person to lead them.

'Our motherland deserves better than what we have right now and you are going to help me give it to her. My dear citizens, America deserves better. God bless the United States and God bless her children.'

Thursday, March 1st 2007

'Vijay Saxena entered his house.'

'Copy that. Wait for my command to pursue,' said Sushanth through his Government Issue untraceable mobile phone.

'Roger that.'

Sushanth immediately buzzed in Coleman and asked for authorisation.

'Give it a minute,' said Coleman and assessed the video feed in the surveillance room at PiCorp New York.

PiCorp New Delhi received video feeds from the cameras installed at the Warden's residence. The feeds were then processed at PiCorp New Delhi and streamed to the United States through a VPN (Virtual Private Network), the function of which was to encrypt and reroute the Internet access and effectively replace the Internet Service Provider.

Vijay entered his house and called out for his wife, but there was no response. He thought that she might have turned in, and so he walked to his bedroom, but he couldn't find her. He took his mobile phone out of his pocket and called her mobile, but it was switched off.

'Now,' said Coleman, and instantly Sushanth had the same relayed to his associates.

Amrutha jumped out of a smokey black Tata Winger and walked towards Saxena's residence and hesitantly knocked on his door.

Distant footsteps were audible and she could sense the warden approaching. She turned around and looked at the minivan apprehensively, as Vijay opened the door and said, 'Amrutha, what's the matter? What are doing here?'

'We need to talk. It's something important. Can I come in?'

'Sure, come on in.'

'Thank you.'

Amrutha looked over her shoulder and entered the house as Vijay shut the door behind her and asked, 'So, what is the matter? Does it have something to do with Rajiv?'

'Where are Kavya and Apoorva?' she asked, not wanting to answer that question.

Vijay shook his head and said, 'I don't know. Her phone is switched off. Maybe they went down to get...'

There was another knock on the door.

'Maybe it's them. I'll go get it,' said Vijay and turned back.

'I'm sorry, Vijay,' whispered Amrutha and injected his neck with dexmedetomidine, a sedative. Vijay passed out immediately and Amrutha sluggishly had him laid out on the carpeted floor.

'He's out. Knock again,' said Sushanth, looking at the feed.

The associate outside the house followed the orders and knocked on the door again. Amrutha immediately rushed to the door and opened it, as three men wearing black jumpsuits stormed inside the house.

'We're in,' said one of the three men as Amrutha locked the door behind her.

'Okay, detach all the devices and retreat to the safe house.'

'Roger that.'

Sunday, April 3rd 2005

Anastasia was shocked to see Mrs. Sedokova at the United Front.

Her fiancé, Sieger, broke the suspense and told her that Mrs. Sedokova had been a staunch proponent of the *Führer* and of the Fourth Reich. He introduced them both and had them exchange excerpts about their trials and tribulations.

During their discussion, Mrs. Sedokova told Anastasia that she and the *Führer* were stumped when Anastasia had shown up at her doorstep on the day before. She told her about reporting Dr. Norbert's blunder to Schüler and having her abducted in order to retain their clandestineness. Subsequently, they pondered over the topic of Anastasia's wedding, with Mrs. Sedokova gaping at her in awe as she narrated her first tryst with the *Führer* at the Berghof.

During lunch, they got down to the topic of Wasyl's death. Anastasia learnt that the *Führer* had Mr. Sedokova and Abu al Khayr murder Wasyl. Mrs. Sedokova told her that the *Führer* had the heroin planted in Wasyl's house and forcefully had him administer it before having the forensic experts remove the undesired trace evidence. They pondered over the details until they were done with the first serving of braised beef with *spaetzie*. When they were offered the second serving of the same course, Mrs. Sedokova had her know that the stalker next to Wasyl's cabin was an associate of the *Führer* and she was ordered to take pictures of Wasyl receiving an envelope from Abu al Khayr. She then explained the girl's background, and Abu al Khayr's association with the *Führer*. During desserts, Anastasia asked her about the money laundered by Mr. Sedokova and found out that the *Führer* had indeed had Dr. Norbert see through the laundering, but it wasn't a mode of payment for having her husband murder Wasyl, but it was genuinely for their son's pediatric cardio-vascular surgery.

After lunch, they discussed Mrs. Sedokova and her family. She told Anastasia that her grandparents lived in the Third Reich and were resolute followers of the *Reichshanzker*. She explained to her about the greatness of the *Reichshanzker's* regime and the fame Nazi Germany had achieved just before the World War II. They spoke about the treaty of Munich, German invasion of Poland, *Blitzkrieg*, tripartite pact, invasion of USSR and eventually moved on to the Pearl Harbor tragedy, with Mrs. Sedokova conspiring that Franklin D Roosevelt indeed had prior knowledge of the attack and that he himself was responsible in cajoling the Japanese forces to bombard the U.S Naval Base. The discussion then drifted to the battle of Stalingrad, Dwight Eisenhower's Allied Expeditionary Forces, fall of Berlin, bombings on Japan, the fall of the Third Reich, Grand Admiral Karl unconditional surrender to the allies and the end of Adolf Hitler's physical existence. She strongly insisted on the words 'physical existence', for according to her, Hitler and his principles were immortal, and that the Fourth Reich was born with the purpose of fulfilling the *Reichshanzker's* legacy.

That evening, they went down to Schüler's residence, where the *Führer* and the Kiev *Gruppenführer* joined them. They casually had dinner, and then they moved to the study to discuss the Wasyl case screw up.

They thought about having the agents abducted, but Anastasia told them that the agents were a part of a big network and they really didn't care about lives. So it wouldn't really make much of a difference if they abducted a mere six men. It might just prove to increase their chances of getting caught. They then talked about turning the agents against their agency, but that seemed a little far-fetched and too risky. So they deliberated over it for a few minutes, and then the criminal mastermind, Joseph Schaub shared with the team the solution he already had in mind.

According to Schaub's Kiev Plan, Anastasia was to tell the team that she got certain info regarding her husband from Mrs. Sedokova. Meanwhile the *Gruppenführer* at Kiev would contact an associate at Afghanistan and have the key planted in Khayr's locker and heroin stuffed in his shoes. Since Wasyl and Khayr weren't alive to confess anything, they absolutely had no problem. Also, since Mr. Sedokova was in fact with Lyaksandro before coming to Wasyl's party, no further supcisions would be raised on that front. So, mischief managed.

She'd then go to Kiev and report the same to the agents, who'd presumably simply put two and two together and find out that it was Wasyl who was responsible for his own death. If the plan didn't work and if the agents turned out to be extremely brilliant, there was always a person to rely on for inside information.

CHAPTER 15

Monday, January 7th 2008

Mark Griffiths would never leave the confines of his room on Friday, and no one was ever allowed to enter his room.

But the day on which Nahiossi was sentenced to serve fifty years at the Attica Correctional Facility was an exception. Mark returned from the United States District Court for the Southern District of New York with tens of news reporters chasing after him. The NYPD had set a perimeter around the Phoenix villa and kept the reporters at bay.

Captain Blunt escorted Mark inside the villa and informed that his men would be guarding the perimeter until the mob died down. Mark thanked him, and before having him sent off, called the butler and the maidservant and asked them to take a leave of absence for the weekend. Captain Blunt gave Mark his calling card and then walked out of the villa with the butler, Dick and the maidservant, Maria.

The phone kept buzzing and Mark ignored it. He didn't want to deal with the reporters and their tormenting questions.

What would happen to the airline industry? Would Phoenix retract to Europe? Who would be voted as the new chairman of the Phoenix Music

Company? Would people lose jobs because of the decline in the company's economy? Was it true that Nahiossi and Juliette were dating? Would he stay in the US or go back to the Netherlands...

While Mark was listlessly pondering over the chain of events, his cell-phone buzzed. The display said that the caller was Reverend Sean. Mark cleared his throat and answered the call.

'Mark, I just got the news. How are you doing?'

'Not good, not good,' he answered, crying.

'Listen my son, the Lord is near to the brokenhearted and saves the crushed in spirit. Believe in him and trust his judgment. Cast your burden on the Lord, and he will sustain you; he will never permit the righteous to be moved.'

'But I never thought that Nahiossi was capable of murder. Why did the Lord do this to him? What wrong made him incur the Lord's wrath?'

'The Lord isn't responsible for the actions of his children and the Lord will never hate his children. Nahiossi was solely responsible for his consequences, for the love of money is the root for all evil. His greed for money made him lose faith in God. He never visited the church and he never once submitted himself to our Lord. The Almighty is beyond our reach and exalted in power; in his justice and great righteousness, he does not oppress.'

'Praise the Lord. I have no authority to question His judgment and I have no doubt that He loves my child. All I ask of Him is the well-being of my son. He is alone in the midst of criminals and even though he too is a criminal to the rest of the world, he is not to me. He will always be my son and the Lord's child.'

'Keep your faith in Him and He shall take care of Nahiossi.'

'Amen.'

'Okay Mark, I'll see you at the church on Sunday.'

'I'll be there, Reverend,' said Mark and hung up.

He then stood up and walked to his room. He locked the doors and windows and switched on the air-conditioner. He went to the bathroom, took a cold shower and slipped into a satin gown. He then walked into his closet and opened the locker in one of the cupboards. The locker housed no cash, or jewels or gun, but it housed a human skull.

Mark slowly and carefully carried the box to the bedroom and kept it on the table. He undid the locks and held his brother's skull in his hands. He then placed it on the table and knelt in front of it. He stared at it with devotion and said, 'John, why isn't the Lord forgiving my past sins? Talk to me, John, please talk to me. Please brother, forgive me. You know I didn't kill you, right? Jesus killed you. Not me. It was all Him'

Mr. Singhania had laundered almost 4.5 thousand crores to Lombard, Brian and Celt over a span of ten years. The *Führer's* financial advisors and espionage unit learnt about this from their confederates in the Swiss Federal Department of Finance, and had Schüler order the abduction of Mr. Singhania to Germany.

Schorsch Sieger met with Singhania, explained his ideology of the Fourth *Reich* and of the conceptualisation of Germany being the World Leader, and had him indoctrinated to their prospect of domineering. Singhania assured his allegiance to the *Führer* and returned to India, not just as the leader of the Janlok Party, but also as the turned associate of the *Führer* and a partisan of the Fourth *Reich*.

Singhania maintained an alliance with Lombard, Brian and Celt, as he had done for almost a decade, and had them cover his tracks. His transactions were authenticated under a phony identity and the chairman of Lombard, Brian and Celt had the identities of Singhania and the *Führer* copiously veiled.

The Chairman, Johan Poli, had obediently hidden the account since the day Kevin was arraigned. He'd assured to keep the account sequestered until the *Führer* asked him to revoke it or have the funds transferred.

A week after the analysts were presented with the task of framing Rajiv, they came up with an airtight plan and had Schüler approve it. The *Führer* was informed about the *Gruppenführer's* plan and accordingly, he sent a few *Schutzstaffel* (SS) from the financial wing of the *Reichssicherheitshauptamt* (Reich Main Security Office) and *Sicherheitsdienst* (Security Service), with the SS-*Standartenführer*, Dr. Hans Gernot, overlooking the operation.

As per the plan, Poli had to hand over three quarters of Singhania's illegal money to the SS and float the remaining quarter back on the company's official grid. Poli had to then morph Singhania's phony account details and annotate for the thousand crores in such a way that upon scrupulous investigation, it would point to Rajiv. Meanwhile, the Indian *Gruppenführer* had Singhania acquainted with Adithya, who now had the task of framing his brother.

Adithya was supposed to shadow his brother and insidiously move the thousand crores to an offshore account in the Bahamas. He had to tenaciously tail Rajiv because the cell-phone to which the TANs would be sent had to be in close proximity with Rajiv. So when the CBI officials had the service providers track down the phone, it would unassailably lead to the locations where Rajiv had actually been at the said times. So in accordance to this plan, Adithya effectuated six transactions - two from Rajiv's house, two from his party office and the rest from his farmhouse. All transactions were made at irregular intervals and the Swedish Krona was skeptically moved to Bahamas. After this, Adithya went to Rajiv's farmhouse alone, and hid the iPad through which the transactions were initiated and the cell-phone that had received the TANs. Two mornings after the devices were planted, Singhania had Shekkar inform Kevin that he could take the prosecution's deal and help them catch the bigger fish, Rajiv.

'Mr. Kashyap, we have bad news,' said Warden Saxena, on the day after Amrutha had him abducted to the PiCorp safe house.

'Your son...' he said, and gazed at Rajiv, as thoughts of his own son, Abhishek, clamoured in his head. PiCorp had Abhishek and his mother abducted from Delhi and restrained at one of PiCorp's safe houses in Mumbai. Well, only that the warden didn't think that it was safe enough.

'...met with an accident this morning. Hit and run case.'

Rajiv dramatically dropped his plate and turned around.

'His condition is deteriorating and your wife wants you to go down to the hospital and...'

'And what?' yelled Rajiv.

'Mr. Kashyap, you need to calm down. I too have a son and I truly understand how it feels when your only son's life is at stake.'

'Truly understand, sure,' mumbled Rajiv sarcastically as the warden continued,

'I have personally acceded to your wife's request, and I am permitting your escort to the Mediwave right away. Sub-inspector Reddy and Harshith are going to be brief with the security procedures and will have you transported to the hospital ASAP.'

Rajiv silently gazed at Vijay and the two sub-inspectors, and simply said, 'Thank you.'

Tuesday February 13th 2007

'Isn't Morgan joining us?'

'I'm afraid not. He had to go down to Kimberly.'

'He didn't mention anything about it. Is there a problem?'

'No, absolutely not,' said Sieger and patted Vaughn.

'If you say so.'

'Martini?' asked the banker, Sieger, as he traipsed towards the starling bar inside the Isak Suite at the Frälsare, Stockholm.

'On the rocks.'

'Coming right up,' mimicked Sieger and smiled.

Vaughn lit another Cuban and puffed it nonchalantly, as the *Führer* played the bartender.

'How is it going at Luxembourg?'

'Dr. Wendel assures me that he has everything chalked out. I'll have to meet with the Grand Duke sometime next week,' said Sieger, with his voice growing louder and clearer as he inched closer to Vaughn.

'Cheers to that,' said Vaughn, as Sieger offered him the drink.

The two buddies sat down and chatted for a while, as they drained their glasses and smoked up the cigars. They then moved into the den and settled in to talk business.

'Julie and Nahiossi have…' he said, and cleared his throat before saying, 'fallen in love with each other.'

'So? You don't want to take over his industry?'

Vaughn looked at Sieger and said, 'What makes you think that I don't want to take over? You know I have no regards for illusions like emotions and affections. I know only loyalty and I am loyal only to the Reich *Führer*.'

'I'm glad to hear that, Vaughn,' said Sieger, and smiled at his comrade.

'Heil Hitler,' said Vaughn and added, 'As I was saying, Julie and Nahiossi are in love and I am going to have them married by Christmas…'

Sieger raised his eyebrow, but said nothing.

'… In two years' time, Julie would become a Dutch citizen and hence she would be legally permitted to hold Nahiossi's holdings in the industry. So we'd have Nahiossi transfer his holdings at Phoenix to Juliette, and as usual, we'll have the schmuck killed.'

'By schmuck you mean Nahiossi, right?'

'Of course.'

'Okay, go on.'

'Once Nahiossi dies, Julie would inherit his possessions and she would be unassailably eligible to invoke the voting clause. But she isn't dynamic enough to handle the pressure. So I'd have her select a member of your choice to represent her and contest in the election. We'd have him win, and *voila*, you'll have a new puppet in the house.'

'It's not about just one person. We need the entire board to back us. We need the unconditional loyalty of the board and we can't achieve it by just threatening people. When you have men coerced to do something of this magnitude, at least one of them will trivialise their pressure points and go public with what we intend to do.'

'Well, what if we kill those who are fiddly?'

'Have you read about the Reichstag Fire?'

'Yes I have, but I don't know how it is relevant in this context.'

'Hitler encountered a political stalemate - ' began Sieger and stood up. He fetched a cigarette from a box on the coffee table and said, ' - when NSDAP's opponents grew in number and held a major ground in the government. Hitler asked President Hindenburg to dissolve the Reichstag, and as a consequence, he had elections scheduled for early March. Six days before the elections, the Reichstag was torched and Göring blamed the communists. Hitler had Hindenburg issue the Reichstag Fire Decree, which suspended civil liberties, Habeas Corpus rights and allowed detention without trial. The activities of the German communist party were suppressed and over a thousand communist party members were arrested. As a result, the majority in the government against Hitler deteriorated and two thirds of the remaining parliamentarians voted in favor of the Enabling Act, which gave Hitler the right to rule by decree. Now he could have just had the members from the opposition threatened or killed. But that wouldn't serve the purpose of the big picture. That would just make the communists ferocious and that would mean disaster.'

'I get it. So what do we do?'

'We have to go about the situation in a…' said Sieger and let the sentence hang, as his private phone began to vibrate in his pocket.

'I'll be just a moment, Vaughn,' said Sieger and answered the call.

'We have a situation. Cortez knows the truth about Huritt and Sarah.'

Sieger chose not to respond to that question in front of Vaughn. He resolutely walked into the bedroom and locked himself in. He then entered the restroom and asked, 'How?'

'Jamie didn't divulge that information. He wants to meet you in person before the situation blows out of proportion.'

'Have Mendez informed about my departure to New York. I'll go down to the airport in forty five minutes.'

'What about the meeting with Hyun Woo?'

Sieger let out a sigh and pondered for a while before saying, 'You fly down to Pyongyang. Discuss about the military and put the idea of the missile in his head. I'll address the other issues when we next meet.'

'I'll do that. And Morgan just delivered the consignment.'

'Good. Did you dispatch it yet?'

'It's been done. Ghaffar will have it delivered to the Sheikh.'

'Good,' said Sieger and flushed the toilet. He exited the restroom, and then the bedroom.

'Sure. Heil Führer,' said Schuler and hung up.

'I'm sorry, Vaughn, I have to leave the country immediately. Something important has come up.'

'What's the rush?'

'Well the Iranian President announced that his administration is open to negotiations regarding its nuclear program. So Schuler thinks that it is necessary for me to go and talk to Manssor.'

'In that case, I think it's best for you to leave. We'll meet again when I come up with something else.'

'Excellent,' said Sieger and shook Vaughn by the hand. 'Now that you are going to be alone all night long, why don't you have some fun? I'll have Walter informed.'

'You see right through me.'

Chapter 16

A man cloaked in black parka pointed his gun at Mark and fired a bullet. Mark screamed as the bullet cut through his chest, while the man in the black parka laughed zestfully. Blood spilled all over the floor as Mark fell on his knees and then collapsed on the carpeted floor of the Phoenix villa. Then the man in the black parka hovered over the body and removed his ski mask to allow the dying man to know who his killer was. He slowly removed the mask, and when he was done, Mark widened his eyes in disbelief and died instantly. The man in the black parka, Nahiossi, shot his father and watched him die in agony.

As Nahiossi shut his father's eyes for the last time, the man whom Nahiossi had only heard about, but never seen slowly walked towards him from the rear and slit his throat. Nahiossi jerked and widened his eyes, just as his father had done mere moments ago.

Nahiossi jolted and woke up from his nightmare. But his reality was more torturous than that of the agony in his nightmare.

He was honoured when the people had him epitomised as the Phoenix. But never had he realised that he'd one day be caged, and that there would be no way, unlike the phoenix, for him to rise back from the ashes.

Twenty three days of confinement in a cell that was no larger than the desk at his office, and no contact with other human beings made him go haywire. There were no group activities at Attica: no work, no educational opportunities, no eating together, no sports, no getting together with other people for religious services, and no attempts at rehabilitation. Phone calls and visitation privileges were strictly limited. Books and magazines were denied, and TV and radio were prohibited. All these factors took a toll on his mental condition. Nahiossi was destabilising, and experiencing hallucinations and delusions.

Nahiossi stood up inside the dark cell and shouted for the guards to turn the lights on. The control booth officers heard his cry, but they did nothing. They simply feasted on his agony.

Like a caged rat under fire, he scampered into the hole, but with every couple of steps, he encountered cold concrete. He craved to catch a glimpse of the outside world. Even the glimpse of a tiny blade of grass would suffice.

The Correctional Officers watched his frenzy for some time and then shot out commands that made him realise that there was nothing he could do to improve the condition. In fact, if he kept on with his perturbation, he would be immediately transferred to the strip cells, where the guards would have him chained spread-eagle and naked to concrete beds in even smaller cells.

Nahiossi breathed heavily and crouched in between two concrete walls. Stewing in his own filth and stripped of all hope, Nahiossi prayed for the Lord's mercy.

Friday, March 2nd 2007

President Nolan Bush pined to visit Rajghat not just to pay homage to the Father of the Nation, Mahatma Gandhi, but also to visit the nimbus precincts of the memorial, where his father had planted a mango sapling during his visit to India in 1984.

Meanwhile Rajiv Kashyap restlessly waited – as the laborious prisoner transport procedures were being perpetrated – and yearned to visit Mediwave, not just to see his apparently dying son, but also to go AWOL.

The Presidential motorcade started from the Maurya Sheraton Hotel, with the USSS, FBI, Indian Intelligence Bureau (IB), the Delhi police and a couple of other private clandestine security agencies - including PiCorp - providing multiple layered security.

Meanwhile Rajiv Kashyap was being escorted to the Mediwave, with Sub Inspectors Reddy and Harshith providing him not-so-sophisticated security.

The traffic enroute to Rajghat was diverted, and every destination on Nolan's itinerary was cordoned off. Politicians, journalists and big shots who were primeval to the upper berth of the society, ceremoniously headed towards the Hyderabad House, where the Dubya was scheduled to meet the Prime Minister, Manmohan Singh.

Owing to the traffic constraints, the minivan in which Rajiv was being transported was diverted to unfrequented roads, where the agents from PiCorp waited in two unmarked Toyotas and a lorry, neatly quipped to abduct Rajiv.

The President's Limousine maintained its steady course for about a half hour, after which it came to a scheduled halt at Rajghat. Once there, the agents spread out and checked the vicinity before having the President disembark from his limo.

As the 43rd President of the United States arrived at Mahatma Gandhi's memorial, the 26th Corporate Affairs minister of India emerged on Gandhi Marg. Immediately after spotting the minivan, Sushanth eased his vehicle into the concerned lane and pursued it.

Rajiv slightly bent down and looked at a lorry that was docked just a few metres away from his present position. He closed his eyes and prayed Lord Vishnu, asking for nothing but freedom. He then let out a gasp and opened his eyes, while the lorry casually pulled into the road and maintained a steady course ahead of the minivan. The minivan was now sandwiched between the lorry and the Toyota.

Meanwhile at Rajghat Nolan was sandwiched between a pious politician and an overly patriotic law enforcement officer, being continually bothered with renditions regarding the nitty-gritty of the memorial. Even though he mentioned nothing, very much like Rajiv, he was eager to be put out of misery.

The lorry slowly decelerated, and so did the minivan and the Toyota. A few seconds later, the lorry came to a sudden halt. The driver, wearing a turban and flaunting a bushy beard, sporadically jumped out and walked towards the rear, while SI Reddy stepped out and proceeded to ask the driver to park the lorry off the road.

As SI Reddy approached the lorry, three men wearing ski masks popped up the cargo space and aimed their SIGs at the minivan, as the driver held SI Reddy at gunpoint. Simultaneously three more men wearing ski masks and completely cloaked in black jumpsuits, busted out off the Toyota and ambushed the minivan. Two of them had the driver and the constable keep their hands off the radio transmitter, while the third agent forcefully opened the rear door and held SI Harshith at gunpoint.

Rajiv said, 'I hope the Gandhi in you supercedes Bose,' and ran towards the Toyota parked on the opposite lane. Amrutha opened the door for her client, and then quickly whisked off.

Meanwhile Nolan was whisked away by members from the MEA (Ministry of External Affairs) office and the Chairman of the Rajghat Samadhi Committee to the serene garden, where around two hundred distinguished visitors right from the days of Dwight D Eisenhower, had planted mango saplings during their visit to Hindustan.

Two of the three agents jumped down the cargo space and strapped both the sub-inspectors before having their weapons confiscated. They then strapped their legs and dumped them inside the minivan's rear. The driver and the constable were none the wiser.

The agents retracted with military agility and dispersed from the scene. The Toyota and the truck were then taken down to a garage and methodically remodeled.

Two agents from PiCorp dressed in the traffic police officer's uniform removed the *'No entry, take diversion'* signpost from either sides of the lane and quietly drove away from the scene. Wolf never believed in chance or luck or karma or anything of the like. Everything was planned.

'Does Nolan think Gandhi would bless one of the main purposes of this trip -- to promote nuclear aid to India?

Wednesday, February 14th 2007

'With Vaughn dead and Nahiossi jailed, there would be chaos in the industry. Almonte would no longer want to carry out operations in Europe. The Vice Chairman of Almonte, Mrs. Clearwater, would go public with Nahiossi's Black Knight story and would implicate the European Board of Directors on a series of allegations. The industry's shares prices would hit rock bottom and they would undoubtedly be Fire Sales. We would then have our confederates purchase all the shares that come up on the European market, while Cortez will buy the shares coming up on the American Stock Exchange. The European Board of Directors would eventually lose the majority holdings in the company'

'I presume that is where I come in,' said Sieger.

'No, not yet. The Board would be losing control, but the Dutch Government and the European Union wouldn't yet allow you to take over. Always make your presence felt by generosity, never make them catch a wind of your desperation. After all naturalisation is the best form of infiltration.'

'You have reassured me of your commitment to the Reich, Jamie. I shall see to it that you will be most generously rewarded once we have established The New Order.'

'I most certainly will be honored, *Führer*.'

'Glad to hear that, Jamie. Now please do continue.'

'Okay, so in order to achieve what I just said, we would have the SS ignite riots in Netherlands. We shall have them protest against the industry and against its functionality. The movement would be a peaceful one and the people protesting aren't going to resort to anything violent. But we shall have the person guiding the attack killed and have one of the Directors of Phoenix pinned for it.'

'Just like Goring framed the communists.'

'Precisely. Also, since the SS is involved with all this, we needn't be precise about the planning. Any of us would welcome death for the betterment of the Reich.'

Sieger silently nodded, signalling the VP to move on.

'Obviously this would further decline the influence of the Board and the fall would be catastrophic. The support against the industry would elope and the Board of Directors at Phoenix would be fiddling with desperation and anxiety.'

'So this is where I come in.'

'Exactly. You approach the directors and extend a helping hand. Tell them that you will take over the company and run it under the same flagship. Then go public with your proposal and confess that you are doing it for the betterment of the countries and of its citizens. The disclosure would get undivided attention from every corner of every country and Cortez's board would debate it for a few days, and then announce its solidarity to the United Front. Soon after this happens, you will go to Attica Correction Facility and have Nahiossi accede to your takeover.'

'That is brilliant, Jamie. So I get to have total control over Phoenix Almonte.'

'That is correct. Now it doesn't end there. I will run for Office in 2008 and when I become the President, I will have a new deregulation act passed which would ensure flexible perimeter rules and slot allocations, commercialisation of Air Traffic Control, user driven ATC system, better procurement methods, increase in the number of regional jets, elimination of federal restriction on airport access, permission to set up commercial airports and, best of the all, autonomy over the routes.'

'So I will have total control over the airlines and can have them routed wherever I want.'

'Yes. That's what you asked for.'

'Brilliant!' said Sieger enthusiastically, and hugged Jamie. He kissed him on the cheek and boisterously praised him.

In between the praises, Sieger asked Jamie, 'Why won't he just have Nahiossi captured in the States?'

'Two reasons. One - it will ruin my purpose of becoming America's favorite hero, and two - if he were captured here, he would be sentenced to life without parole. But now his maximum sentencing limit is fixed by the extradition treaty, and so he cannot be sentenced till death.'

'But why does he care so much about Nahiossi's life?'

'Because he is Huritt's son.'

'So Julie and Nahiossi are...'

'Exactly.'

Minions In The Well

CHAPTER 17

June 19, 1979
Sebastian's office, *La rue Joseph-Kessel*
Paris, France

5:00 PM.

'*Oscar, vous irez sur le plan avec Sebastian. N'est-ce pas?*'

'Definitely, Mr. Achak. First up, I will sequester the periphery within a fifty-metre radius with the restroom as the point of reference. No spectators, no media personnel and no one from the staff will be allowed inside the periphery – ' said the burly man with hooded eyelids and sneezed. ' – Excuse me, without my permission. Next, I will instruct the cheerleaders to stay put on the other side of the track up until the last participant leaves the restroom. I will also have the security personnel stationed on the outer side of the compound wall and lastly – ' continued the man with coiled black hair and sneezed again. ' – Sorry, I'll arrange for distractions.'

'Be specific.'

The awfully blanched Irish immigrant looked at the lawyer and said in his wobbly voice, 'About what?'

'About the distractions.'

'Right! Okay, Mr. Sebastian. The distractions will include pretentious media personnel, flashy cheerleaders in minimal clothing, women lifting their skirts, fireworks and the spectators on tenterhooks.'

'Lemonade?'

'Yes. Well, it is not so much of a distraction. It is more of world-weariness, agent.'

'Same difference. Pray, continue'. *Fuck you!*

Oscar shifted a smile and said, 'I will have Chlorpromazine mixed with lemonade – '

'– No, Mr. Oscar, you will have lemonade mixed with Chlorpromazine.'

'Same difference,' said Oscar and winked at the thirty-three-year old stiff-necked lawyer.

Chlorpromazine, marketed in the United States as Thorazine and elsewhere as Largactil, is a typical antipsychotic. First synthesised in 1950, it was the first drug developed with specific antipsychotic actions. These drugs are homologous to tranquilisers that are capable of strongly reducing awareness to and mindfulness of one's surroundings. It works on a variety of receptors in the central nervous system, producing anti-cholinergic, anti-dopaminergic, anti-histaminic, and weak anti-adrenergic effects.

'All right, continue,' said Sebastian impassively and wiped the sweat off his slick, bald head. He picked up his sterling silver cigarette off the table, coughing as he did, and lit himself another unfiltered Gauloises.

Huritt looked at him sternly and thought, *why the hell do you smoke so damn much?*

The husky-voiced, red-complexioned lawyer in Charvet Place Vendôme's white long-sleeved shirt undid another button of his blue velvet waistcoat and said, 'I'm a patriot! I'm contributing to the national good. I'm ameliorating our deficits.'

'Faire taire!' said Huritt disgustedly and turned back at the thirty-two-year old evicted Londoner, who was fairly good at speaking French. His five-year stay in Paris and his signature French beard made first-timers believe that he was a French national. But then he wasn't all that good with the language and the accent. Regardless of the language barrier, he was proficient in workman lingo, and his knowledge in HR management was far beyond description.

Oscar uncomfortably shifted his weight onto his left buttock and said, 'I will go to the VIP lounge and stay there until 7:45. Then, I'll go to restroom 1 and survey its vicinity. After assessing the situation, I will call the volunteers. I will then drive back to the VIP lounge at the starting point.'

'Perfect.'

'I will wait for Ricardo's call, and then I will drive back to Gate 1 and repeat the same errand.'

Huritt's chuckle was a tenor, expressing his disagreement with Oscar's narration. But unlike the Irish immigrant, Sebastian failed to display any sort of precipitance.

How did he understand? He doesn't know English! Oscar thought and peered down his gold-framed spectacles.

'He wants you to elaborate it. He doesn't want you to rush. He wants every stone unturned,' said Sebastian and sighed, cunningly steering Oscar's attention. He then added the official boisterous motivational dictum, 'Our future depends on tomorrow's events. Our laborious efforts will be cast out in the open and we have to be diligent through and through. Remember, if we succeed tomorrow, everything will change. Everything. You know the magnitude of our pursuit. I needn't remind you about the severity now, do I?'

Sebastian might have hinted something. He is right. I needn't scratch my head over trivial issues. I need to focus my attention. I need to pull myself together.

'Sorry, I do, I do understand. And I definitely won't let him down, because that would mean letting myself down and I would never do anything to disgrace myself.'

'Good to hear that, Oscar. Please, continue.'

Oscar sneezed again, only this time he felt the need for a handkerchief, and sadly he didn't have any. 'I-I'm sorry, I forgot to – '

' – *Prendre cette,*' said Huritt passively and handed over his handkerchief.

'Thank you, Mr. Achak. I-I buy you a new one,' said Oscar and intently waited for him to reply. *Do you know English, do you know...* But Hurrit turned towards Sebastian and asked what Oscar had said. Sebastian translated Oscar's statement to French and then retranslated Huritt's reply to English. 'He says he'll subtract the handkerchief's cost from the ten million.'

He doesn't know English. He definitely doesn't. 'Sure!' said Oscar and gave Huritt a thumbs-up. He sneezed again, wiped his nose on Huritt's handkerchief and then continued his narration. 'After receiving Ricardo's call, I will drive back to Gate 1 and survey the rear side of the restroom 1. Then at ten o'clock, I will call the volunteers and have them collect the cartons again. Once that is done, I will drive back to the VIP lounge near Arc de Triomphe.'

'Est-ce tout?'

'Is that all?'

'With regards to the Triathlon, yes.'

'Parfait.'

'Merci, Mr. Achak,' said Oscar and smiled. He sneezed again, ruefully retrieved a pill from his wallet, poured himself a sip of whiskey and sent the pill down his throat. He sat quietly for a brief minute, and then he said, 'At eleven o'clock, I will drive down to my apartment and pick up my wife and son. I will drop them off at Charles de Gaulle and thereupon drive down to Bondy.'

After thorough discussion on the details for ten more minutes, the international attorney stood up lazily, pulled up his black trousers and limped towards Oscar. He took an envelope from Huritt and handed it over to the Irish immigrant saying, 'All the best, Oscar. Here you go, it's time for you to re-enter the *Smoke.*'

5:30 PM.

'You almost lost it there. Oscar looked at you with suspicion!'

'I know. Fuck! I know,' said Huritt Achak, the noble son-in-law of Sir Edgar Fermont, as he paced around Sebastian's dimly lit den. Even though he was confident about the practicality of his plan, he just couldn't shake off the trepidation. He went over the plan again and again with his *compadre* and he trained immensely. His mind was so fixated on winning the Triathlon that he simply couldn't keep his mind contained. 'Too much pressure, Sebastian. Too much pressure.'

'I know, buddy. But we cannot afford mistakes now. We've been extremely cautious and we have crossed so many hurdles. We cannot fail after coming so damn far. We have got to endure it. We must win.'

Huritt collapsed on the couch, poured himself bourbon and gulped it hurriedly. 'I-I'll try to be more careful. Er, sorry.'

'No problem, *amigo*. No problem. Keep your faith in God and everything will be just fine.'

'God! What God? You son-of-a-bitch! Don't tell me you are a believer!'

'From time to time.'

'From time – you know what, fuck you!'

'I'm sorry, my parents bred me in praise of the Good Shepherd. Not my fault. I just can't stop believing in Him!'

'Why?'

'Because...because I don't want to,' said Sebastian and lit himself another Gauloises.

'You know what? It's fine! I don't care!'

'I'm glad that you don't.'

The two of them let the silence sink in and let their minds dwell on something less trivial. Huritt thought about Pam, the petite brunette he had fucked on the previous night, and Sebastian thought of buying himself a new cigarette holder. A diamond studded piece. Or perhaps platinum...

'Sebastian, why don't you go out and smoke? This place stinks!'

'Smells like heaven on earth,' said the green-eyed lawyer ecstatically. 'Don't forget, *Mon frère*, your compulsive smoking addiction supported our claim at *Cour d'assises.*'

'What claim?' asked Huritt, as if he didn't know what Sebastian was talking about.

'Erectile Dysfunction, the case of *Huritt Achak vs. Montego Cortez*, October 16, 1978! That sexy racked Veronica!'

'Ah! The lady with the breasts of a Greek Goddess!'

'Goddess? You said you don't believe in God. Looks like you make exceptions for Goddesses. For Greek Goddesses. For Goddesses with big breasts!'

'I used it metaphorically, asshole!'

'Metaphorically? Wow! I've trained you so well! I should have been an English professor. I would have been illustrious!'

'Only if all your students were smart.'

'All right, boss! Let's call it even then,' said Sebastian as he slumped right next to Huritt and placed another cigarette between his lips. He took in a couple of drags, and then the doorbell jingled.

'That must be Felix,' said Sebastian and stood off the couch. He limped along the long corridor and then sluggishly opened the door.

'Ah! Mr. Tom Felix.'

5:45 PM.

'The man of the hour!' exclaimed Huritt in French as Felix entered the den.

'I'm sor - ' began Felix, but before he could complete that sentence, the tobacco hit his lungs and he began chocking. He patted his head and walked back into the corridor, unable to breathe. He felt like he had just entered the gas chamber!

Huritt hastily eyed Sebastian and snatched away his cigarette. 'Come with me!' he said, and dragged the lawyer to the dining room. He made him sit on a chair, like a child being punished for not doing his homework, and then he poured water in a wine glass and offered it to his loyal driver.

Felix drained the glass in one shot and entered the dining room to face his master, Huritt.

'I'm sorry, Sir, I didn't mean to - '

'It's quite all right, Felix. He doesn't really mind,' said Huritt and sat behind the teak wood dining table. 'He deserves to be... punished. The next time he smokes so damn much I'm going to set his pubic hair on fire!'

The trio sat quietly for some time and tasted some wine. Huritt spoke about Pam, Sebastian about a platinum cigarette holder, and Felix about buying clean clothes and all the food that he liked. The mood was upbeat for a few minutes. They cleared their minds and then they then got down to business.

'Felix, let us go over your assignment,' said Huritt, and pounded his robust fist on the table.

'*Oui,*' said the short, groundnut-brown complexioned, wavy-haired driver who looked like one of those ancient French actors with long sideburns and centipede-like moustaches. 'I'll drive you to *Bois de Vincennes* at half past five and I'll make sure that the car attracts the crowd. I'll wait there for ten minutes and then head straight to Mark's garage. I will then escort you to *Chateau de Fermont* and wait there for your command. I shall then go back to the garage and take some pictures - '

' – *Réel sexy,*' chipped in Huritt.

'Take some pictures,' repeated Felix in his squeaky voice, choosing to ignore Huritt's comment.

'*Sexy et érotique,*' muscled in Huritt.

Felix gave a disgusted grunt and caved in. 'Fine! Take some sexy and erotic pictures with *your* wife and then drive down to Gate 2 near Arc de Triomphe.'

'Excellent!' said Sebastian and collected another envelope from Huritt. He held it in his palm and walked closer to the driver. He stood at an arm's length from him and said, 'Felix, if everything goes as per plan, on the day after, you will have enough money to buy whatever you want. You can shop at Charvet Place Vendôme and you can dine at Le Meurice. Felix, you are very crucial to us. No matter what she does, don't even think about ditching us. If you do, I'm sure that you won't get away with it. You know me well enough to deduce the extent and credibility of my work. Don't make me your enemy. You won't like the bad me. He is pure evil. He is extremely selfish and sadistic. He will crush your bones and eat your flesh out. Is that clear? I'm not trying to threaten you, my dear Felix, I'm just trying to make our intentions clear…for the better good...All the best, Felix. Here's your flight ticket to *the Smoke*.'

'I-I won't let you down…I won't let master Huritt down. No, I won't.' *But the moment after everything is done, I'll have Mark put a bullet through your bald head. Asshole!*

6:15 PM.

Ricardo Frasco, the garbage truck driver at the Paris municipal corporation, was Huritt's Clemenza. He was five-foot-ten, obese, greasy haired, tanned and nicotine-scented, just like Sebastian. He waltzed inside the den, kissed Huritt on the cheek and said, *'J'ai de se précipiter maintenant. Je vais dire aux points clés.* I have to rush now. I'll just tell the key points.'

'Oui,' responded Huritt with a tone that clearly conveyed empathy.

'One, pick up Mark and load the boxes at seven-thirty. Two, drive down to *Route de ceinture du Lac Daumesnil* and unload the boxes with Oscar's assistance and stay there till eight-twenty. Three, drive you to the garage and make necessary arrangements for the photo-shoot. Four, take you down to the restroom 1 on route *de ceinture du Lac Daumesnil* at around ten-fifteen. Five, load the boxes. Six, drive to the yard and seven, go to *Banshee,'* muttered Frasco in a flash and stood up to leave.

Banshee was Oscar's mini-trailer that was chained to a forsaken part of Paris on the poorer side of the city, the side where the crooks and felons dwelled. It was a haven for molesters, prostitutes and drug dealers. In spite of Sebastian's repetitive persuasions, Ricardo, a man with towering self-esteem, refused to move to a better locality in the city. He stood strong among thieves and maintained a good relationship with the prostitutes and drug dealers.

'Bonne nuit, Frasco,' said Huritt.

Ricardo just stood up and walked towards the noble son-in-law. He patted Huritt's back, stroked his salt and pepper hair, and walked away, whistling a random tune.

CHAPTER 18

July 27, 1979
London, England

'Huritt, we better hail a cab. Neither of us is capable of driving!'

'Eloy, stop being so goody-goody, come on! We managed to smuggle seven billion francs out of France! We deserve the celebrations. We owe it to ourselves, don't we?'

'And, we are quite acquainted with taking risks. So, well, why not try driving under the influence of...of all the crap we administered tonight? You know, take a shot in the dark.'

'I don't know. I mean...' *Fuck you! You can't drive when you are this high! It's illegal!*

'Just get in, officer,' said Sebastian and shoved him inside the rental car with the registration plate number OZ 9347.

Huritt took the wheel and turned the radio on. 'Hey cry-baby! We go now, can't we?' asked Huritt and stared the engine after receiving a 'Whatever!' He stepped on the accelerator nervously, thinking, *I'm going to be rich! Filthy rich! Just this one last hurdle. Just this last one.*

Night is draggin' her feet

I wait alone in the heat

I know, know that you have your way

Till you have to go home

No is a word, I can't say…

'Sing along, guys!' said Huritt ecstatically.

'I-I haven't heard this…'

'O bloody 'ell!' mimicked Huritt and gave a sluggish laugh.

'Priming yourself aye, Huritt? Becoming a Brit already.'

'I don't know, Uncle Eloy. I don't know.'

'Uncle Eloy? Please!'

'So, Eloy, what is your plan now? After going back to Paris, I mean,' asked Sebastian inquisitively.

'I'm going to resign the department. I'll find myself a teaching job, I guess.'

'Too guilty to stay in the department, are we?'

'Well, something like that. Never mind. What about you?'

'Oh! I'm a lawyer. I come guilty. Guilt is my middle name.'

'So you'll stay back in Paris then?'

'Na. I'll be heading to the Home of the Brave. I've been offered a job at the Almonte Research Lab. This asshole's bosom bud, Cortez, and his colleague, Vaughn, who kind of looks exactly like Huritt, founded this Research Lab last week. They are recruiting new and trained professionals to each sector and they want me, rather, Cortez wants me to head their legal department.'

'Kind of looks exactly? That is so not lawyerly!'

'Why should I always be "lawyerly"? Can't I just be normal?' asked Sebastian.

'Fine! So this guy Vaughn kind of looks exactly like Huritt, aye?'

'Yep. Kind of looks exactly. Here, take a look. It's a picture of Vaughn and Cortez with Senator Jamie Edwards. Last evening, the Senator donated one million dollars to Mr. Fletcher. A very noble and a generous man he is,' said Sebastian and handed over a copy of the Washington Post.

'Wow! Almonte is off to a good start!'

'Precisely! And I'm going to make it great.'

'Well, good luck!'

'Was that sarcasm?'

'I don't think so.'

'Good for you, Inspector. Good for you.'

'Anyway, Huritt, what about you? How do you intend to spend your time in London?'

Huritt didn't reply. He stirred in his seat and he stepped on the accelerator. His hands flailed about the steering and his eyes kept drifting off the streets.

'Huritt! What's happening? Slow down! Huritt!' exclaimed Eloy, worried.

'Huritt, why are you going so fast? Please, slow down. I'll drive instead.'

'Fuck you! Fuck you all! I don't want to live. I have nothing to live for. No family, no money, no job, no identity, no respect! I'd be better off dead!'

'Huritt! What the fuck! Stop the car!' yelled Eloy and put his hands on the steering wheel. 'I told you not to let him drive.'

'Huritt, that's enough! Pull over,' said Sebastian, his heart pounding.

'Pull over? Pull over?' said Huritt and depressed the pedal harder.

'Sebastian! Do something! He is going out of control!'

'Huritt – '

'Huritt! Look ahead! We are going to…Huritt!'

The car rammed against a metallic sidebar and jumped off the cliff.

'Noooooo!'

'Oh God!'

Chapter 19

September 27, 1992
Henry's office, Roulette Construction Site
Amsterdam, the Netherlands

5:00 PM.

Henry Douglas waited at the entrance of his office, timidly clutching a bouquet of lilies. *She loves lilies. She had given me that look of hers when I gave it to her the last time.* He shifted his puffy eyes off the dewy pathway and feverishly stared at his Rolex. *6:36...She isn't on time, as always. Hope she hasn't changed since our...she is here! She is here!*

The steel fence gate opened with a screech and through it entered Veronica. *I'll give that bloody bastard a taste of his medicine. I told him a million times!* Veronica thought, as she walked on the muddy terrain towards the cabin, where she and Henry had parted on a doleful note.

'That's him over there. Don't get me wrong, but please, be... be nice...don't do anything – ' fumbled Henry's driver, wiping the sweat off his forehead. *Bitch! Don't mess around with him. Just be done with it and get the hell out of here!* Screamed a voice in his head, but then, he just couldn't say it out loud. Not to Veronica.

'Just get your wacky face out of my sight!' shot Veronica, bitterly.

'Please, madam. He isn't his old self now. He is – '

'I know what I have to do, all right? Now shut your bloody mouth and get lost! You hear me?'

Dillion looked at Veronica's tacky eyeglass, trying to somehow catch her eyes, and said, 'Just – ' before he turned around and trudged his way back, his baggy pants brushing the ground and turning browner with each step.

And stay out! Screamed Mrs. Griffiths, with her mouth shut.

You are a dead man walking; you have nothing to fear, ruminated Henry as he adjusted his tawny flat cap and straightened his necktie. *You were man of style, Henry. Now look at you, hiding yourself behind bedraggled fabric!*

The sun had just kissed the earth and the bats were blatantly zooming about, hunting for its prey. Veronica lifted her head and looked at the thick clouds masking the moon. *Should I or shouldn't I remove my scarf?*

'Veronica, you-you look – '

My face is covered! What are you looking at! 'What the hell do you want from me?'

'I just...' muttered Henry and handed over the bouquet. 'Please, take it. I know you like them.'

The clouds rumbled and the wind howled, adding credence to the gloomy notch.

'Henry, I'm not the same person. I'm not in the trade anymore. I'm out! I have told you to stop pursuing me...begged you. Now please don't make me do this in Mark's way. You won't like it.'

Veronica undid her dotted scarf and pulled down her glasses. She stuffed them both in her purse and pushed back her silky blonde hair, which brushed against her petite buttocks.

I can die right now! Henry thought, as he saw her dainty seductive face. *Those eyes! And lips!*

'Please, take this.'

To hell with you! Veronica snatched the boutique off his bony fingers and tossed it on the floor. 'Henry! I am here to warn you. I am here because you have helped me immensely. Now, stay away. Go back to your wife and leave me alone!'

Henry broke down and began to tear. He simply turned back and walked inside the cabin, leaving the door open. He collapsed on a gray wooden chair and buried his face in his hands. Veronica stood where she was and pondered whether or not to enter the cabin. *Why do you care? You came here to give him a warning, that's all. Now just turn back and leave!* She gave in to the voice in her head and turned back, only to slap her face against Dillion's rough palm.

The two hundred and fifty pound saggy-breasted ox of a man wrapped his arm around Veronica's puny waist and lifted her off the floor. He pressed his other hand against her mouth and forced the *"Help! Somebody help me!"* down to the place from whence it came.

Veronica pounded the Ox with her soft hands and swayed her feet about, trying hard to kick herself free. She was like a little bird, dolefully crimped by an anaconda's muscular body. 'You bitch! Shut up or I'll fuck the life out of you!' yelled Dillion as he thumped his feet against the murky ground and walked towards the pint-sized wooden cabin. They could now hear a plane rumbling, slowly and steadily descending, with fresh drops of rain beating its metallic wings…

She doesn't like me anymore! I'm going to die alone. I'm going to die in this very cabin…she left me at this very place. She –

Henry was pulled back from the Remorse Island as Veronica fell at his feet with a loud thud. 'Help! Somebody help!' she yelled, the voice in her paving its way out to the open.

The clouds rumbled again and the rain came down harder. Henry angrily stood up and threw himself at Dillion. He flexed his bony weak fist and thumped Dillion on his cheek. 'How dare you touch her! You freak! Get out of here you scumbag! Get...out,' spit Henry and pushed him out of the flimsy door.

Veronica quietly stood up and wiped her tears off her heart-shaped face. *Why is he fighting? Is he fighting because Dillion hurt me? Or is he trying to pull off something to...*

Henry slammed the door on his loyal servant's face and turned around apologetically.

Outside, the gratified loyalist pulled out a cigarette from the top left pocket of his wornout trench coat and slid it in between his broken lips. He put his right hand in his pant pockets and searched for the lighter. *Shit! I must've left it in the car.* He scratched his bushy grey beard and pulled the cigarette off his nozzle.

'Veronica, I'm-I'm really sorry...I didn't ask him to...I'd never hurt you...' said Henry, and sprinted towards her, like a mad dog. He held her face in his hands and kissed her lips. Shocked, Veronica pushed his face and slapped him hard. Henry's weak legs gave in and he collapsed on the dusty carpet, as blood ran down his nose and kissed the dust. His cap flew off, revealing his frayed hair. *This is it*

CHAPTER 20

September 12, 1978
Chateau de Fermont, Le Septieme
Paris, France

'"Anyone charged with a crime is presumed innocent until proven guilty". This is precisely what the prosecutor will tell you...even the President. But believe me, Huritt, the truth is, "Anyone charged with a crime is presumed guilty until proven innocent". Now that is the truth and the whole truth.'

'But then, there is no need for you to worry. It might as well be quite advantageous to us. You know, no man can ever prove your innocence. It just isn't possible. But it is happy-go-lucky to prove that you are "not guilty".'

'Mr. Huritt Achak, how do you plead for the murder of Ms. Sarah Bibiana?'

'Ha-ha-ho...Not guilty.'

'Atta boy!'

CHAPTER 21

October 29, 1992
Amsterdam, the Netherlands

'Your grand pappy was a car mechanic, just like me. He lost his wife when my brother was five and I was two. So he was pretty much our only parents!' said the man in the jet-black three-piece and smiled.

But the boy with the bald head sat quietly and gazed at the wall on which his mother's portrait hung.

'Well, you can listen if you want to. But I'll just keep going…'

The boy with the bald head was still irresponsive. He just wanted his mother back and he wanted his guilt to disappear. *I'm sorry, mama, I'm so sorry.*

'…My elder brother, Jay, was just like you. He was highly intellectual and a big time believer in God. He had a keen desire to learn and to get educated. He was so not like me. I just wanted to be like my papa. A mechanic. I loved working at the garage, repairing and fixing stuff. You know, the engine, the shaft, the battery, the axel, the radiator…anyway, the point is that Jay and I were always at odds with each other. But if you see from an outside perspective, he was the odd one, you know, because my papa and I were alike.

As we grew up, the difference in opinions between my papa and Jay also grew. They weren't all that comfortable with each other. They quarreled about everything. How shabbily my father dressed, how badly he spoke, how stingy he was with his money and well, everything. So Jay left home and went on his separate way. He ditched me and my papa.'

The boy shot a glance at his father and then slowly turned back towards the photo. The father smiled, he was relieved to learn that his son was paying some attention to what he was saying. That was enough. That was plenty progress.

'My papa was shattered! He was deeply hurt and he started feeling insecure. I was his only son now and he wanted me to stay close to him. So in order to keep me with him, he borrowed a lot of money and used it on me. He refurbished the garage, he taught me everything there was to learn about repairing cars, he gave me lots of pocket money, he let me watch movies every alternate day and he also let me booze and smoke.'

The boy didn't take his eyes off the photo, but he lightly nodded.

'Gradually, I extended my reach and I frequented brothels. I did it with a woman once every week. My dad didn't ask me anything. He was just happy that I would go back home every night and have dinner with him over a portion of laughs and a pint of pleasantries. Back then I thought he was a fool. An insecure maniac. Back then I didn't know what despair meant. I didn't know what being lonely meant.'

The boy's eyes moistened, and he began to bite his nails. *I killed you, mama. I killed you! I know what lonely means. But you weren't good either. Even you did bad things.*

'Son, that's enough for today. Off we go to sleep now.'

CHAPTER 22

July 26, 1979
The Frälsare
London, England

4:40 PM.

Morgan tepidly walked towards a private elevator installed at the end of his exquisite lobby. *No one will ever know about us! It will remain within these walls! And even if someone speculates...no, that wouldn't work. Okay, so, I'll say, "No one will ever know about us..."*

The door split open with a chime, and Morgan immediately stepped inside the car. He mundanely pressed the only other button on the pad and returned to his thoughts, as a melodious yet monotonous music filled the car.

We have been together for over two years now and you have to agree, we've never been happier. What happened at the Royal Opera House wasn't just...

The music died down and the bell chimed, throwing the door open. Morgan took out the keys from his Gieves & Hawkes trousers and returned to his mental self.

What happened at the Royal Opera House wasn't just coincidence. It was meant to happen. We were destined to meet, and so we did. And now, I think it is time for us to take a little leap...

The key met its mate and the Royce clicked open. He stared at the jet-black wall next to him, and reflected, *We need to...we have to get intimate. I promise it will be discreet. No one will ever know what happened inside these walls. And I assure you, we'll be happier.*

He smiled, looking at his refection on top of the Royce before flexing his back and strapping himself behind the wheel. 'My love,' he whispered and pulled the glove box open. He retrieved a package marked "confidential" and slid it inside an inner pocket of his single-breasted jacket with notch lapels, roped shoulder and working cuffs. 'You will love.'

The car started with a roar and Morgan smoothly drove it out of his private parking lot. He switched on the up-to-the-minute music system and emerged out of Femhörnig's headquarters on James Street, as the security at the check post yanked the horizontal iron barrier and let the Royce pass.

Morgan turned a blind eye to his surroundings. He was the least bit interested in knowing what was happening around him. He synced his thoughts with the person singing on the radio and swiftly drove towards Frälsare.

Twenty minutes later, the security at the humongous hotel's parking segment devotedly disbarred the barricades and allowed him to dock the Royce in the most secluded area of the basement. Morgan hid the Corniche in shadows and then briskly walked through the steel doors that said, "Authorized personnel only". Once inside, he stepped into the car on his left and placed a call to the Isak Suite.

The Isak Suite was the permanent residence of Morgan's lover, whom he called PI. The suite was named after PI's grandfather, Walter Isak, who first started the Frälsare during the World War II. When PI took charge of the establishment, the board of directors and the leading shapers of the foundation deserted the establishment with a fare share and migrated to the west, fearing that under PI, they might lose everything they had held dear. All of Morgan's meetings with the underworld, smugglers and his eroticism were safely guarded inside the walls of this very suite, without the slightest trace.

Upon PI's authorisation, the lift propelled upward and quickly opened up to a lobby that featured marble floors and stark white walls with black accents. Morgan slightly brushed his smooth chestnut brown hair and patted the package through his ethereal Italian fabric.

As Morgan stepped into the lobby, two surveillance cameras, one positioned inside the lift, and the other, camouflaged in a Swedish coat of arms wall clock, captured his movements and pushed it to PI's PC.

Just say it Morg...just tell PI what you have in mind, Morgan thought and punched in the four digit passcode on a numeric keypad.

1933.

A few clicks and clanks followed, and the door finally opened to one of the finest suites ever built. The Isak Suite housed a drawing room with the state-of-the art technology, a fireplace, fine antique furniture, a home theater, a marvelous boudoir, two comfort stations, a kitchen, a store room, a conference room and a den that was secluded from the conference room, a rooftop outdoor garden, a sun deck, and a small surveillance room skirting the sun deck.

As Morgan entered the chamber, Philip Isak was seated in his den, smoking on his pipe and staring at the ceiling. Morgan stealthily tiptoed toward him and brushed his head. *This is it. Just do it.* 'PI, it's so good to see you!'

'Good to see you too, Morg,' replied Philip and kissed his partner's forehead. 'Did you hear about our babies?'

'Yes. They are coming in tomorrow.'

CHAPTER 23

The Resistor Sir Edgar Fermont was a prominent member of the Free French Force under Charles de Gaulle. In a decade long scintillating career, he played an active role in the liberation of Corsica, Normandy landings, liberation of Paris, and in bringing de Gaulle's Fifth Republic to the fore.

In 1960, Prime Minister Michel Debré appointed him as the French Foreign minister, owing to his war decorations and yeoman service to the FFF. He served as an uncorrupt, dedicated and loyal minister for four years, during which time he cautiously knitted Europe in a cultural weave. He envisioned European unity through a cultural boulevard, and as a consequence, on the twentieth of June 1962, he broached the Grand Triathlon. Thereupon it morphed into a major European annual sporting event and served as a coliseum for the collaboration and exchange of foreign relations and cultures.

In 1962, Robert Avril assassinated The Resistor and with it came to an end a magnanimous era in de Gaulle's Fifth Republic. Serious repercussions followed the assassination, and in less than a month, the Avril family was exterminated in its entirety.

Gradually the political stability was restored and the need for foreign influx became dire. And so, Michel Debré's new Foreign Minister rebooted the Triathlon, and renamed it, in honor of Sir Edgar, The Fermont Triathlon...

CHAPTER 24

June 20, 1979
The Fermont Hospital
Paris, France

1:30 PM.

'Keep your eyes open, Huritt. Look, look over there. You made it. Don't close your eyes,' repeated Kramer, time and again, as the siren slowly died down. A myriad of hospital staff rushed towards the ambulance and jerked the door open. Coach Kramer and Sebastian lifted the stretcher off the ambulance and passed it over to the ward boys. 'Did I…Did I win?' asked Huritt, opening and closing his eyes, gradually losing his senses. 'You did more than that, kid.'

Numerous doctors joined Huritt, as he was stormed into the operation theater. 'This looks plenty bad, Dr. Martin…'

'Ah! This is nothing! He has been through worse, right Mr. Achak?'

'I can do better…I've seen worse,' said Huritt feebly just before shutting his eyes.

'Sebastian, come with me, quick. The media needs some answers. Better put the boy in the spotlight while he is at the hospital. A lot of sponsors will come crawling to the hospital with their big fat checkbooks,' said the flat-voiced Draconian, Coach Kramer, once the red light over the OT lit up.

'But-but he just went in. I mean…'

'Listen to me, prick, listen to me very carefully. That bastard over there is as cunning as a shithouse rat and as brave as a lion. He'll live to see tomorrow, that's for sure. He still has a lot of money to make. Daddy needs his pockets full. I won't let him give up on me. Not so easily, no. So just shut the fuck up and come with me.'

Chapter 25

September 27, 1992
Henry's office

Thin beads of sweat trickled down Veronica's smooth skin and then seeped into her satin V-neck. She bit her lip nervously and whispered, 'Henry! Henry, wake up. I-I need to go, now. Henry… get up!'

But he didn't. *I can't stay here any longer. I have to go!* Veronica said to herself, and quickly stood up. She nimbly walked towards a window hidden behind an old gaudy curtain, and slightly lifted it, hoping not to see the Ox.

But she did. He was sitting on one of the two muddy steps, his pants still brown, tearing up the cigarette in his hands into pieces and tossing it out into a scraggy stream that had formed right in front of him.

The clouds were still crying, resonating her cry for help, and growing intense with each second. Distant noises of prime movers shutting down, and the factory horns blaring at the top of the audible human range sent a shiver down her spine. *The siren! Damn it! The workers would be leaving any minute now. What if someone…this prick is sitting right outside...the rain. Mark! Shit! I'm trapped with his... with this...*

She let the drape fall back into place and walked back towards Henry. She took out her dotted scarf from her purse and wrapped it around one of her hands. She picked up a glass of water from Henry worktable, and with her clothed hand poured it on Henry's face.

Herny's face twitched at the touch of water. He coughed, blowing dust particles off the ill-vacuumed burgundy Persian carpet. Veronica placed the glass on the couch and walked towards the door.

'Ver-Veroni...please,' muttered Henry, as he struggled to fight the pain. 'I need you-need you to...' he continued, and writhed towards his worktable.

'Henry, I really have to leave! Please ask your...your dog to let me go!'

'Veronica please, just...just read...just read this,' he said, and pulled a file off the table. 'Read this,' he added, and held the file in her direction.

'What is it?'

'Take it, please!'

'What the hell, Henry! Why are you being so melodramatic? You want to have sex with me and I don't want to fuck you. It is as simple as that. Nothing that you do will change my mind!'

The Ox knocked on the door. 'Boss, everything all right?'

Veronica quickly moved to her right and picked up the glass off the couch. She held it again in her clothed hand and smashed it against the dull colored wall. The glass broke into shards and scrambled all over the floor. She held her newly-crafted weapon tightly and stared at Henry.

'Ask him to let me go.'

'Veron – '

'Just do it, Henry. Don't make me want put this thing in your chest.'

Henry just stared at her, shocked. His legs were shaking uncontrollably because the impact had sprained his dangerously weak hamstrings. There were bloodstains below his nose and on his chin, and the side of the head had turned a tinge of bluish black. His voice cracked as he slowly and apprehensively said, 'Dillion, your work is done here, get out! Take the car and go home.'

'But sir, I – '

Henry strained every sinew and mustered the strength to stand up. He aggressively walked towards the door, opened it, and pushed Dillion out of the porch.

The Ox stood under the weeping skies and watched his *Vader* go wild. He slightly bowed to Henry and walked towards the exit gate, recollecting the thoughts from when Henry had fought with his biological parents and brought him out of the purgatory where he had burnt his entire childhood.

'T-thank you,' said Veronica, as she watched a light turn on and then go off in Dillion's car. She didn't want to leave when the Ox was at the gate. No she didn't. *I won't leave until he gets the hell out of here!*

Henry walked inside, his footsteps heavy, and bent down to lift the file off the burgundy carpet. A stream of blood gushed into his head and he felt heavier. He was tired. Exhausted. He had too many factors weighing him down. Too many. *I can't take it anymore.*

As Veronica stood on the porch and watched Dillion light up his cigarette, she *smelt* Henry coming closer. Henry was a captive of his own consciousness. He had chained himself to the confines of his cabin and had so far lived like a decrepit animal.

Veronica turned around and looked at Henry's harrowing walk. Henry bowed down his head and despondently handed over the file to Veronica. She tilted her head, saw the Ox drive away and then snatched the file from him. *If that's what it takes to leave me alone!*

She held the plastic file over her head and stepped out into the rain. She picked up her bizarrely expensive fur coat and maneouvered across the yard with all its puddles, thinking about how she would narrate all of this to Mark, and how he would react.

Meanwhile Henry stood at the shrine of his captivity and watched his only want walk away. *She hates me! She...I'm going to die alone,* thought Henry, as he heard the grill bang against the iron frame.

*She isn't coming back again. She is gone...you have nothing left in your life...*said Henry to the air around him and screamed, 'I don't want to live anymore!'

He walked back inside the cabin as fast as he could, his thoughts keeping pace with his legs and his eyes moistening. He knew that he had finally reached the end zone and there was no way he could ever again be with Veronica or with Albert. He was rid of family, love, respect, dignity and every emotion that makes people want to live in spite of the many harships. His hands shaking but his mind firm, Henry picked up the broken glass off from the place where Veronica had left it and moved towards the mirror. He looked at his reflection in the mirror, *I'm a ghost,* and placed the sharp edge of the glass on his saggy skin.

I'm a ghost!

Chapter 26

October 20, 1978
Cour d'assises
Paris, France

The *Cour d'assises* (Assize Court) is composed of *La Cour* - a President with the rank of counselor to the court of appeal and two judges, a jury composed of nine jurors, ushers and clerks. *La Juge d'instruction* (Investigative Judge) gathers the information and facts regarding the case and the defendant's and plaintiff's history, and then compiles it in a report called *Dossier* and sends it to *Cour d'assises.* The information will be taken into purview during the trial and the President will base his judgment based on both the arguments and the dossier.

'M'lords, the jury is ready,' said the *Huissier assermenté* (Sworn Usher), a few minutes after both the plaintiff and the defendant unanimously selected the nine eligible and neutral jurors. He then walked to the *Greffier* (Clerk) and informed the same.

'Usher, escort the jury,' ordered Justice Lorenzo, as the clerk began to record the proceedings. Justice Lorenzo, 65, was a brown, brawny man with thick grey hair. He had served as a successful barrister for about six years in the United Kingdom, where he earned a law degree from one of the finest universities in the world, Cambridge. He then worked as a solicitor for about four years with "Parsons & Co", one of the leading marketing firms in the United States, before he returned to his hometown of Paris, where he was appointed as an honourary member of the bar. He gradually made his way up the legal machinery and ascended to become a highly regarded magistrate.

The Sworn Usher walked towards the door behind the *barre des temoins* (Witness box) and shouted out loud, 'The president invites you to the courtroom.'

The jurors, a teacher, a medical secretary, a businessman, a retired police officer, a librarian, a housewife, an author, a priest and a philanthropist walked single file and took their seats next to the President and the judges. Four on the left and five on the right. The audience, as a rhetorical custom, stood as the jurors entered the hall.

The Sworn Usher handed over a file furnishing the details regarding the jurors, the attendance list concerning the summoned defendant, plaintiff, their respective lawyers and witnesses to the *Greffier*, who checked the contents, validated them and then passed them on to the typist seated beside him.

As the typist noisily typed the required content under the supervision and advice of the *Greffier*, the assistant ushers laid out papers and pens, glasses and bottles, and detailed reports of the pre-trial motions in front of the jurors. The journalists, sitting in a box behind the plaintiff, were also handed over a copy of the pretrial motions and a case-study dossier.

At 12:30, that is three hours after the three judges had arrived, four-and-a-half hours after the jurors had arrived, two weeks after Huritt was taken into custody, six months after Sarah Bibiana was found dead and seven months after Huritt had deserted Sarah and married Lucy Fermont, the trial of State v. Huritt Achak began.

Judge: Is the counsel ready to proceed?

Prosecutor: Ready, Your Honour.

Defense: Ready, Your Honour.

CHAPTER 27

June 20, 1979
Ile de Bercy
Paris, France

5:30 AM.

'*Bienvenue à tous au Triathlon Fermont.*'

'*Mesdemoiselles et Messieurs*! The Fermont Triathlon is not just a sport, as it is a cardinal aspect of the European cultural conglomerate. This day, *Mesdemoiselles et Messieurs,* celebrates the impetus of the long-standing dream of unified Europe. Ergo, the course of this majestic event diverges from the rules of the conventional Triathlon. The participants, representing each of the ten member-countries, travel through Paris's neck of the woods in virtue of three continuous and sequential endurance events, which include a 3.5 km swim across *Lac Daumesnil,* a 100 km bike ride and a 20 km run on the majestic streets of Paris, finishing the race at Arc de Triomphe. Participants will be allowed to change into their respective gears at the concerned Changing Rooms only. They are allowed to rest nowhere else throughout the event. If they happen to do so, they are as good as disqualified. Entering the Change Rooms is purely based on the participant's choice, for the time will be ticking without pause for the entire event. At the end, the winner takes home one hundred thousand francs and the admiration of all the ten countries,' said Aimon, grumpily uttering each and every word with the utmost stress.

The huge display board commonly used for advertising purposes was now displaying the rules for the day's event.

RÈGLES/RULES:

- Il / Elle doit respecter les règles sanctionnées ci-dessous. Tout manquement dans la conduite de l'adhérent doit être traitée comme immorale et est soumise à de graves répercussions.
- Le participant ne peut reposer que sur les toilettes stationnés à la jonction

Aimon sipped a glass of water and surveyed the crowd, as they shouted, cheered and applauded with inexplicable enthusiasm. Aimon put the glass down and looked towards the Project Manager, asking him if he was good to go. Oscar confirmed John McKenzie's status with his personal secretary, and upon receiving the green signal, gave Aimon the "Go".

'Mesdames et Messieurs, put your hands together and welcome our chief guest Señor John McKenzie.'

John McKenzie, aka the Big Mac, was the former foreign minister of Great Britain and the present finance minister of the Union. His ministry was responsible for the annulment of tons of restrictions concerned with the European trade and commerce, which were unfortunately amassed by his predecessor governments, straining inter-country relationships.

The Big Mac emerged from the right wing surrounded by a dozen armed guards. He walked straight towards Sir Edgar's massive portrait and performed a grand salute, as he vociferated Sir Edgar's slogan, *"Un pays, un nom, un seul peuple!"*

John was greatly influenced by Sir Fermont's groundbreaking achievements, and seventeen years after the great visionary's demise, his ministry swore to realise Sir Fermont's unfulfilled vision. He actively participated in the many socio-cultural events and dreamed of creating a synergy of European countries on grounds of unity and compassion.

The audience and other dignitaries repeated the same slogan, over and over, the clamour growing each time. The Big Mac slowly walked across the stage and sat down at his designated seat, which was placed adjacent to Lefèbvre Delacroix, Minister of Foreign and European Affairs.

Having been born and brought up in England, he was a hard-core fan of "the gentlemen's game". In 1978, he had personally aided the construction of a massive cricket stadium in Essex. It had since then hosted a number of international cricketing tournaments and spiked an increase in the economy.

The Big Mac, clad in an expensive three-piece brown suit, waved to the crowd and then folded his arms. Observing this, Oscar signaled Aimon to continue.

'Keep the applause going, Mesdames et Messieurs and welcome our very own, Michel Serrault.'

A boy wanting to be a circus clown was curbed and forced into a seminary by pious parents, who wanted their son to take up priesthood. But it wasn't long before the boy dropped out and took up acting, and he never looked back again. Thus began the journey of Michel Serrault, one of the most acclaimed actors of all times. Of his bountiful accolades, *La Cage aux Folles* was the most commercially successful and critically acclaimed movie. The movie had run for well over a year at the Paris Theatre and the Art House Cinema in NYC. It won the Golden Globe Award for Best Foreign Language

Film, and for years remained the most successful foreign film to be released in the United States.

The monomaniacs roared and jumped with zest when Michel voiced, *'vous devriez essayer* tout une fois.' (You should try *everything* once). They just couldn't contain their excitement.

'Also welcome, General Bernard le Blanc, Ministre de la Défense et des Anciens combattants, The Bolt - Pierre Cioran, and Manquer Europe, the breathtaking Yasmine Faye.'

'Je t'aime Yasmine,' shouted a French maniac.

'Marry me Yasmine, please,' cried a Londoner.

'Vous êtes si sexy!' exclaimed a Spaniard.

Every other member on the stage turned towards her and gasped at her beauty. Her slender long legs, alluring eyes and long braided hair blended perfectly with her elegant wardrobe, making her one of the most attractive women in the history of French cinema.

The London Times would add the caption, *"Yasmine - A great solution to bring Europeans together"*, below her sensational picture.

The august members also included ambassadors from the participating countries, secretaries of various departments, the editors-in-chief of different agencies and dignitaries from vast sectors of law enforcement. The entire gathering of celebrities was seated on one of the three islands *in Bois de Vincennes,* a magnificent park in Eastern Paris.

At the north end of this park stands the *Château de Vincennes,* which used to be a favourite second home to the French kings. In the southwest wing of the park stands the *Redoute de Gravelle,* a military redoubt constructed under the reign of Louis-Philippe. In the eastern part lies a *Hippodrome* specialising in trotting races, *Avelodrome,* and the French national institute of sports and physical education. The Bois de Vincennes also houses four lakes, fed from the Marne River: *Lac Daumesnil* in the west, *Lac des Minimes* in the north-east, *Lac de Saint-Mandé* in the northwest and *Lac des Gravelle* in the southwest.

The Lac Daumesnil forms two islands: *Ile de Bercy* (The Bercy Island) and *Chalet des iles Daumesnil* (cottage islands Daumesnil). The *Préfet de Police* had chosen *Ile de Bercy* as the ideal location for the event, for the simple yet smart reason that the island could be easily cordoned off with no more than two helicopters guarding the perimeter. The civilian choppers would escort dignitaries to the island directly from their respective embassies and then chopper them back to the point of pickup.

As planned, *Ile de Bercy* was guarded like a fortress, with numerous PPs rigorously securing the perimeter. There were hundreds of volunteers, fire engines, ambulances and maintenance trucks throughout the arena. Passes were issued to a few limited guests, and to the rest, tickets to enter the island were sold at sky-high prices.

'Now amigos, get ready to welcome the stars of today.'

The competitors from various clubs were hustled in numerous boats, with each competitor being accompanied by a glamorous woman wearing the traditional outfit and clutching a flag of their respective country. The athletes enthusiastically waved and sent flying kisses to the spectators on the bridge and on the island.

France: Black with the *Fleur-de-lis*.

Spain: Yellow with the naval insignia, *Pabellón de la Marina de Guerra*.

Italy: Azure with the insignia of the Royal House of Savoy.

The Netherlands: Orange with the insignia of the Grand Cross of the Order of Willem.

Denmark: White with the Scandinavian cross.

West Germany: Gold with the *Bundesschild*.

United Kingdom: Navy with the Red Cross of Saint George.

Belgium: Amber with the Leo Belgicus.

Ireland: Green with the Cross of St Patrick.

Sweden: Elephant grey with the Scandinavian cross.

The colour and the symbols brought to the fore the national flags of the respective countries.

As a practice, contenders were recognised based on the color of their trunks. Accordingly, black was the most sought after club. It had housed the trophy for three consecutive years and it intended to do the same even in the present tournament.

'France, Spain, Italy, The Netherlands, Denmark, West Germany, United Kingdom, Belgium, Ireland and last but not the least, Sweden,' announced Aimon, as each club made their way towards the pulpit.

'Hold on to your seats and prepare yourselves to witness one of the most gripping events in the world of sports,' screamed Aimon, and waited for the crowd to settle. He then clutched the microphone again and said, 'But before that, let us convey our gratitude to the founding fathers of the union.'

The audience stood up and so did the dignitaries. The musicians prepped their instruments and a group of trained singers intoned the Anthem of the European union, "Ode to Joy", composed in the 18th century by Friedrich Schiller as a celebration of the brotherhood of men. The audience eventually joined the singers and the whole island resounded with the joyous anthem. It in a way also urged the Spaniards and Swedish nationals to be a part of the glorious Union.

'Marvellous,' whispered McKenzie blissfully, and closed his eyes, wanting to picture the serene thought behind the song. The press from all the 10 countries ran every which way, shooting numerous pictures, replacing films and flashing blinding lights. The news channels, newspapers and magazines were going to have a field day!

'Está usted listo?' shouted Aimon at the top of his voice through the microphone. 'Are you ready?'

'Oui!'

'Si!'

'Yes!'

'Ja!'

'Nay!'

John McKenzie could sit no more. He stood up hysterically and snatched the microphone from Aimon, as he hardly managed to say, *'Please welcome Monsieur John McKenzie, The Bi…'*

'Wow! Look at this! The women showcasing our culture, the participants portraying the national flag and the national symbol, the crowd enthusiastically intoning their national anthems, the sponsors and businessmen collating from the ten countries, the union of the press, conciliation of the citizens, our conglomeration, the leaders, three separating sporting events endured in one race, the amazing race. *This* is what Sir Fermont dreamed of. A melting pot! He sure was a visionary, there is no denying it,' said Big Mac, as he glanced around the arena. It was 6:45 AM and he could see people gathered all around the island, wide-awake, lively and enthusiastic. The island could house no more.

Numerous press reporters zoomed their cameras, clicking pictures, extending the microphones, recording the audio transcript and jotting down whatever was said.

'He saw the future; we are striving hard to fulfill his vision, and it is for you, the formidable citizens to think big; to think for the whole of Europe, work for Europe, and to die, with honour, for Europe.'

He paused for a brief second and added, 'Yesterday is history, tomorrow is a mystery, today is a gift and that is why it is called the present. Do your best every day and don't live each day thinking that it is your last, for in the face of death today you will lose sight of a better tomorrow. Dream big. Achieve bigger. Hail Europe.'

The last part of his short but enigmatic speech was translated and the response was beyond words. All the flags shot up and everyone, for the second time, recited the Ode To Joy at the top of their voices, as the wave passed onto the bridge and the other side of the island.

Big Mac walked to his seat and sat to the praises of the honoured members on the dais.

Aimon clutched the microphone and shouted, 'Êtes-vous prêt? Are you ready?'

The crowd shot out their response, as the competitors marched towards *Lac Daumesnil*.

Each competitor stood at a separate sector of the lake, with 500 metres of strong ropes connected from the island to the other side, the finishing side.

'Êtes-vous prêt?'

The crowd, with soaring enthusiasm, cheered in unison.

'Êtes-vous prêt concurrents?' shouted Aimon once more, only this time the question was directed to the competitors.

'Yes,' said each contender one after another in his respective language, raising his hand high up in the air.

The competitors stood beside their respective diving boards and gazed at the channel, rubbing their hands and jumping up and down in order to relax their muscles.

'À vos marques.'

The competitors bent forward, clasping their hands in front of their chest, so as to pave way when they plunged into the cold water.

'Preparer fixé.'

They began shivering, not because of the cold, but because of nerves, for they knew that the "Fermont Triathlon" was about to begin, in just a second, to be precise.

People were chattering about the participants on the two bridges, the rowboats, motorboats (with its motor switched off) and peddle boats (without peddling).

'Aller!' yelled Aimen, firing the gun in the air above him.

At 7:30, Black, Yellow, Orange, Gold, Azure, White, Navy, Green, Elephant Grey and Amber jumped into the *Lac Daumesnil*'s clear blue water, flashing vivid lights and reflecting the bright sun.

The Fermont Triathlon, and thus the journey of Huritt Achak, had boisterously begun.

CHAPTER 28

June 20, 1979
Ile de Bercy

8:30 AM

The Sikorsky SH-34 Seabat, one of the last piston-powered military helicopters, landed on the *Ile de Bercy* at half past eight and escorted John McKenzie, Michel Serrault, Lefèbvre Delacroix, General Bernard le Blanc, Pierre Cioran, Yasmine Faye and their primary associates to *Hôtel de Ville*.

Once they were put in place, the ambassadors from the participating countries, secretaries of departments, the editors-in-chief of various agencies and dignitaries from various law enforcement departments were also choppered down to the City Hall.

The personal secretaries, bodyguards, advisers and numerous assistants, whom the high-brows fancied, were driven in shuttle buses that were chaperoned by two police wagons.

As the SH-34 Seabat kissed the skies, the delegates peered down to see the competitors hustling in their bikes and entering *Av. Robert-André Vivien.*

They would have a fine day, they knew, and their international tryst would be rewarding, they hoped.

CHAPTER 29

I'm a bad person, Veronica. I'm cruel.

I have fucked many women. I've cheated on my wife. I've not been caring father. I've betrayed the trust of people. . I'm selfish. I'm not kind. I have no friends. I've never respected anyone. I've never loved anyone and no one loved me.

My money gave me women. It gave happiness, it earned respect, and it gave power. My money is my friend and I love money. But my money also betrayed me.

My money cannot cure cancer. My family, my wife took my money. I have no money. I have no friends. I was thrown out. I'm alone. I'm scared.

I don't want to die.

I love you. Not money.

Please stay with me because I will die soon.

I need you.

Chapter 30

October 17, 1978

Cour d'assises

La Cour, Jurors, Advocate general, *Greffier*, *Huissier assermenté*, *Huissier*, *medias*, *demandeur* (plaintiff), *intimé* (respondent), *procureur* (prosecutor), *défendeur* (defendant), *informateur* (informant), *témoins* (witnesses), *la famille de la victim* (victim's family), *la famille de la intimé* and *la public* had assembled at 9:30 AM in *Cour d'assises*.

The Greffier announced the commencement of the case, the *Hussier* brought the court to order, the President took the jurors' oath, the plaintiff prayed for justice, the prosecutor dreamt of another victory, and the media worked on the dynamic description of the day's proceedings.

Once the formalities were completed, the President of the court began his trial.

'What you will hear in the next few moments are the opening statements of the lawyers. I caution you that what you hear in the opening statement is not evidence. The evidence will begin when the first witness begins to testify, and the judgment will be pronounced accordingly, taking into account the various exhibits,' said the

President, Lorenzo, and waited for the words to sink into the public minds. He then eyed Reyes and said, 'Now, the prosecution shall present its opening statement.'

The clinking noise of the typewriter faded, as did the scratching of the pencils. The media personnel seated on the first two rows in the *boîte publique* (public box) shifted their gaze from the jotting pads to the prosecutor, Nicolas Reyes, 51. He was white-haired, brown-complexioned, unpleasantly slim and squeaky-voiced.

Nicolas jubilantly rose from his desk and gave a slight nod to a few "known" jurors. He then gazed at the defendant/accused for a split second, and then began his well-rehearsed opening statement.

'Good morning, ladies and gentlemen. Mr. Huritt here,' he said, pointing at the person seated behind the defendant in the *Box de accuses*, 'emphatically proclaims that he is "not guilty" of murdering Ms. Sarah Bibiana, housewife, aged twenty-nine.' He observed a change in expression on one of the juror's faces (who happened to a housewife). Even his junior observed the same and circled the name of that particular juror on his scrapbook. 'And I am here to emphasise the contrary. Let me walk you back to the fourteenth of August, Monday. Ms. Bibiana was found dead in my client Mr. Montego Cortez's "home"...which, I'm afraid, won't ever be what it once was.' Two jurors, an author and a librarian, and one of the two judges smirked, which Reyes managed to observe. He slightly nodded at his junior, who circled their names. 'Her body was recovered at around 11:00 AM that very day, and was immediately sent to the morgue. The coroner conducted his tests and stated in his report that asphyxiation was the cause for her demise. Her recent medical reports suggest that the deceased pious mother of the unnamed three-month-old child – '. The priest and the philanthropist looked at Cortez with pity and Reyes managed to observe their change in expression. ' – Was rid of all spruces of respiratory ailments. With this observation enumerated by a handful of exhibits, my deterred client, a well-educated chemistry graduate from Imperial College – ', said Reyes and saw the teacher on the jury raising his head to see Cortez. '– Filed a complaint on the day after she was cremated at St. Mary's. The police decided to investigate the case and commissioned its best investigators on the task. The commendable police investigators, as always, found enough evidences to pin Mr. Huritt on the charge of murdering Sarah Bibiana.' He now conquered the retired police officer. 'To this indictment, the defendant pleaded not guilty. Now if we prove him guilty, you must find him so. We will prove this as particularly as it can be, that this man here murdered this innocent man's fiancé – ', he said, pointing at Huritt and Cortez respectively. 'You will see from the reliable testimony and hard evidence that the defendant had the motive, the opportunity, and the means to commit the crime. In addition, we have firmly established the identity of the criminal offender to be that of the defendant in this case, through circumstantial evidences. Now you will repeatedly hear the defense barking that the State's case rests on circumstantial evidence, implying that the absence of an eyewitness merits an acquittal. Please don't give much heed to this trickery. Law does not require eyewitnesses, and in fact, they aren't even made to swear the oath. So whatever they testify need not be "the truth, the whole truth and nothing but the truth".' Now the other judge chuckled. *The businessman and the President.* 'Guilty verdicts can and should be reached on circumstantial evidence, and I trust you, the Jury, to take into account the concrete circumstantial evidence and find the accused to be guilty on all counts. That is all, my Lords.'

Reyes peered down the list furnishing the names of the Jurors, the Judges and the President, and found that only two names had not been circled. *Eventually I'll have them as well,* Reyes thought, and shifted his gaze at the Jury box. Reyes desperately wanted to impress the Jury. He wanted to hook their emotions and steer them through the trial. He knew that emotions were the key for his victory. Not logic, but emotions, for the lawyer he was up against was a singular person of considerable experience and shrewdness, and who seldom mated with defeat.

Theodore Sebastian had crucified defeat through deceit. Nevertheless, he was a lawyer of towering honour and he was the one person in whom Lorenzo saw his own youth. He was a man of methods who always believed in the concept of jotting down almost every syllable that the prosecutor and witnesses had in store. He shrewdly used their own statements against them and he managed to barge out of the dark alley by shedding light on some minute procedural glitch and blinding the prosecutor's case. He never cared about truth or justice. He was a singular person with a remarkable knack of manoeuvring through any case in a way that his opponents were drowned in the most tangible loop, while his ally walked out of the court merrily, regardless of whether he or she was guilty or not. In economic terms, the odds of the case collapsing under his head were minimal.

'The defense may present its opening statement,' said the President and looked at Sebastian.

Sebastian straightened his coat, visibly kissed the crucifix on the chain that was cradled around his neck, and then slowly rose, smiling at Lorenzo and brushing his bald head. He shook hands with his client and he bowed to the prosecutor and his client. He then limped towards the Jury box, placed his hand on the deck, making sure that his Rolex was visible, and closed his eyes. He remained like that for a brief moment and then he began his opening statement.

'Ladies and gentlemen, the Lord has brought us here together today to render justice to a tragedy that occurred on the fourteenth of August, 1978. An innocent, unsuspecting, young mother unfortunately breathed her last. You or I could just as easily have been involved in the situation leading up to the events that brought us here today. But there is a second tragedy in this case. My client, an outstanding member of this community, who has attended our school system, contributed to our economy through the Fermont Constructions and Fermont group of hotels, raised a family, attended church, served the poor and the needy through the *Fermont Hospitals* and participated in tons of charity events around the world, stands here today before you, wrongfully accused of a horrific crime. Try to imagine, if you will, what it feels like to be falsely accused of the kinds of things the prosecution wants us to consider. How would you react?' he gave some time for the words to sink in and then added, 'I just need to state some facts. Nothing more. No presumptions or suggestions,' he said, and shot a sharp glance at the prosecutor before adding, 'My first point is that Ms. Sarah Bibiana, as quoted by the prosecutor, was found dead –' continued Sebastian and kissed the crucifix again. ' – in the complainant, the unfortunate victim, Mr. Montego Cortez's humble abode. Mr. Cortez left his house, as always, at around 10:30 AM, leaving Sarah and the infant at home. At 1:30 PM, when Mr. Cortez returned from work, he reported her death to Inspector David Felipe at the local police station. The inspector visited Mr. Cortez's house at fifteen minutes to two, with another police constable, and scrutinised the house. He sent the –' said Sebastian, and shook his head. ' – Sarah was sent to the Homicide Forensic Department. Dr. Denis conducted her autopsy and then reported that the cause for her death was asphyxiation. Her body showed no signs of strangulation, to be precise, no evidence leading to anything skirting the obvious yet unfortunate suicide. Certainly there were ill feelings between my client and the unfortunate victim in this case, but that is and should not be convincing to you or any other group of reasonable people. Ladies and gentlemen, we cannot bring the poor, unfortunate victim back to tell you what happened. The state may claim to have some "circumstantial evidence", but I humbly request you to keep asking yourself the hard questions, and remember there's always another side to every story. As you listen to the prosecution's case, remind yourself that they will not tell you the whole story. It's not their job to do that. Ladies and gentlemen, I implore you to listen to the whole story, and prevent another tragedy from occurring…the wrongful conviction of an innocent person. May the Lord guide you through this darkened alley,' said Theodore Sebastian and slowly sat down, buying more time for the jurors to see him.

CHAPTER 31

October 30, 1992

Amsterdam

'Your mother was gorgeous. I-I met her during one of my escapades. She was the new girl at the brothel. Still a virgin. Young and sweet and innocent. She-she...every man going up there wanted to...to, you know. So her handler, I-I don't remember the name exactly. He put her up for auction...as if she was a commodity!' said the father in a muffled tone.

The boy still stared at the wall where his mother's picture once hung. *Mama, I don't know why papa threw you out. I want to see your face, mama. I want to...*

'After doing it with another woman, I came out and saw your mama being auctioned. She looked at me with fear in her eyes, as a fat monstrous pig *bought* her. Hell! I couldn't do anything. I didn't have that kind of money. I didn't have the courage to take on a mountain of a man. No, I didn't.'

'Mama,' said the boy, opening his mouth for the first time in days.

The widower was thrilled and filled with joy. But he didn't let it transfer onto his face. He buried his joy, and continued, as though nothing significant had transpired.

'Mama went with that man, Ricardo, he was called. Fat Pig Ricardo. I vividly remember him standing up with exaltation after the final bid. He looked at all of us with a sense of pride, and sloppily walked towards your mama. He laughed loudly...wickedly. His greasy hair was all over his porous face and his sweaty fists were the size of your mama's head. Fat Pig Ricardo strummed his crotch and smiled savagely at your mom. That bloody pig!'

'Mama,' weeped the boy feebly.

'You mama gave me one fleeting glance. I was probably the only young man in the room and I was probably the only man who had something good for a face. The others had crap plastered across their damn faces!'

'Mama.'

'She looked at me in the eye. She wanted me to do something. She wanted me to save her...to protect her.'

'Mama. I killed.'

Chapter 32

1. The couple, Huritt Achak and Lucy Fermont Achak, shall live in harmony for one full year, with effect from the 20th of June 1978.
2. With regards to the above-mentioned condition, I accredit Eloy Dufort and Theodore Sebastian as the legal benefactor (1) and (2) respectively. It is the benefactor's duty and responsibility to validate the above-mentioned condition regularly (Every alternate day at the least).
3. Should the clause (1) be at any point of time be breached by either party, the Benefactors have the authority to dispose of the property to the Fermont Family's trust (Reg.No. 22483).
4. Further, if the benefactors/court, finds/proves Huritt Achak as liable/guilty of any misdeed/crime, then the trustees have the authority to transfer the property back to Lucy. Should it be the other way round, Huritt Achak shall be given 20% of the conglomerate. But he shall in no way be entitled to the property.
5. Eloy Dufort and Theodore Sebastian should directly govern the funds and incentives required for the Fermont Hospitals, Hotels and Constructions.

6. The benefactors will look after the financial interests of the family. A separate joint account should be created in the name of the two benefactors and the benefactors alone should be given the authority to duly supervise the familial finances.
7. If the clause (1) is satisfied, Lucy Fermont Achak should be named the legal heir to the Fermont Family.
8. Should unprecedented circumstances arise with the validation of clause (1), the property and everything therein will be transferred to the rightful heir in the bloodline of the family.
9. With the onset of clause (6), Lucy Fermont Achak will have the authority to transfer the enterprise only to her child and no one else.
10. In case a child is adopted and legally recognised by law, Lucy Fermont Achak has the authority to transfer the property to the adopted child.
11. The Honorable Magistrate Franklin is given the responsibility of protecting the Will until and unless the transfer of enterprise is executed.

CHAPTER 33

June 20, 1979

7:45 AM
Mark's garage, *Rue de Confians* (The Conflan Street)
Paris, France

'*Mark! Le 7:45 train à Barcelone vient de passer par. Dépêchez-vous!'* said Ricardo Frasco, waving his right hand in the direction of Barcelona.

'Una pequeña Corrección,' shouted Mark from his cramped bedroom trailing the garage. The masquerader looked at the mirror one final time before the grand showdown, and then slowly and confidently emerged out of his bunk. He looked at the twenty-four-year old beefy man and said, *'No Marque...Huritt.'*

'Fils-de-pute!' said Tom Felix amazedly and walked closer to *le faux patron*. The fake boss.

The kid from Bondy, who had just taken his first steps on the other side of the Teenage Avenue, was still impish. He called everyone by their nicknames and he was highly superstitious. He went to the church every alternate day and he had never touched a woman in his life. He wore cheap uncomplimentary clothes and always spoke of becoming a movie star. Typical kid!

'Stupéfiant!' exclaimed Ricardo and walked closer to the masquerader. 'You look exactly like Huritt! Brilliant!'

'So you accept defeat?' asked Mark merrily.

'With all my heart,' said Ricardo and patted Mark with his oily hands.

A few weeks ago, when Sebastian had proposed the grand solution, Ricardo wasn't all that convinced. He was highly skeptical about the whole masquerader hoopla. But today, after seeing Mark on the other side of the final curtain, his beliefs had taken on a different tune altogether.

'Great. Well then, what are we waiting for? Let's go get some action,' said Mark in his smoky voice and marched towards Ricardo's maintenance truck.

With only a couple of minutes to eight, Mark climbed into the rear of the *camion à ordures* and closed the husky steel door shut. Ricardo quickly smoked the fag end of his cigarette and threw the stub on the floor. He neatly stamped it with the giant foot and then locked the door shut, saying, 'Fuck them nice and neat, Marky, nice and neat.'

'I will, *mon frère*,' said Mark confidently from behind the door. *I hope I will.*

'*Capitaine porc*, please be careful at the checkpoint. Don't be too overconfident,' said Felix worriedly and shook hands with him twice.

'Kid, two mistakes with that sentence. One, I am always careful, and two, you cannot use too,' said the maintenance truck driver grumpily and smiled at Felix. 'Do well, kid. Make Huritt proud. You remember what Sebastian said, right?'

'I heard it loud and clear, *capiraine porc*.'

'All right. I'll see you soon,' said Ricardo and climbed into the driver's seat. He switched the engine on, shifted the handbrake, and just before lifting his leg off the brake pedal, he put his fist out of the window, spread it out wide and said, 'Poof!'

8:05 AM
Restroom-1, *route de ceinture du Lac Daumesnil* (Ring Road Lake Daumesnil)
Paris, France

'Morning, officers, care for some lemonade?' asked Oscar O'Donnell, in gibberish French, as the zoo clock chimed eight times. He then quickly handed over the jar to Gendarme Emeric and sneezed. 'I have the handkerchief!' exclaimed Oscar with childish innocence and took his jar back.

All the five PPs stationed at restroom 1 with clear orders to maintain a shielded precinct before, during, and after the event, replied with the affirmative, as expected, but with a little apprehension, owing to Oscar's running nose. But then they just couldn't say no to the Project Manager.

'Here you go, Gendarme Emeric,' said Oscar, pouring the refreshment into a plastic cup in Emeric's hand.

'Many thanks to the wife, *Monsieur* O'Donnell.'

'Thank you, gendarme, she'd be really glad to hear it. Just holler if you need more, okay?'

'I know the word, *Monsieur*.'

'Perfect.'

On the day before the event, the restroom 1, which was constructed to the south of *Lac Daumesnil* and to the north of *Bois de Vincennes*, was tenaciously cordoned off. None except the authorised personnel were given the nod to enter it, and every person entering/exiting the restroom was thoroughly checked and the logs were meticulously maintained. All of this was, as planned, happening under the supervision of the Project Manager, Oscar O'Donnell.

'Gendarme Fulbert, on whom are we betting today?' asked the six-footer, sneezing again, and moving on the next law enforcer.

'Black, as always. The Unbeaten,' replied Fulbert, pressing his ear against his transistor radio.

'Ha! Good luck, *Monsieur.*'

'Merci, patron.'

'What about you, Gendarme Geoffrey?'

'No more shots in the dark, Oscar, no more shots. I lost a few wads at the French Open. I wagered on the bloody Paraguayan,' answered Geoffrey hastily and drained the glass in one gulp.

'I'd bet on the Swedish chap, Bjorn Borg. He had six grand slams under his belt, while Víctor Pecci had just four. Geoff, don't you study their track records before putting your money on the table? Only a fool would bet for Pecci!' said Gendarme Lou.

'Well, I'd bet you are right,' said Oscar, handing over a glass to Lou.

'And you would undoubtedly have your hands full!'

'You mean, he'd have that redhead's *sein*?'

'Pierre! No! I have a granddaughter of her age. Jesus!'

'Lou, age is no barrier to admire beauty,' said Gendarme Pierre, the eldest, toughest and most astute of them all. He was doggedly staring at the well-made red-haired cheer girl, who was preparing herself for her act during the arrival of the competitors.

'Well said, Gendarme Pierre, well said,' said Oscar and stood right next to him.

He saw the cheer girls prepping themselves up, the gypsy musicians, dancers and fortunetellers prancing around the pavement while the visitors feasted on French fries, kebabs, *cocido, horchata,* sherry wine, marzipan and *turrón.* He saw the kids who were engrossed in playing *El bote, Zapatitoinglés, Los tresnavíos* and scores of other games lined up explicitly for keeping them thoroughly entertained.

'Paris is full of life! Isn't it?' asked Oscar.

'Full of beautiful women sucking the life out of you,' replied Pierre.

Oscar took a long deep breath and asked, 'Audrey is beautiful, isn't she, Gendarme Pierre?'

'What! You know her?'

'I was the one who *hired* her. Of course I know her.'

'Would you...never mind!'

'I will,' said Oscar and handed over the entire pitcher to Pierre.

'Drink up, Pierre. I'll have you pulled out immediately after the contestants pass by.'

'*Merci,* Oscar, *merci,*' said Pierre and drained the entire pitcher.

The CPZ immediately hit his nervous system and he instantly began to throw up.

8:05 AM
Avenue de saint Maurice (Avenue of Saint Maurice)
Paris, France

'Carte d'Identité,' asked Claude, officer at the Sub-directorate of operational management, DOPC (the organizational management of public order and traffic), *Préfecture de Police.*

'Oui Monsieur,' replied Ricardo and handed over his identity card to Claude, as he lit up a cigarette and looked at the security arrangement. It was exactly like how it was in Oscar's drawings. The layouts were perfect and the security arrangements looked like they were taken straight from Oscar's notes.

Oscar, you bloody bastard!

Claude passed on Ricardo's ID to his colleague who cross-referenced the name and identity across a stream of names in the "permitted personnel register".

Ricardo Frasco, age 24, Paris corporation municipal, Fanuco Lorenzo. In time – 8:10 AM.

Claude returned from the check post and jogged towards the truck, saying, 'Get down man, open the rear door.'

'Sure, *monsieur*, just a minute. You see, I'll need some time to, um, you know, carry my weight and get off this moth-eaten truck!' said Ricardo as he handed over a cigarette to Claude.

'No problem. I can wait.'

'Thank you, *Monsieur.*'

'Frasco, right?'

'That's what my parents used to call me.'

'Right. Anyway, why do you have this "moth-eaten" truck? Where is the one that the PMC issued?'

'Oh that bitch is at the garage. Apparently I'm too heavy for the PMC issued axle!'

'You don't say.'

'And, touchdown!'

'Say Frasco, which garage are we talking about?'

'The one near the post-office.'

'Does it have a name?'

'No. People just call it "the post-office garage".'

'Seriously?'

'You can enquire if it pleases you.'

'Control, this is Officer Claude from Saint Maurice. We have an unpermitted truck at the check post. The driver, Mr. Ricardo Frasco, claims that the PMC issued truck is at a post-office garage. What should we do with him?'

'...Copy that.'

'Well?'

'Stay put, the PM is on his way,' said Claude in a low voice and lit up his cigarette.

'So did you get to see Yasmine?'

Claude took a puff, blew a ring with the truck at the backdrop, and then said, 'No. I was here all morning. Didn't get a chance.'

'Oh man! Isn't that the worst? Being so close and *still* not being able to see?'

Claude took another drag and said, 'No.'

'What do you mean no? There is something worse?'

'Maybe.'

'Oh! That was...a lot of information. Highly substantial. Thanks.'

'Can we please cut the loose talk and wait for the PM in silence?'

'Maybe,' said Ricardo, and then the two men smoked in silence and waited for Oscar.

A whole minute later, Oscar arrived at the check post in the gendarmes' Chevy and asked Ricardo to show him inside the cargo area.

Ricardo immediately undid the bolt and helped Oscar climb up into the cargo compartment. He then took a few steps behind and stood next to Claude as he watched their first trick unravel.

The officers will just let you pass. If they don't, Control will take care of it. I will take care of it, thought Ricardo as a smile crossed his face. He just couldn't help it.

'Why are you smiling?' asked Claude.

'I was thinking about doing it with Yasmine.'

Claude just looked at him for a brief second and then scoffed.

'Okay, you can pass this through,' said Oscar and sneezed. 'Excuse me,' he said for the millionth time and jumped out the docking bay. 'You better report it to us from next time. Have your PMC issued trucks checked beforehand. Is that clear?'

'Yes, *Monsieur*. Thank you, *Monsieur*,' said Ricardo and locked the door shut.

'And stop saying *Monsieur* so many damn times!'

'Yes, *Monsieur*.'

You stop sneezing so many damn times!

CHAPTER 34

The *Château de la Muette* is a château located on the edge of *Bois de Boulogne,* a park located along the western edge of the 16th arrondissement of Paris. The Château covers an area of 2000 acres, which is 2.5 times larger than Central Park in New York and comparable in size to Richmond Park in London.

Three *chateaux* have been located on the site since a hunting lodge was transformed into the first château for Princess *Marguerite de Valois*. The Château has been the military Headquarters of the Germans and the Allies, and presently it serves as the Headquarters of The Organization for Economic Co-operation and Development.

The OECD originated as OEEC back in the fifties, and since then it has provided the framework for negotiations aimed at determining conditions for setting up a European Free Trade Area, to bring the European Economic Community and the other OEEC members together on a multilateral basis.

On the fifteenth day of April 1979, three terrorists opened fire on El Al passengers in the departure lounge of Paris-Orly. The French military immediately infiltrated the airport and neutralised the situation. But this attack made the local government deeply concerned regarding the security at the Paris-Orly Airport, and the security of their motherland. Hence all activities at the Orly Aerodrome were immediately halted. All major domestic flights were routed to *Charles de Gaulle* and the rest to *Le Bourget* Airport.

On the 20th of June 1979, about twenty similar French charter planes landed at the Orly under the pretense of running tests on the radio, the runway and checking the state-of-the-art security systems on the aircraft. The planes didn't taxi for long. The delegates were quickly picked off the tarmac and driven to *Château de la Muette.*

By 7:00 AM, all the invitees were gathered at the chateau to discuss, renew and update various matters regarding Free Trade Area, economy and alternative sources of energy, and to amend some provisions pertaining to the Soft Law.

Soft Law refers to quasi-legal instruments that do not have any legally binding force. Soft law instruments are often used to indicate how the European Commission intends to use its powers and perform its tasks within its area of competence. With the passage of time, soft law instruments hold much potential for morphing into Hard Law, which will then be incorporated into the legal framework of the various countries.

Soft law is a convenient option for negotiations that might otherwise stall if legally binding commitments were sought at a certain point in time when it is not convenient for negotiating parties to make major commitments for political or economic reasons, but they still wish to negotiate something in good faith in the meantime. Soft law is also viewed as a flexible option that avoids the immediate and uncompromising commitment made under treaties and it also is considered to be a potentially faster route to legal commitments than the slow pace of customary international law.

With the passage of time, the content of declarations and commitments made at international conferences is spread throughout the world through umpteen number of means. In doing so, these aspirational non-commitments often capture the imagination of citizens who begin to believe in these soft law instruments as if they were legal instruments. In turn it is felt that this ultimately impacts governments who are forced to take into account the wishes of citizens, NGOs, NPOs, courts and even corporations who begin to refer to these soft law instruments so frequently and with such import that they begin to evidence legal norms.

The Foreign, Home, Finance and Trade and Commerce ministers of the European founder countries of the OEEC were gathered at *Château de la Muette* for a diplomatic incognito meet to discuss and incorporate a soft law relating to the topics under discussion. Owing to the rapid industrial growth and ever increasing economic cooperation and stability in the Union, the member nations were more confident than ever with regards to making and amending new and effective laws. It was less likely that they would not receive support from their home governments, considering the fact that each member nation had joined the union wholeheartedly and that they had elected a President, one among them, to lead them and pave way for the realisation of the concept of United Nations of Europe.

The laborious security measures that were otherwise necessary were greatly reduced. Since the meeting was incognito, no one knew anything about it, and since it was convened during the Triathlon, the attention was greatly diverted. With the city overflowing with tourists, foreign and local celebrities, diplomats from various embassies and politicians, not much concern was given to the proceedings of the OEEC. The speculation was much more relieved by giving permission for the organisers to choose *Rue André Pascal* as a potential road for the bike circuit.

CHAPTER 35

The Baron of the Roulette Airlines was a man in his late fifties. He was divorced with a son, whom he met only four times a year. He was a very reserved man. He seldom met his relatives and friends. After the devastating failure of his first marriage, he had stopped believing in relationships, and detested all familial relations. He needed no relatives and always chose to be a lone warrior in his illusory land of isolation.

The lone son from Voorburgwal however attracted his attention. Henry saw his own younger self in Albert. Albert's thirst for knowledge and his formidable fervour towards the metallic kites sparked Henry's advertence right after their first conversation. He had introduced Albert to a mechanic and a foreman, and had them train him at the apron, de-icing area, runway, touchdown zone, holding position, air base, inventory and R&D.

The muscular man with a fat mustache and eyebrows that dwarfed his eyes would talk to Albert once every two days. They would discuss everything about the industry, the stocks, the shares, the projections, the assets, the financing, the revenues and the agendas.

At sixteen, Henry's protégé knew almost everything about the industry. Henry would bring the boardroom debates to his chamber and call upon Albert to present his views on the pertinent issues. The duo formed a prodigious partnership. They would write the matter under discussion on a huge black board in Henry's chamber and stare at it for hours. In small doses it would morph into heated discussions at the end of which, more often than not, they would have the wall smothered by chalk dust and from the dust, they would fathom their inkling that would grow into the tree of revolution.

But even though they spent hours together, they would not once speak about their personal lives. Both individuals repelled social afflictions, and this very factor made them comfortable in each other's presence.

As the sixteen-year-old aviation wizard upped a year, Henry was diagnosed with leukemia. He had no family, no friends, and feared that after his demise, the industry might fall into incapable hands, hands that weren't Albert's.

The General broaching the badge of almighty dollars wanted a Brigadier like Albert to head his platoon, to lead his regiment into soaring heights and to keep his banner fluttering high up in the skies.

But upon hearing the news of his illness, all his relatives came closer. He and his wife got back together again and he hardly visited the office anymore. So as to say, he was being held captive by the people he despised. Meaning, his meetings with Albert decreased. At one stage it reached rock bottom.

Soon sick old Henry's so-called relatives forcibly made him sign his Final Will and Testament, transferring his 45% share in the Roulette Airlines to his only son, William. The wanton wife raced out of their condo soon after the will was drafted and William soon followed suit.

Henry was a loner again. But Albert stuck on to him. He gradually started embracing the reality. He grew closer to Albert and he was presented with a new challenge, a new purpose. He yearned to train Albert to the fullest. He wanted to imbibe in him all his tactics, schemes and skills regarding the industry. He wanted to better the life of the poor orphan, who was given the gift of brilliance but rendered limbless in the realms of economy.

Nine months after his diagnosis, three hundred days after his excruciating chemotherapy and familial torment and four months after his splendid training sessions with the person he knew as Albert, he was told the news he had long waited for, but always told himself, "not today".

The doctors told him that he was in his final run and that his chances of survival were hanging by a fine thread. He was told to spend a few days in the company of his dear ones and then putter away his last days at the hospital, as they ensured a less painful cessation.

In this moment of sheer desperation, he decided to contact the two people he really loved and cared for, Albert and Veronica Griffiths.

CHAPTER 36

October 17, 1978
Cour d'assises

The court livened up again after a brief recess.

A few cameras were focused on *barre des témoins* as the trail was about to begin.

Lorenzo: Is the state ready to proceed?

Reyes: Yes, Your Honour.

Lorenzo: Very well then, the state may call its first witness.

The Usher shouted the name of the first witness, Edgar Dominique.

Edgar rose and slowly walked towards the witness box. The walk from the public stands to the box appeared to be the longest walk ever, since every pair of eyes moved with the walker. As Edgar reached the witness box, the usher held the Bible and walked towards him.

'Do you swear to tell the truth, the whole truth, and nothing but the truth, so help you God?' asked the Usher.

'Yes. I do, Sir,' replied Edgar earnestly.

Reyes: Mr. Dominique, could you please introduce yourself to the court?

'I am Edgar Dominique. I work at *Bien Guérir,* a medical shop at #434 *Avenue de Laumière.* On the 14th of August, Tuesday, I saw this man – ' he said, pointing at Huritt, who was sitting in *Box des accuses* (the box of accused), '– getting out of a taxi and banging on Sarah's door. After some time, she opened the door and the two of them immediately got into a fight. Sometime later, she slapped him, and then he forcefully nudged her to go inside the house. About a half hour later, he came out hurriedly…agitatedly, hailed a taxi, and departed.'

Reyes: Thank you Mr. Dominique. Now, I would like to call my next witness, *Monsieur le president.*

Lorenzo: The witness can be seated now. Usher, call the next witness.

Usher: Mrs. Sylvie Absolon, please approach the witness box.

As always, the oath was taken, and after Reye's queue, she began to testify.

'I am Mrs. Sylvie Absolon, Ms. Bibiana's neighbor. On the 14th of August, at around 1:00 PM, I was watering my plants when I saw this man getting out of a taxi and then banging on Ms. Bibiana's door. Once she answered the door, there appeared to have been a fight between the two, for a short duration of course, after which they went inside. That is all I saw. I can testify that this man definitely went to her house that day. Then at around 1:30 PM, Montego came and enquired about Bibiana. I told him what I'd seen and then we went together to his house and used a spare key that was with me, and went inside. We-we then found her – ' said she, her voice trembling, ' – lying on the bed…dead!'

The next person in the box was Cortez. He passively faced the court and said, 'I am Montego Cortez. I-uh, I was…I was Sarah's fiancée… On the day of the murder – '

Sebastian: Objection! *Monsieur le president.*

Lorenzo: Sustained!

Cortez: Sorry… On the day Sarah was found dead, I returned from work at around 1:30 PM. I happened to have forgotten to take my key that day. So I rang the bell and waited for a couple of minutes…but no one answered. I then went to Sylvie's and asked if she had seen Sarah. She told me everything about what she'd seen, but Sarah's act of stepping out of our house is a…a very unlikely event. She doesn't even answer the door for me. I always have to carry my key!

Anyway she was really scared for the past couple of days. I asked her what the matter was, but whenever I did, she simply used to walk away. I then decided to take her to a psychiatrist. But she protested. I asked if we could speak to her brother. But she resisted. I didn't know what I had to do. She always stayed confined to her room and her condition worsened when the baby became ill.

Sebastian: Okay, Mr. Cortez. Now, could you please tell us what happened after you met Mrs. Absolon?

Reyes wanted to object, but Cortez began before he could stand up.

Cortez: After I spoke to Sylvie, we entered my house using her key. Once inside, I found Achille, sitting right next to his mother's corpse and crying out loud. It…It was a terrible sight.

Many jurors were moved, picturing the dreadful scene in their minds. Reyes smiled and shot a provocative glance at Sebastian, who seemed to be undeterred.

Cortez: I immediately called the police, and Inspector David Felipe answered the call.

Reyes: Thank you, Mr. Cortez. *Monsieur le president,* I would now like to call the informant, Inspector David Felipe.

Felipe: Mr. Cortez called me from his residence at 1:28 PM and reported a death. I immediately informed the HQ and took off to the scene with my constable, Jean. On my way, I noticed that there were no signs of break-in, implying that no one had busted into the house. I then found Ms. Bibiana lying on her stomach, with her face tilted to the side and facing the door.

There were no signs of fight and no sign of blood. She was clutching a picture of herself and Mr. Huritt in her hand, and also, there was a bottle of Midaxolac on the table right next to her, beside an empty glass.

I observed that her skin was swollen at a few places, so I thought that she might have been poisoned. I then cordoned off the room and called Homicide. They arrived at around 2:05 PM. And there ends my participation. That is all.

Reyes: Inspector Felipe, could you please hand over your report to the *Greffier*?

Felipe handed over a detailed police report of how the information was received and a brief description of the scene.

Reyes: *Monsieur le president,* from the testimony of Felipe and Jean, it is affirmable that the accused, Mr. Huritt Achak, did enter the house without breaking in. Meaning, he let himself in.

Sebastian: Objection, *Monsieur.*

Lorenzo: Sustained. Proceed.

Sebastian: Thank you, *Monsieur.* Maybe she herself let him in.

Reyes: But we also have two witnesses testifying that Mr. Huritt and Ms. Sarah fought at the doorstep. Meaning, she didn't like him being there and she wanted to drive him away without letting him in.

Sebastian: Or he just came to inform her about something, which we will discover shortly, and she asked him, rather dragged him inside the house, against *his* will.

Reyes: Learned counsel, you have the burden of proof. I can presume any scenario I want. You can rebut it while you present your defense case-in-chief. *Monsieur le President et Monsieur l'Assesseur,* I would kindly request you to allow me to present my witnesses.

Lorenzo: Granted.

Sebastian sat down and asked his assistant to make a note or two.

Reyes: Inspector Felipe, is what I'm stating valid as per your primary investigation?

Felipe: Yes, Sir. It corroborates with the evidence.

The President ordered him to sit, after which Jean gave a similar kind of testimony. Sebastian didn't object. Reyes then called the forensic expect.

Dr. Denis: We found fingerprints, shoeprints, hair samples, fabric and tire tread evidence at the scene, which are identical with that of Mr. Huritt's.

We dusted for prints, scanned for evidence and collected every possible exhibit at the scene. We then sent the body to our lab for further analysis. The microscopic pathological analysis revealed that her nervous system had collapsed, and among the many effects, the prime cause for her death was respiratory arrest, more precisely, asphyxiation.

There was no fabric inside her nose, meaning she wasn't chocked by stuffing a cloth or by pressing a pillow or other such means. Also, there were no signs of strangulation.

Now the toxicological analysis of the blood, urine, hair and saliva consistently revealed signs of a Benzodiazepine. There were no signs of intravenous shots on her body. So we analysed her stomach and found the residue of the drug. The drug found in her stomach was of the same composition as that mentioned on the bottle found on the table next to her bed.

Reyes: Yes, Mr. Denis, now what made you think that Mr. Huritt was responsible for the death of Ms. Bibiana?

Dr. Denis: Respected, prosecutor. It's not my job to think. I just assert that there is more probability for Mr. Huritt to be involved with her death, as I have found his fingerprints on her face, four fingers to be precise. Clearly proving that he slapped her. Also, when Mr. Huritt was called down for interrogation, I observed two inundations on the frontal portion of his neck, the analysis of which proved that it was caused from Ms. Bibiana's nails. Plus, the shoe prints near her room were scrambled, implying a distinct possibility of a fight. That's all I have to say.

Reyes: Dr. Denis, I'd like to rephrase my earlier question. What, according to you can be the probability of Mr. Huritt's involvement in the death of Ms. Bibiana?

The doctor fumbled for a bit and then with visible apprehension said, 'More than 50%'.

Reyes: Respected jurors and the learned court, more than 50% probability. Thank you, Dr. Denis.

Next, Reyes's seventh witness, Sarah's brother, Bayol, was called to the box. He calmly introduced himself and gave an account for the motive. Then somewhere down the line, he lost his temper...

Bayol: Sarah and that fucking bastard...

Lorenzo: Abusive words shall not be encouraged in the court! The prosecutor has to brief his witnesses regarding the rules of this courtroom or else the witness shall be declared hostile and will be in the court's contempt.

Reyes: I apologise for his behavior, *Monsieur*. It won't happen again.

Bayol: Sarah and this guy lived together for almost a year. I never approved of it...I never like Huritt. Not one bit. The more I advised, the closer she grew to that scum!

Sebastian: Objec –

Bayol: And one terrible morning, she deserted me. She walked out on me...I always told her that this man wasn't right for her. She never listened to me. In fact, she saw me as her enemy!

My sister was a really brave girl. She wouldn't go to the extent of suicide. She wouldn't take such drastic decisions.

Reyes: Very well, Mr. Bayol. But why didn't you approve of Mr. Huritt?

Bayol: He didn't have a good background. His parents were felons and they were sentenced when he was of young age. Since then he grew up at that orphanage. Let me tell you, Mr. Reyes, he was born to criminals and he was brought up at a lonesome place. He is a sociopath. Relations mean nothing to him. In fact, it was my sister who stuck up for him and forced me to accept him. He didn't care to come and talk to me. He may look all gentle and elegant on the outside, but on the inside, he is a devil. Once he had the opportunity to marry a woman from the Fermont family, he ditched my sister and pounced on that poor lady. Of course he wouldn't have told Mrs. Fermont about Sarah. My sister probably tried to hint to her about his sadistic character, and Huritt, discovering this unpleasant act, wanted to shut her up before she could spill the beans.

Reyes: So, respected jurors, you have the background of the accused, and you have the motive.

Sebastian didn't move. He was saving up everything for the cross-examination.

Reyes: Is there anything else, Mr. Bayol?

Bayol: This sociopath should be punished. He should be hanged and...

Sebastian: Objection! *Monsieur le President et Monsieur l'Assesseur.*

'Sustained.'

Reyes hastily dismissed Bayol and called his penultimate witness.

Usher: Sub-Inspector Joseph!

Joseph: Steve, a constable, and I went to the court, obtained the warrant, and went to *Chateau de la Fermont*. We spoke to the security and learnt that on the day of the alleged murder, Huritt arrived at the *Chateau* only a few minutes past 1:30. Then we spoke to Huritt, read him out his rights and asked him if he had been to Sarah's. But he flatly denied it. He said he had never left home that day.

Reyes called the constable, who confirmed the same, and he then ushered in his last witness, the security guard, and he too, confirmed Joseph's and the constable's statement.

Reyes: Respected jurors and the court, let me sum up all the testimonies. Mrs. Absolon and Mr. Dominique saw Mr. Huritt fight with Ms. Bibiana. Mr. Dominique saw him exit, and while he exited, Ms. Bibiana didn't come to close the door. Inspector Felipe and *Gendarme* Jean testify that there was no sign of a break-in, supporting Mr. Dominique's and Mrs. Absolon's statement.

By clutching the picture of Mr. Huritt, she was pointing out her murderer. Dr. Denis testifies that there was more than 50% probability for Huritt to have murdered Ms. Bibiana. Ms. Bibiana's brother, Bayol, testifies against the credibility of the accused's parents, who themselves were felons, and also tells us about Mr. Huritt's opinion about emotions. He also gives us the motive.

Sub-Inspector Joseph, a gendarme in good standing, and Huritt's security affirms that he was lying. So the deluding sociopathic son of felons, who had a traumatic childhood, went against the wishes of the innocent woman's family, carelessly lived with her, gave her a child and pounced upon the rich. Then in order to hide his past life so that he could live lavishly, he heinously murdered a mother, an innocent citizen of this law-abiding country and a great human being, in cold blood.

That is all the witnesses I have, respected court.

The court was adjourned for the day and the defense was to cross-examine the witnesses on the next day, the eighteenth.

CHAPTER 37

October 31, 1992
Amsterdam

'I couldn't shake her from my head. I couldn't stop thinking about her. I didn't want to help her or anything. I just didn't want her to be with him. I couldn't let that happen. I don't know why I thought that way, but I wanted to free her from the Fat Pig!'

'Mama, free.'

'Yes, son. I went back to the brothel and found out Ricardo's address from the owner of the place. I then tracked him down and knocked on his door. But there wasn't any response. So I went around the house, found a window, broke into it and searched the house.

I found your mama in one of the rooms, on the floor, her body and face bruised. I knew she deserved better and I knew that I couldn't just leave her there. So I picked her up and carried her outside. She simply looked at me and then she closed her eyes. She knew she could trust me. She knew that I would protect her.'

'Mama, protect. No.'

'Yes son, I-I failed to protect her. I-I was helpless.'

CHAPTER 38

September 13, 1978.
Alexis Hospital.
Paris, France.

'Hello honey, I am Stephanie from Pascal Medical University. I urgently need your help. Please…' said Veronica and moved a couple of steps ahead, so that she was at a nail's distance from Denver's ear, and whispered, 'in return I shall ensure that you are pleased…'

Veronica was Mark's favorite *pick*. He would always ask for her at *"La Rojo"*, a prostitution club in Paris owned by a Spaniard. She had a dainty seductive face with alluring skin, a broad forehead with gleaming deep-set eyes separated by a straight-edged soft nose, paunchy, red, gleaming lips (she achieved it by mixing lipstick with a pinch of sugar in a few droplets of water) and long straight blonde hair that brushed her perfect round and juicy cheeks. She never wore bikinis, and men would die to just sit and admire her elegance.

On the 13th of September, at the Alexis, she chose to wear a satin, white, slim fit, V-necked top, revealing a significant part of her back and her firm, soft, perfectly gapped breasts, even as her kinky nipples protruded through the satin. She wore a condensed black skirt that was barely visible. Her long sturdy legs were stacked in gauzy nylon stockings, while her feet were dressed in red high-heeled shoes and nails were colored black. But for her economic condition, she wouldn't have ended up as a prostitute. Her elegance and grace would have surely rendered her as a star in the movie trade, not the body trade. When you see a woman with such charisma, you tend to question the insanity of the creator and the very fabric of human nature.

'Do you have the dean's authorisation letter?' Denver sternly asked, trying hard not to stare at her alluring eyes, resplendent lips, stacked breasts, cockeyed nipples, tempting long legs, pinchable, seductive butt and captivating, tempting figure.

'No sweetie, I don't,' said Veronica, swaying her arms and legs, as she moved closer to Denver, a short, yet slim man in his mid 30s, with silky black hair and a pale face. He had expressionless eyes, for he didn't like his job. His lips were blackened, thanks to the smoking. His nose was a bit crooked, thanks to a bar brawl, and his pockets were not filled to the brim, thanks to the poor wages. He was a familial man, married with four kids. A man full of debts and unsatisfactory progress in life.

Denver forcibly controlled his urges, while Veronica forcibly let the same go.

'I can't help you, Miss. I'm the only person in charge of the records section, and should there be a problem tomorrow, I will be the first person under scrutiny. I'm so sorry ma'am,' he said reluctantly, staring at the ground below her red heels.

'Honey, I consulted the Dean before approaching you. He demanded the authorisation letter from the college. Bloody bastard!' she said with force, so that Denver could see her breasts move harmonically behind the satin cloth, forcing him to get aroused.

'Today is Sunday, stupid! The office at my college isn't open!' she shouted, and then added, 'Sweetie, I have my project submission tomorrow and I don't want to blow it. I shall blow something else for you," she said, whispering the last few words as she seductively bit her lips and held his penis through his trousers, while her breasts almost pressed his chest.

'I've failed continually in most of the exams. This assignment submission is my last resort to stop them from detaining me, and I shall do anything to stop them from throwing me out of the institution. I mean anything,' she said, pressing his trousers near the crotch,

His voice trembled as his penis began shooting up. He babbled on, knowing not how to react. He alternatively opened and closed his mouth a few times, sweating and swallowing all the words, and letting only a few gasps escape his mouth.

'I won't tell anyone about anything that is going to happen between us,' she whispered, sending moist waves through his ears.

'Okay, okay. You wait here and bolt the door. I'll go to the records section and get you the required case files,' said Denver as he marched from his minute cabin towards the records section, forcefully distracting himself from further advances.

'Write down whatever you want and pass it on to me quickly,' he added, removing her hand off his penis.

'"Erectile Dysfunction" – Dr. Martin Leroy, "Cardiac arrest" – Dr. Christine and "Lung congestion"- Dr. Edwige,' she mouthed, as she jotted down the same on a sheet of paper.

'How do you know all these doctors?'

'Considering the fact that I am a medical student and also the fact that these people are well-acclaimed doctors in France, it is customary for every other student studying medicine to be aware of these names.'

'Dr. Leroy would have been so happy to hear that from you. He always loved and cared for young and passionate students. Thousands of young minds came to this place in his company and reached great heights. May his soul rest in peace,' said Denver and closed the door behind her.

'And by the way, I also need to create a case report of my own. So if you could please get me a few formatted sheets without anything filled in them. Dr. Leroy's is most preferable, "Erectile dysfunction" is a fairly easy topic.'

CHAPTER 39

June 20, 1979

8:12 AM
Restroom-1

Gendarme Fulbert, Geoffrey, Emeric and Lou assisted Pierre to the Chevrolet Nova Police vehicle and thrust him on the rear seat. Lou quickly took his place behind the wheel and drove away, trying hard to avoid the commotion at the complex.

A few seconds after the Chevy left, Ricardo arrived at the scene of interest with his maintenance truck and entered the restroom through gate B.

The restroom had two entrances that were mutually perpendicular to each other. The gate facing *route de ceinture du Lac Daumesnil* was gate A, and the gate facing west was gate B. Gate A was smaller and accessible only to the *Préfecture de Police* and the competitors, while gate B was larger and dedicated primarily for the entry/exit of the commissioned vehicles and personnel. Five guards, three at Gate A and two at Gate B were assigned to carry out the ordeal assigned by the DOPC.

Lou and Pierre, who were supposed to be stationed at the west end, were now absent. Hence Oscar took the charge of guarding Gate B, while Fulbert, Geoffrey and Emeric took their positions at gate A.

'Welcome, Ricardo,' said Oscar gaily and let them enter the restroom.

All these acts were pre-planned and practiced extensively. The problems that might arise were considered and necessary changes were immediately implemented. Accordingly, the compound walls were raised to twenty feet and people within a 50-metre radius were cleared off, so that no one from the outside could see what was happening on the other side of the concrete curtain.

The truck was manoeuvred swiftly inside the compound and finally brought to a halt right below one of the ten Change Rooms.

'Mark, quick,' whispered Oscar and banged twice on the wall of the truck.

Mark immediately jumped towards a door on the top of the container and stealthily crawled out of it before lugging himself in through the restroom window.

The restroom was a 20X40 structure, with the forty-feet-wide wall containing a door on the rightmost corner. The space towards the left was left void, save the three seven feet long wooden benches lined next to each other, and the wall on the opposite side was divided into ten equal blocks. Each change room had a lavatory and a changing area that were separated by a curtain.

'Ladies and gentlemen, navy reaches the finish line surpassing all his competitors!' announced Aimon at 8:14 AM.

At the precise moment, Mark entered the restroom through a square, three-foot wide window, which originally had three vertical iron bars.

A few days before the construction of the restroom had commenced, Huritt had told Oscar, *""If he had to escape, he had to pass through the iron rods""*, that is what I want the people to think. And by people, I mean anyone who is suspicious. But then we really needn't bother much about it, because I'm sure that no one in Paris will be suspicious as long as I am winning. We are patriots, you see."

Oscar had devised a way for what Huritt wanted, and both were happy about it.

The Londoners started applauding, cheering and waving their flags as their man rushed to the restroom, comprehending the fact that he was about 6.68 seconds behind Anouk Fermont.

Mark, wearing a full-head latex mask, black goggles, black shorts, black long-sleeved T-shirt with the yellow *fleur-de-lis*, black leather gloves, white socks and white tennis shoes, helped Huritt climb out of the restroom. Huritt crawled out of the window and said, *'Bonne chance, Huritt.'*

Mark immediately screwed the detached iron rods and sat on the commode seat, with his hands clasped tightly together and heaving monstrous gasps of air through his lungs. He pulled his left sock as high as he could, pulling at every strand of cotton. He then securely donned his helmet and confidently walked out of the restroom.

'Reporting Black, Fleur-de-lis, from restroom-1, *Route de ceinture du Lac Daumesnil*, exit at eight hours, eighteen minutes, 57 seconds. Over.'

'Black, 08:18:57, affirm, black, 08:18:57.'

'Positive.'

'Reporting Navy, red cross of Saint George, from restroom 1, *Route de ceinture du Lac Daumesnil*, exit at eight hours, twenty minutes, 02 seconds. Over.'

'Navy blue, 08:20:02, affirm, Navy blue, 08:20:02.'

'Positive.'

8:15 AM
Route de ceinture du Lac Daumesnil

Huritt swam the three-and-a-half kilometre loop like a whale, sweeping back copious amounts of water. *Money, new life, fame, power. Money, new life, fame, power.* He sporadically eyed the skies embossed in gold and etched in blue, as he drew small amounts of air through either sides of his mouth. *Money, power. New life, fame.* His legs vigorously paddled the waters of *Lac Daumesnil*, producing white foam as each leg met with the liquid surface. *Money, new life, fame, power. Money, new life, fame, power.* Contrary to most sportsmen, he didn't really care to see where he stood, for he was well aware of the fact that he was well ahead of all his competitors. As always. *Money.*

Huritt beat his previous record by 2.48 minutes, finishing the circuit in 54 minutes and 11 seconds. He had of course a big race ahead of him. The race of his life. A race that would make the God of good fortune sternly stare at him, a race that would give him a sundering leap in the days to come, a race that would render him free from running for the rest of his life.

'Black! Mesdames et Messieurs,' shouted Aimon, as Lefèbvre Delacroix and General Bernard le Blanc smirked at each other.

Money, new life, fame, power.

'Alors Huritt. Vous pouvez battre tout le monde.'

'Come on, Huritt. You can beat them all.'

'Fleur-de-lis!'

'Blazing Black!'

'The Unbeaten!' shouted the proponents of Huritt, as he sprinted along the path heading towards the restroom on *Route de ceinture du Lac Daumesnil.*

Now that the contestants were approaching the restroom, the police had a hard time controlling the mob. The traffic had been diverted and only the vehicles concerning the *Organisateurs de l'événement* (Event organisers) were allowed on the course roads.

Gendarme Fulbert, Geoffrey and Emeric broke the discussion after sending the other two gendarmes away and ran to take their positions outside the restroom compound. They stood in front of the high compound wall, at a distance of ten feet from each other, and gripped their rifles firmly.

'Reporting Black, Fleur-de-lis, from restroom 1, *Route de ceinture du Lac Daumesnil* at eight hours eighteen minutes sixteen seconds,' announced one of the volunteers standing at the entrance to the restroom.

'Black, 08:18:16, affirm, black, 08:18:16,' relayed a voice from the records office on *Avenue de Saint Maurice,* in response to the volunteer's transmission.

'Positive.'

Money, new life, fame, power.

CHAPTER 40

June 20, 1979
8:30 AM - 03:00 PM
Aid-station 1

'*Bonjour, Monsieur Huritt.* I'm a great fan of yours. I really want you to win today! Please sign my bra, would you?' asked a young lady volunteer, lifting up her shirt and thrusting a pen towards a Mark who had his head bowed.

At the aid stations, as far as possible, try to keep your head bowed. Don't make eye contact with anyone. Never remove your glasses. Remove your helmet only when no one is around you. Don't fold your sleeves. Never remove the gloves, they might notice your fingers. Wear tight socks. Keep them as close as possible to your knee, but without attracting undesired public attention. The only completely exposed part of your body should be the knee. That won't really attract suspicion. Keep all this in mind, Marky. Don't talk to anyone. Don't eat anything in front of the volunteers. Avoid anything and everything that draws undesired attention and suspicion.

I won't draw any "undesired attention". Stop saying that a million times!

The event organisers provided long-sleeved shirts, tights, shoes, gloves, helmet and socks to every athlete. Generally people preferred to wear minimal apparel, but Oscar O'Donnell, the Project Manager, had insisted on the use of sheathed vestment for two prime reasons. One, the national symbols could be better recognised and two, it would protect the participants from intense UV burns. The Sports Ministry took a liking to the first reason and sanctioned its approval.

The participants' shoes had GPS trackers designed to track their instantaneous positions. The chips were programmed to collect the data pertaining to each athlete and send it to the Saint Maurice base station through Yeux. The data would then be buffered and transmitted to the City Hall, where the delegates would observe the exact location of the competitors once every 1.618 seconds.

The competitors had two devices planted on them, but were told that as per the statute, they were required to wear "a" tracking device. In case a competitor was to indulge in trickery, as in take short cuts or take assistance of propellers or even tamper with the device, the analysts at the Saint Maurice would recognise the glitch and inform the same to the DOCP, who would see to it that the particular competitor was apprehended and disqualified from the event.

Mark turned sideways and shook the girl's hand, as he wiped his face on his t-shirt. He showed his face long enough for the volunteer to recognise him as Huritt, but not long enough for her to feel suspicious.

He collected the "snacks and the energy drinks bag" from the counter and walked as far as possible from the crowd, volunteers and fellow competitors. He breathed in measured sequences and composed himself. He then slowly drained the energy drinks and the power bars and quickly dashed out to the track.

At 09:06 AM, he left the Aid Station 1, which was located at a distance of 16 km from the restroom 1, and headed towards *Chateau de la Muette*.

Chapter 41

8:27 AM
Mark's garage

Almost nine minutes after they had left restroom 1, Ricardo banged twice on the steel wall behind him. 'We are out, *Monsieur*. We crossed the first barrier,' shouted the greasy haired driver gleefully.

The twenty two year old blue-gray-eyed ace athlete emerged out of the false steel wall and elatedly jumped off the truck. He hugged Frasco, patted him on the back and kissed him on the cheek. Huritt then walked hurriedly towards his Jaguar XJ Double-Six 5.3 and climbed into it without delay.

'I'm psyched! *Patron*. You kicked them all in the ass! I was all "Awe sooky sooky" when you beat the crap out of *Lac Daumesnil*. 4-sho man! It was crazy!' said Felix excitedly as the five-point-seven-five footer climbed inside his car.

Bloody kid. 'Thank you, Felix. But let us reserve all the merriment for the end. I want you to be serious, Felix, I don't want you to be impish. Please concentrate on your assignment. I'm requesting you. It's clear, isn't it?'

'Oui patron. Désolé.'

'Good luck, *patron.* May the force be with you,' said Ricardo, closing the door shut.

'To infinity and beyond,' replied Huritt and lifted the rear seat that was custom modified. The seat was hinged along the axis on the inner side of the region joining the backrest to the seat base, giving access to a void that was designed suitably for single occupancy. *La Patron* prostrated inside the rectangular coffin-like box, his head facing the roof of the Jag, while Felix replaced the rear seat back to its initial position and clamped it in such a way that it was perpendicular to the backrest.

'Froom Breetish weeth love,' said Frasco and patted the car's head.

'Chateau de Fermont, Monsieur.'

CHAPTER 42

24th June 1979.
Bibliothèque de sciences humaines et sociales Descartes (CNRS - The Human and Social Sciences Library Paris Descartes)

7:00 PM.

The European Economic Community (EEC) was established with the idea of bringing about economic integration, including common market, among its members (Belgium, France, Germany, Italy, Luxembourg, the Netherlands, Denmark, Ireland, Norway and the United Kingdom). The Schuman Declaration's call for the pooling of coal and steel resources under a common High Authority served as the inception for the unification of the member countries. EEC is looked up as the forerunner of several other European Communities and also what is now the European Union (EU).

During the tenure of President Jenkins (President of European Committee), elections were held in France, Italy, Netherland, Denmark, Luxembourg, United Kingdom, West Germany, Belgium and Ireland, and the new Parliament formed, galvanised by direct election and new powers, started working full time and is now more active than the previous assemblies. The parliament became the first Community institution to propose that the Community adopt the Flag of Europe.

Also, the aim of the Council of Europe is to achieve a greater unity between its members for the purpose of safeguarding and realising the ideals and principles that are their common heritage and facilitating their economic and social progress…

CHAPTER 43

November 26, 1992
Amsterdam

'So, we came to Amsterdam on the day after my brother died. But when we came here, we had nothing. No money, no job. For the purpose of getting a job, I lied that your mother and I were born in Amsterdam.'

'But you guys were born in – '

' – Belgium. Like I said, your mama's bloody father had forced her into prostitution, right from when she was thirteen.'

'Just like Tracy!'

'No, not like Tracy. No one forced Tracy. She volunteered!'

'She volunteered to be a prostitute?'

'...Son, if your mama were here now, she'd kill both of us. She always said, "I'm not a prostitute. I'm a sex worker. The only non-taxable and highly pleasurable source of income".'

'Papa! Stop! Gross!'

CHAPTER 44

stop bothering me. I don't care
I no longer destroy
ur family Sarah. Y ver I tel
Don't you dar If y
sobey me, you ession
again. I hope that you don't wa
to be responsible th of Cortez and
our child. Burn this letter rightaway.

CHAPTER 45

Red sanguine fluid tricked down the surface of the yellowish sheath. *I'm sorry,* said Henry to his reflection on the mirror and tightly closed his eyes. *You have no other option but to die.*

His hands shivered and his heart pounded as the thought of slitting his throat exacerbated in his head. The sharpened glass pressed against his skin, again, forcing out more blood. But Henry couldn't muster the courage to complete the swing. He put down the knife, again, and cried, again, and splashed more water on his neck. He padded the blood with a clean white cloth and he threw it back into the sink. *I can't do it. Not this time...*

He rubbed his eyes and reflected, *Henry! How many times do you want to try? You have no reason to live! You are a liability to all. No one cares about your existence. Be brave, Henry. Be brave.* 'Be brave, Henry. Be brave,' whispered Henry and wiped off his tears. 'You cannot let them *choose* how you die. You cannot let them win again. You have to be the best of them all. You have to do what is best for you. And right now, *this* is the best thing you can do.'

Henry exhaled as all the thoughts gushed out of his system and simply looked at the knife. He stared at it for a few seconds, thinking, *Life is all about making the right decisions. So pick up the damn knife and make your life less painful. Just end it…*

The wretched billionaire airliner gave in to the Lord of the Inner Voices and picked up the knife. He then turned on the tap and washed the bloodstains off its silvery surface. He slowly wiped it clean and held it tightly in his hand. Fear again took over and he tried countering it by rapidly inhaling and exhaling, and chanting, *Do it, Henry, do it for yourself, do it for respect, do it for freedom!*

'*Het leven is wreed!*' shouted Henry and again closed his eyes. Silence took over, again, and Henry fixed his eyes on the darkness that his life resounded. He let out a deep sigh and clasped his other hand over the knife handle. The tickler was cradled in his hands and he was all set to go through with the plunge.

'*Het!*' screamed Henry and pointed his hands in the direction of his neck.

A splitting sound echoed through the cabin as the telephone jingled. Henry's concentration was disturbed, and he was forced to open his eyes. *No one ever calls me at this hour…except…shit!* Henry thought and sprinted towards the phone, with the knife still grasped in his left hand. He picked up the receiver and said, 'Albert?'

'Uncle Henry, can I drop by your cabin now? I need to tell you something very important. I-I need to confess about…I can't do it over the phone.'

Henry's voice cracked as he opened his mouth to say, 'I'll meet you in ten?'

'Fifteen, Uncle Henry, make it fifteen.'

'Okay, I'll be…waiting,' said Henry and glanced at the knife in his hand. 'See you soon,' he continued, and dropped it on the floor. *Someone cares about you. You still have a purpose.*

Henry slowly put down the receiver and froze, staring blankly at the door. He heard the rain receding and he could hear wind howling through a small gap in the window. He looked around the cabin, thinking, *I could have been dead by now if not for Albert,* and let out a profound gasp.

He then looked at the phone, again. *Should I call Veronica and apologise? No, no. She wouldn't…she might…Mark might…no!*

He stared helplessly and aimlessly looked at the door yet again. Out of the blue, the door swung open and Veronica stepped in. Her thick coat of fur had disappeared and she was now clad in a wet satin V-neck. As she pushed back her soggy hair and walked closer to Henry, he could see her nipples pressed against her dripping blouse and her slippery breasts jerking up and down behind the satin curtain. In one clean sweep she removed her blouse and pressed her squirmy breasts against his coat. She immediately held his face tight and kissed him on his lips.

Henry was stupefied! Before he could even comprehend what was happening, she unbuckled his belt and pulled down his trousers. She then took his hands and put them on her waist, as he closed his eyes and tried not to ejaculate.

Veronica, striking a balance between empathy and exasperation, removed his coat with suppleness and dropped it on the carpet. Henry moved his hands down her waist and pulled down her skirt, as she undid his shirt and pressed her perfectly rounded silky breasts on his naked chest.

A few seconds after being pressed against the tender bosom of the woman whom he desired the most, Henry put his hands on her shoulder and pushed her down. She nimbly unbuttoned his shirt and dropped it right next to the coat. Once he sensed his penis in her hand, he took his hands off her shoulders and put them on her head, even as she grabbed his penis and thrust it in her mouth. She moved her head in and out a couple of times, and then she held his hands and had him kneel on the burgundy carpet.

She agilely turned around and bent, pointing her face towards the door. She pushed her hips towards Henry and stuck his penis into her vagina. She slowly moved front and back a couple of times, and then Henry slowly held her hips and let his lungs open. He began to moan and he began to cry, turning aggressive and quickening the motion. Meanwhile Veronica bit her lip and tried to keep quiet. But then, as the motion quickened, she let her lips free and managed to gasp...

'Uncle Henry, where is Dilli...Mom!'

'Albert!'

'Nahiossi!'

CHAPTER 46

Cortez's dealer Nathan was associated with the diamond smuggling mafia gang in South Africa. His people, the *verlossers,* meaning the saviours, as they called themselves, were the people of prime influence in the diamond business. They had *Vennotes,* meaning partners, in about 15 countries including the USA, Switzerland, France, London, Saudi, India and Spain. They worked with such efficiency, secrecy and stealth that they were not once suspected in a career spanning more than six decades. They worked under the leadership of one of the leading diamond establishments of the time, Femhörnig.

Femhörnig was a Swedish company with mining establishments in South Africa. Since the British had its stronghold over the country and considering the fact that there were many foreign establishments all over the African land, the imports and exports frequented and thus the flow of money in and out of the country was fairly easy. Just before the inception of the World War II, the company had established itself tactfully in South Africa without much intervention. The country needed funds, and Femhörnig needed the mines. They struck a deal with the local government and Femhörnig established a firm footing in the Kimberly mining business. Right from day one no common person ever knew that Femhörnig was involved with smuggling.

To the outside world, it was a landmark establishment. It made generous contributions during the Apartheid and also backed a few politicians back at home. So it was evidently politically and legally fortified and free from all hindrance.

Unlike many illegal organisations, they never feared the usage of names. As Shakespeare quoted, "What's in a name?"

3:30 PM.
Ryk Douglas, SA.

A few minutes after Cortez had bid *adios*, Nathan went to the Femhörnig New York and called the Ryk Douglas, Northern Cape…

Chapter 47

August 1979 – August 1980

The *Oudezijdsvoorburgwal* is a street and canal in the Red Light District of downtown, Amsterdam. The OZ Voorburgwal runs from the *Grimburgwal* in the south to the Sea Dike in the north, where it merges into the *Oudezijds Kolk*.

Voorburgwal is rich in contrasts, with sex shops, window prostitutes, peep shows, brothels, bars and coffee shops on one side and monumental canal houses from the Golden Age and the remains of monasteries from middle ages on the other.

The Phoenix Cassettes, #44, OZ Voorburgwal, was the new amalgamated postal address of Mark's and Veronica's.

The move from Valencia to Paris to Amsterdam wasn't quite a jolly ride. Especially for Mark. The fact that he wasn't with his brother when he breathed his last was excruciating. He simply couldn't assimilate the fact that his dear brother, John, was dead. He forced himself to forget the past and to move on with his life... prioritising his family. But he couldn't. Images from the past haunted him and kept him from moving on. He was constantly reminded of his days in Valencia...in Paris. He wanted to go back to the past. He wanted to spend yet another childhood with his brother…with his only family.

If not for Veronica, Mark would have ended up at a mental institution. She showed him the meaning of life. She gave him the motive to live. She presented to him the greatest gift ever…sense. She held his hands firmly and pulled him out of the pit. She made him realise that they now had an all-new reason to live…that John's passing was a message, telling them to bury the past and to start fresh. She reasoned with him that he wasn't responsible for John's death. She had him work at the post office during the day and every night, she kept him busy and entertained. She didn't leave him even for one second. The nightmares ebbed and he slowly recovered. Slowly came back to reality.

Mark became quite convinced that neither he nor Huritt were responsible for his brother's death. He learnt from the newspapers that Huritt and Eloy were in London on the day John died. He also learnt about Huritt's death and he couldn't but settle for the unsubtle truth. John was no more. Yet he had these daunting feelings, dreams and non-volatile subconscious, always hinting and pointing him to Huritt.

Nahiossi?

No. How could he possibly know?

Or did he?

Nah. Huritt is dead! Sebastian is somewhere in the US and Ricardo is in the Caribbean.

'John. John! Stop daydreaming, you son-of-a-bitch!' shouted David Butler, the supervisor at the Birmingham Central Post Office.

'Oh! I'm sorry. I…I had a rough night yesterday,' said Mark, brushing his hair as he gave a slight wink.

David was well aware of Veronica and her sensual elegance. Just a fortnight ago, he had a taste of her sensuality prior to bringing out John's official documents from the Paris Post Office and giving him a fairly modest job at the Birmingham Office.

Why would an assistant-postmaster at Paris settle for a lower job in Birmingham? David thought many times. Nevertheless, Veronica had made things easier and clearer to David. He couldn't care less as to why John came down to Amsterdam. *With that sort of a woman, he could legally make millions in Amsterdam.*

David and Mark shied off from the urban areas and crashed into many clubs in and around the suburbs. They drank out their souls and drove madly with pimps and slipshod hookers.

Two months after Mark had got the job at the post office, David and Tracy, a raunchy fifteen year old from Kennington High School, were doing it behind the bushes at a private property that was located just off the state highway.

Mark let them be and rushed to the nearest telephone booth to report the incident. A few minutes later the night patrol police drove up to the place where David's car was parked and they headed in the direction from whence the moaning noise originated. The cops slowly went around the bushes and caught the two in the middle of their sensual act. Tracy and David were heavily drunk and when one of the cops split the two apart, David, who was almost climaxing, spat his semen on the officer's face…and then they began laughing uncontrollably.

Since Tracy was *unused,* they gave her a few warnings and sent her home. But they took David into custody and escorted him with them. The following day, Tracy, in the presence of her attorney, testified at the magistrate's office that David had *forcefully* picked her up after school, *forcefully* got her drunk and *forcefully* driven her over to the site. Tracy's attorney filed a complaint about David on account of deviate conduct, child molesting, child exploitation, vicarious sexual gratification, child seduction, sexual misconduct with a minor as a Class B felony, kidnapping, criminal confinement and possession of child pornography.

David invariably confessed to all the charges except rape and child pornography. But who was to believe him? Tracy's testimony was all that mattered. She begged the judge to keep the issue off the media and to see to it that David was dispatched to some place where he would learn to respect women and feminism.

After David parted with the post office, Mark bribed an official, even blackmailed him with explicit pictures, and took David's position as the assistant postmaster in Birmingham.

Tracy was appointed to babysit Nahiossi and the trio, Mark, Veronica and Tracy, formed a formidable team. Their motto, "More Money".

September 1980

Veronica hadn't quite lost the nudge of prostitution. She...she practiced the act often and she considered it like any other profession. *Hard* work pays.

By the dawn of October, she and Tracy had fucked a herd of men from the Amsterdam elite, and had three sergeants, two inspectors, one superintendent, half a dozen lawyers and a secretary to the DA in their pockets.

October 1980

Commiting felonies were much easier than it was before.

The pictures of high-ranking officials, as Mark proclaimed, were safely hidden in three different bank lockers. If he, Veronica, Tracy or Nahiossi were harmed, the pictures would immediately be handed over by his people to the magistrate, the media and the chief office of the DA.

"By harm, I mean assault, threat, and kidnap, lawsuit, trickery and any sort of activity that would even minutely damage the sanctity of my family," said Mark to every one of those big shots who were on their film. He always kept them on his leash and ensured that they were served extremely well.

Eventually they hired four more prostitutes, two male and two female, and in totality they had six workers. Six sex workers.

November 1980

Veronica was excluded from the act of posing for hidden cameras.

Their associates grew gradually, but at a slow and well-controlled pace. They only dealt with the moneyed lot. Never messed around with the commoners.

Through their mechanised and centralised workforce, they developed a lot of contacts. The blackmailed officers gradually morphed into their acquaintances and friends.

They relished the services offered at *La Roja* and they had their colleagues join Mark's establishment. They reasoned that there really wasn't anything wrong with what Mark and his crew were doing for a living. They saw no reason to have them reported or to shut down their business. They were being served well and they were also being paid well enough to keep their mouths shut.

The associates helped in laundering small amounts of money inside the Netherlands and were in turn rewarded with a hefty share.

December 1980

Tracy was sent to the Controller of Publications, Ministry of Urban Affairs and Employment, and Department of Publications, where she filed for an RFI (Request For Information), posing as a potential research student.

Usually the tenders were received a month or so after the date of publication. So until then, Mark would do some fieldwork and sniffing around. A week before the submissions, the snitches at the Department of Publications would have the names of the top two rivals competing along almost the same lines. Mark would then filter out the post in transit to the Department of Publications and steal them for a few minutes to the men's room. He would copy the final quote of both companies and slip it inside the heap of other letters. If the result were obvious, Mark would withdraw himself from the ordeal and move on to his other errands.

Otherwise, he would go his workshop at the cassette studio and call the top contender. Among all other qualities, Mark was invincible in trying to convince and lure people. He would thus persuade the shortlisted company to pay him a sum, not even superficially comparable to the profits they would make, and upon receiving the advance, he would hand over the details.

He would say, 'Look, mister. I am not after money. I do this for a living. So just give me an advance, how much ever you find convenient, and take the quotation. If the information I have given you is true, you can pay me the rest. Else you can shove it up my ass. Should we call it a deal?'

The answer was rhetorically, 'Yes'.

The result was obvious.

Mark would wait for a few days, collect his payment and then re-establish his contact, now as the blackmailer. He would give the person an option to pay another half or to go to the prison on account of perjury, bribery and fraudulent activities.

If some of the tenders weren't sent through post, Mark would send his workers to the typists and the clerks of the respective companies and have the details extracted. The typists wouldn't open their mouths after the deal. If they happened to do so, they would have charges of deviate conduct, child molesting, child exploitation, vicarious sexual gratification, child seduction, sexual misconduct with a minor as a Class B felony, kidnapping, criminal confinement and possession of child pornography, in addition to which they would be fired from the company and also from their families. It was too massive a gamble. The obvious result being that their mouths were kept shut.

As time elapsed, Mark's contacts grew. He was involved with laundering, forging bank checks and doctor's prescriptions, prostitution, blackmail and an ever increasing list of felonies.

As years rolled on, he became rich. His cassette store grew, its branches grew, and the happiness and the quality of living grew exponentially. But Nahiossi grew too and what were they going to tell him if he asked what their profession was? From where did they get so much money?

In order to account for those questions, Mark retained his job at the post office, while Veronica looked after the cassette shop.

A young man from Mexico had visited the club in 1985 and had fallen in love with Tracy. Just like the way Mark had fallen in love with Veronica. So they let Tracy go.

By 1986, Mark and Veronica had enough money and the couple was content with it. They thus decided to end all their...illicit activities and concentrate only on the future of their son, Nahiossi Griffiths.

CHAPTER 48

9:27 AM.

Rue André Pascal to Lac Daumesnil.

Paris, France.

The bikers were expected to go round the city, covering almost one landmark location in every arrondissement. Accordingly there were two loops, the Outer Loop and the Inner Loop. The Outer Loop was simpler. Minimal manoeuvres and minimal obstructions. On the other hand, the Inner Loop required skilled cycling and excellent proficiency. So both resilience and skillfulness were being put to the test, and Huritt had the advantage of not proving his resilience. His intelligence had taken care of that.

At 9:27 AM, the competitors were raging zealously on the Outer Loop, but most of the participants lacked the concern to overtake the other. They reserved every extra ounce of energy for the Inner Loop…for the thorny leg.

But, as an exception to the case, the Swedish participant was undesirably eager to lead the crew. He demanded attention from the media and wanted to be on the cover of every other newspaper and TV channel. He didn't wheel for his country. He wheeled for his own self. He pirouetted for pride and money. He propelled to please himself. He advanced with the unscrupulous illusion of attracting fame and he impelled, compelling his mind to saunter on far-fetched paths, rather than on the credible path. His lack of concentration made his bike slightly nudge the Spaniard's, who was just a few seconds ahead. The Spaniard's bike swept the ground in a counter-clockwise direction prior to tumbling on the hard ground. The Swedish biker lost balance and he too met the same ground, face down. The two nationals, though not heavily injured, managed to buy themselves a few minor bruises.

'The ground crew has just reported an accident on the Outer Loop. The Swedish biker…' announced Aimon from the Control Station as he was fed with the live news from the reporters' mobile crew.

Undaunted, the Spanish biker rose and dusted himself, after which he offered his hand to the person who had pushed him back to the bottom line. The Swedish biker took his hands, embarrassed, and stood up. 'Are you all right, brother?' managed the Spaniard in his shackled English. 'That decision rests in the hands of our home offices,' replied the other.

'No, it's with us, the people,' said the Spaniard and picked up his bike.

'Sounds about right. Well, let's get going. We have a race to win,' replied the Swede.

'You bet,' said the Spaniard, and they at once hopped on their bicycles and got back on the track, rivals again.

"A spectacular glimpse of the brotherhood," would be in bold capitalised letters in almost all newspapers and below it, *"Competitors keen to coalesce with the Union. What will the home office decide?"* again in bold, but morphed.

At the city hall, the ambassadors of Sweden and Spain exchanged looks. Assuring looks. The delegates at the OECC watched the spectacle on the TV and clapped merrily.

The meeting was adjourned and all the delegates' eyes were on the television as the participants passed on the *Rue André Pascal* and proceeded towards Roland Garros.

France was well ahead and Spain lagged well behind, just a couple of feet from Sweden. A few seconds behind France was United Kingdom, who was toe to toe with Belgium. The rest were monotonously peddling ahead, thinking about nothing but the next aid station.

* * *

Aid Station 2 was located near *Musée Pasteur, Rue du Docteur Rou* in the fifteenth arrondissement.

The museum was established in 1935 in honour of Louis Pasteur, and it preserves his memory in the apartment where he spent the last seven years of his life. It also houses innumerous scientific equipment and the Neo-Byzantine Chapel in which he is buried.

As the herd reached *Musée Pasteur,* Mark was flat out fatigued. The full-sleeved black clothes, the mask and the catch-me-if-you-can act were utterly unbearable and taxing. Even though Huritt had him trained under the guidance of Coach Kramer, a local athlete who hadn't made it to the international arena owing to the fact that he had suffered a grade 3 hamstring, Mark couldn't endure the stretch. It's one thing to practice perfectly in a friendly territory, but it's totally different to perform in a hostile environment with tens of thousands of eyes watching you and the world media following your every step.

Not now Mark. Don't rest now. Huritt won't like it. Come on! No more aid stations. You can go back home. Fuck them, Marky. Fuck them!

Mark quickly drained his energy drink and the solid supplements, and was soon back on track. United Kingdom's biker hadn't rested for long. He'd quickly drained his drink and was back on the track as well, covering more ground than the others.

The statistics had now reshuffled. UK was leading, followed by Belgium. Mark was in the third position, with Ireland struggling hard to keep up with France. West Germany and Denmark had just left Aid Station 2, while Italy and Netherlands had just entered, and Sweden and Spain were yet to reach the aid station.

'Looks like your boy has lagged behind,' grunted the Ambassador from the UK, staring at the GPS tracker and at the LIVE coverage on EUN.

Lefèbvre Delacroix and General Bernard le Blanc grew hot under their collar, as did thousands of other French patriots.

'It's not about how fast you reach someplace, Ambassador. It's about how you reach. Slow and steady wins the race,' said General Bernard le Blanc

'With all due respects, General Blanc, slow and steady wins no race. The fucking rabbit was too ignorant and ludicrous to have rested without paring the finish line. Ignorance and foolishness succumbs the race, not slow and steady wins the race.'

'Well, Mr. Orwell, we aren't so much concerned about winning. We are concerned about the morale behind this whole event and about how this will bring our countries closer,' countered Lefèbvre Delacroix.

'And that's how we expect you bootlickers to be.'

The bikers faced a petite apprehension and demotivation on the course between the landmark destinations en route. There was nobody cheering them on, and the whole environment was kind of depressing. Gloomy.

Three crews followed the participants in their jeeps and were moving at very low speeds. An ambulance moved on the other side of the track with a fire engine, and a few police guards on their tail.

Ireland's biker came next to the masquerader and smiled. Mark's heartbeat escalated rapidly, as did the knot in his stomach. He turned his head aside and peddled faster and more aggressively. Soon he came within a hand's reach of the Pole.

The Irish biker shrugged and moved ahead, aggravated. From then on, Mark maintained his pace in such a way that he was in between the Irish biker and the UK biker.

Meanwhile the Spanish and the Swedish bikers hauled ahead, pushing down the exhausted Italian. The Netherlands remained constantly at the seventh position, tailing Denmark, who was flip-flopping for the sixth and fifth positions with Germany.

At the City Hall, the delegates resumed their meeting and the French Home Minister delivered his keynote address.

Towering hopes; Sir Fermont's dream appeared far from impossible. His vision was being realised, fifty years after his death, and it was honoured and nurtured in an international arena.

'...Let us strive towards creating a synergy and uniting our countries under a common banner. Cheers!'

Forty minutes after the British biker had left Aid-Station 2, he finally arrived at the restroom from where the participants had begun their journeys.

The crowd was huge and so was the cheering. The media coverage was commendable and the security was tight. Nevertheless there were only four guards at the restroom. Gendarmes Fulbert, Geoffrey, Emeric and Oscar. They had decided against informing the superiors about the absence of Pierre and Lou. They feared that the two might be suspended on account of breach of duty, and in any case, no one was to infiltrate the restroom compound. There were bountiful *Prefectures* outside the compound and the surrounding buildings were cleared off. Gendarmes Fulbert, Geoffroy and Emeric were on the outer side of the restroom at gate A, and Oscar took the charge of securing the gate B, again.

Oscar, before heading to the VIP lounge, had persuaded Gendarmes Fulbert, Geoffrey and Emeric against informing Saint Maurice regarding the absence of Gendarmes Lou and Pierre. He told them that he would take the responsibility for all the chaos, and that he would have the back-up gendarmes sent down to the restroom as soon as he had conversed with the Saint Maurice base station. The gendarmes, whom Oscar knew on first name basis, had agreed to comply, and everything was as per the PM's plan.

At 10:20, Ricardo's *camion à ordures* entered the west gate, just like before, and were again welcomed with Oscar's sneeze. Ricardo manoeuvred the truck inside the compound again, and pulled up below the second cubicle from the right corner of the rest room at junction 2.

Like a bat out of hell, Huritt sprang off the cavity on the top of the truck and entered the restroom, just like Mark had done that very morning.

'Here comes Huritt!' announced Aimon, nine seconds after he had announced the arrival of the athlete from the UK.

Huritt had warned Mark against letting anyone enter the restroom ahead of him. *Remember, you can let anyone lead you throughout the circuit. But you should be the first to enter the restroom. What if someone barges in and spots me? We can't afford to take such chances. Don't depend on coincidence, depend only on conscience.*

But Mark had failed to keep up. He had chanced their future on coincidence and let the UK contender enter the restroom first.

Fuck! Fuck! Huritt is going to kill me! Shit! If we get caught, we are most certainly going to prison. Oh God! Screamed a voice in Mark's head as he barged inside the restroom. He ran towards the second cubicle and stood in front of the closed wooden door.

Someone was here before me!

'Reporting Black *fleur-de-lis*, from restroom 1, Route de ceinture du Lac Daumesnil, exit at ten hours, twenty-five minutes, fifty-seven seconds. Over.'

'Black, 10:25:57, affirm, black, 10:25:57.'

Chapter 49

20th June 1979

8:47 AM
Chateau de Fermont

'*Bonjour Felix!*' said the security at *Chateau de Fermont,* before he moved to stop Huritt's Jaguar at the threshold. He quickly snooped inside it through one of the open windows, and then moved on to check the trunk. 'Why are you here? Shouldn't you be at *Lac Daumesnil*?' questioned the guard, as he lifted the trunk open.

'*Monsieur* Huritt forgot to take his supplementary bag,' replied Felix, casually.

'*Oui, Felix,*' breathed the guard and let the Jag gain entrée to the armoury like mansion that offered a magnificent view of the Eiffel tower in the backdrop.

The mansion was islanded by spacious ornamental gardens, centuries old palm trees, shady borders, colorful exotic plants and ancient cypress hedges. The stone-walled mansion comprised of three twin bedrooms, several large terraces, an outside summer bar and a basement for parking ample sorts of wheelers. The heighted arched door paved the way to enter the spacious entrance hall adorned with Sevillian wall tiles. The ground floor harbored a cloakroom, a magnificent main drawing room with center columns, vaulted ceiling, a stone fireplace and a humongous personal library. In addition, there was a twenty-four-seater timber-panelled dining room. The master bedroom was spaciously knit with a canopied double bed, teak wood windows, copper framed iconic mirror and a magnificent fireplace, with many portraits of the ancestors of the Fermont family, the latest addition being Sir Edgar Fermont. On the second floor, there were rooms harboring the only butler in the mansion and two servants. The mansion was indeed an architectural treat, a landmark structure of the fifties.

Felix speeded the Jaguar into the basement and parked it right below the rectangular wooden framed glass window, which gave access to the rear part of the mansion's garden, more importantly, Lucy's chamber.

The driver carefully scrutinised the surroundings and confidently opened the seat-base, paving way for Huritt to exit the coffin-like box. 'Well done, Felix,' said Huritt excitedly and jumped out of the Jag. He swept his eyes around the dimly-lit bedrock as he commanded Felix to 'Get the shutters'.

'Aye,' came the reply, as Felix sprinted towards the mechanical box driving the rolling shutters. *It's time to go* thought Huritt and climbed on top of his metallic cat. He closed his eyes and recollected his mentor's words, *"Domination predicates on power, and power on money. No act of an outlaw and of the deprived in achieving true dominion over the knavish society is amiss. And so reflect the attributes."*

'We're good to go, *Monsieur,*' whispered Felix and extended a "thumbs up" from the shadows.

Huritt simply nodded and jumped at the dusty window located just above the roof of his car. *Nothing is amiss* muttered Huritt and nimbly squeezed himself out through the window. Once out, he looked around the milieu in a flash and then barged into

Lucy's chamber through an ancient bay window, which was visually isolated from the security post at the entrance of the *chateaux*. The compounds and creepers served the purpose of blocking the neighbors' view.

Oh God! Lucy thought on seeing Huritt. She timidly dropped the telephone receiver and was all set to call out for Camila, one of the two servants, who was to Lucy, no less than a mother. She was the sole being Lucy looked up to.

The kindhearted nanny from Dublin was the one who had cared for Lucy and nurtured her right from the moment the little girl lost her mother. Back in those days, Camila was quite the Irish charmer. It was believed that Sir Edgar had her bedded soon after he lost his wife. There were rumours telling that he was having an affair with Camila under his wife's very nose. But then again rumours and gossip are quite the essence of fame!

Camila's ashy-blond bouffant, blue-gray eyes, short and snuggly hourglass figure gave Lucy quite the comely feeling. Lucy had always called out for her, in times of need, and Camila had never failed her. She was always there for her, even when Sir Edgar was assassinated. She had stood by Little Lucy and kept her on her toes. But now, in the face of her satanic husband, little Lucy was helpless. Huritt's forty-five had her limbs tied and mouth shut. She couldn't run to the person behind whom she had stood firm in the face of all her problems, nor could she call out for her, like she had done till then.

'Hold your horses, my dear,' said Huritt sternly, pointing his revolver at her womb.

He ran toward the wall and then stealthily moved towards the door, keeping the gun pointed at Lucy. He quickly bolted the door shut and ordered her to sit.

She walked wearily to her chair, harvesting the fact that she practically could do nothing but to be all ears to her dreadful so-called better half.

'Why-what are you doing here?' A perplexed Lucy asked, hiding her agitation. *If he is here, then who is on the TV?*

'To kill you, of course,' placidly said Huritt, lessening the volume on their CRT device. 'Look at me! I'm in two places at the same time!'

'What are you doing here?'

'My dear little Lucy, you disappoint me. Isn't it intriguing that I'm in two places at the same time? Your question should actually begin with a "How", shouldn't it?'

'What the hell are you doing here, Huritt?'

He slowly walked away from the television and stood in front of Sir Edgar's humongous portrait, with his unforgiving eyes closing in on him like that of a hawk. He confidently put his finger on the trigger and said, 'I'm here to kill you.'

She began involuntarily perspiring. Time and again Lucy opened and closed her small mouth, not knowing what to say, for she was drowning in an ocean of thoughts and fighting hard to breathe. *He just talks big, but he can do nothing! He isn't that capable a man. But why is he...how is he at two places? Who is the other...who is at...*

'I can understand what's going on in that tiny head of yours. After all, I am your "better-half", aren't I?'

She didn't reply. She just stared at him, with rage and fear fighting one another. She still believed that Huritt was no man of action. *He won't kill me! He knows he can't! Father's will...*

'You might be thinking whether or not I will kill you. I'm right, aren't I? Well, I expect no less of you. Anyway, let me ease you a little.

I have a truce with one of your kin, not just "one", it's actually "the one". You know, "the one" who will inherit your old man's fortune, should you be dead,' said Huritt and paused. He wanted her to absorb whatever he said and understand the implications. He then looked at her sternly and said, 'one is to three, my dear.

I've wasted enough time trying to persuade you. Wasted more than necessary. I can afford to waste no more!'

Lucy stayed muted for a few seconds. *How can he know the inheritor? Sebastian? Even if he did know, why will he...*'Why is he going to part it with you?' asked Lucy curiously.

'You can't be so sure about the "he or she", now can you? As regards to your "why is he going to part it with you" part, the answer is quite simple. For anyone to inherit your old man's fortune, you have to die. And in order for that to happen, someone will have to kill you. Well who can be better for the job than your "better-half", right?

Plus, killing you isn't all that easy...no it isn't. No one but *Monsieur* Huritt Achak is capable of plunging a knife into your chest. Well, as a matter of fact plunging anything into you! You get it? Of course you do. Anyway, I obviously deserve a share to acknowledge my tedious...um, pursuit. And my share is one thirds of whatever crap your old man amassed.'

'You won't kill me. You can't kill me. I'm carrying our son! I'm – '

' – stupid? Dumb? Woman! Do I look like a man who cares about children? I fucked you not because I wanted a child! I fucked you because...well, because my penis wanted to.'

Lucy's eyes numbed. Little drops of tears seeped through the lids. 'The note,' whispered Lucy. 'The note.'

'Ah! Who cares about that imbecilic note of yours? The jury won't be able to ascertain anything from that, for at this very minute, I am, um, let's see,' said he and looked at the TV before saying, 'ah yes! I am at *Parc de la Villette*. Beautiful place. Anyway, the point is even if I kill you, God forbid, they can't prove my guilt beyond a reasonable doubt. I can't be at two places at the same time! Can I?'

'Ca-Camila has a copy of the note. I've told her everything about you and your psychopathic behaviour. She will testify against you.'

'I can take care of that. Sebastian is a crackerjack. You saw him acquit me in Sarah's case. They had my fingerprints all over her body, you know, all over! My shoeprints were all over the house, people saw me entering her house, they found my note, and I also had the motive. But you saw how I manipulated all the evidence. You saw how good Sebastian was. Didn't you?"

Well, this is it, Lucy thought and then asked, 'You don't want to leave any murder trails. Do you?'

'Of course I don't…and that is why I won't murder you here.'

Lucy wiped her eyes and looked at her husband. Clearly. She advanced a few steps towards him, smiled and said, 'Why won't men like you finish your "job" quickly? Why do you have to stand and explain yourself to the "victim"?'

Huritt now looked perplexed. 'I'm sorry, what?'

'Oh dear, my dear little doll, aren't you adorable?' said Lucy, approaching Huritt with each step.

'Stand back!'

'You saw me drop the phone soon after I spotted you. Didn't you?' said Lucy, mimicking Huritt.

Huritt silently nodded his head.

'Do you know who was on the call?'

Eloy, thought Huritt, but didn't mention it aloud.

'Eloy!' said she, raising her eyebrows. 'He would have heard everything we "discussed" till this very minute.' Her lips kissed his ears and it said, 'Everything, my dear doll.'

'He will be here any moment…' said she and impulsively snatched his gun away. She clasped it tightly in her hands and paced backwards. She pointed it straight at Huritt and said,

'…and arrest you! Your game is over, Huritt. This…is it.'

CHAPTER 50

9:04 AM.
Chateau de Fermont

'Eloy, listen, Little Lucy is going to shoot me! Please come soon, Eloy! Save me! Save me please,' mimicked Huritt, as he sanguinely walked towards a cupboard on his left hand side.

'Huritt, stay where you are! Stop it right there. Take one more step and I'll blow your head off!'

'Oh dear God! Please protect me from my evil husband. Oh Lord, please protect my son...your son,' blabbered Huritt and extracted a key from a small wooden chest that was carefully roped off inside the cupboard.

'What-what are you doing, Huritt? What are you looking for?' asked Lucy and thought, *Another gun? No, he doesn't have one. Uncle Eloy made sure of it...Or did he?*

'Go ahead, call out for that...that juicy little treat...that wild cougar!'

Camila? He wants me to call out for her?

'Call out for her only if you don't love her,' continued Huritt and closed the cupboard.

'What do you have in your hands?' yelled Lucy, her hands shaking, and with them the gun. *Stop shivering! Stay confident, Lucy, stand still.*

'Nothing!' said Huritt, taking his hands out of his pant pockets and stretching them out wide. 'Although, I wish I were holding on to those beefy teats…Camila's, I mean.'

'Camila!' screamed Lucy. 'Mom, come in here!'

'Darling little Lucy,' said Huritt condescendingly and paced towards her.

'Stay back…stay back or I'll, or I'll…' Huritt didn't stay back. He was almost an arm's length away from her. 'Die!' yelled Lucy and pressed the trigger. The barrel clinked hard and Lucy jumped a step back.

…But no bullet was fired.

'Oh! My bad. I'm sorry,' said Huritt and snatched the gun from her hands. 'The problem…the disease you are facing is eccentricity! You know, immediately after you snatched the gun off of my hands, you could have ran out of this room. You could have, at once, called out for Camila. You could have taken a moment to see if the gun was loaded. But no! You did nothing that would give you a chance to save your precious filthy life. Oh! And our child's. I almost forgot…again,' continued Huritt, and loaded a bullet he retrieved from one of his pant pockets. He then pulled out a silencer from the other and screwed it at the mouth of his forty-five.

'I know you way better than you know yourself. I know your strengths and your weaknesses…your diseases! Well, if I knew you were so capable, I wouldn't have let you come near me in the first place. You see, I've always been a man of humour. I wanted to give you a chance to save yourself and I wanted to show you how powerful I am.'

'Where is Camila? What did you do to her?' asked Lucy with concern.

'She is upstairs, in the storage room. She is helping Felix find my supplementary bag, which I apparently forgot to take with me. You know, your father was a million times smarter than you. He and his associates discussed complex political manoeuvers and policies in this very chamber. So you know, he saw to it that the walls were rid of all ears. Well, that and the fact that he had to confine Camila's moaning in this chamber, you know, with your mom living right next door! So obviously your desperate call for Camila was well confined in this splendid chamber.'

Lucy nervously turned towards the telephone and gave it one futile glance, as Huritt said, 'Oh my dear little Lucy, maybe you were talking to your Uncle Eloy when I came in. But then, that was the end of it. Felix had the telephone connections disconnected. You know, Uncle Eloy is always on the line, and we needed some privacy. After all, this will be the last we stay in this room, as husband and wife. So well the occasion demands some privacy, doesn't it?'

I'm sorry baby, thought she, Lucy, as she touched her belly. Tears rolled down her cheeks as she realised that the end for her and her child was nearer than she'd expected. All her protective shields had fallen between the cracks, the shields that were so intellectually knitted by her father, the shields meant to protect her and the heir of the Fermont family, the shields meant to keep harmony and happiness in the family, when the person responsible for the ordeal failed to do so.

'Eloy is now at *Chateau de la Muette* upon orders from the government. There is no way for him to come here. So you see, on so many levels, this day is perfect and this plan of mine is flawless. So just get that suicide note of yours before I can blow your head off!'

'Huritt, why are you doing this to me? You can have all the money that you want. Please don't hurt my child. Please don't.'

'Lucy, I never meant to kill you. Believe me, I was of the opinion that the gun might be sufficient enough to get the job done...to have you do what I wanted you to do. So you see, I didn't even fill the magazine. You brought this on yourself. You threatened to kill me. You even had the audacity to press the trigger!'

'I'm sorry, Huritt. Please let us go. Please Huritt, for our child… for our child,' cried Lucy and collapsed on the floor.

'The note,' said Huritt grimly and stared at her.

Lucy quickly ran to her cupboard and removed the white wallpaper pasted on the bottom of its inner surface. Then she took out a key from the inner side of a photo frame, and opened the locker that was hidden on the other side of the white wallpaper. She quickly extracted the note and handed it over to her treacherous husband.

Huritt checked its contents, then locked the iron safe, and slid the door shut. He scraped the remaining bits of wallpaper off the surface and threw it in a bag, while she replaced the key in the photo frame and hung it back on the wall.

'Good, now stuff all your jewels in a bag. Quick!'

She did as he said, as the grandfather clock chimed once.

9:30. You have just 20 more minutes.

'Now as to the note with Camila, let's just say I'll have it extracted,' said Huritt,

'She doesn't have it! Please don't hurt her, Huritt. Please. I swear on my child…on our child. She doesn't know anything about us. I-I didn't want to hurt her. So I didn't tell anything to her. You have to trust me on this – '

'– Trust? Well, that is one squirmy bitch!'

'Huritt, please listen to me.'

'I know what I have to do, okay? Now just shut that lying mouth of yours and follow me.'

'I'm not lying, I'm not…I'm not,' groaned Lucy.

'Follow me,' said Huritt and traced his way back towards the window from which he'd entered. 'Should you try to alert anyone, my men out there will render you and your child, sorry, our child, well, you know what I mean, don't you?' grimaced Huritt and pushed her uncaringly through the narrow window, pointing his revolver at her. He then peeped outside the window through which he had entered, and found Felix waiting for them.

'Okay, woman. This is going to be your last push before that wretched child pops out. So make it a point to stay quiet. For the sake of the baby,' said Huritt and pushed her through the window, as her protruding stomach squeezed against the window frame. She put her hand in her mouth and bit hard; streams of blood oozed out of her palm.

Felix eased her off the window and put her inside the car. He then sedated her with a shot and inhumanly dumped her inside the rectangular coffin-like box.

In the meantime, Huritt took a piece of thread from his inner pocket and climbed back on the windowsill of Lucy's chamber. He put the "bowline knot" to the bolt head attached to the latch and maneuvered it over the top surface of the window. He closed the two windows and then linearly pulled the thread through the minute gap between the top surface of the window and the wall right above it. The latch began to crawl up, slow and straight. Owing to the pulling force, it moved feebly through the latch hook on the frame of the window and at a particular tension in the thread, the latch bolted, producing a clicking sound that was distinctly audible to Huritt. He breathed a sigh of relief and pulled the thread with more force. The thread loosened itself and slid through the gap, and finally fell right into his hands. He confidently got down from the sill, wiped his shoeprint off it, disturbed the land below his shoes, clearing it off shoeprints, and slid in through the basement window. He was quickly shut below the rear seat base, right on top of his wife for the last time, compressing the incubating infant and suffocating it with its own mother's blood.

'My sweet Lucy, let me just *taste* you before you go unconscious,' muttered Huritt and pulled at the top of her gown. He thrust his mouth on her breast and feasted on it for one last time.

Felix started the engine and eased the car out of the basement, only to be stopped by the security in order to carry out the usual sniffing. The only difference being that now, a forty-five year old bald and fair-complexioned professional hound, Inspector Eloy, did the sniffing.

'Où est Huritt?' Where is Huritt?

CHAPTER 51

September 27, 1992
Mark and Veronica's residence, #34, Tuinstraat, Jordaan
Amsterdam

The Ox reluctantly pulled up Henry's Cadillac in front of #34, Tuinstraat, Jordaan.

This has to be done…for Henry, said Dillion to the air around him and then pegged his unwieldy feet on the dewy asphalt. He manoeuvred his bulk out of the scant saddle-like seat and cast a cautious glance at his surroundings. *All clear.* He calmly closed the door shut and lugged himself towards the protruding rear of the 1972 Sedan de Ville, jingling his keys that came with an "H" pendant, and whistling a tune that harmonised with the rattle.

She invited trouble. I had nothing to do with it. It is entirely her fault, reflected the Ox and unlocked the trunk. He slightly lifted it, placed his handkerchief in between the two metallic lips and then walked towards the flimsy stairs that led to Veronica's humble abode.

He traipsed a few steps forward, his brown pants still brushing the floor, and stood at the foot of the stairs. He nimbly took the keys in his left hand and installed them in between the fingers of his right. *She hurt my father. She shouldn't have done that.*

He put his right hand, the hand with the key, behind his brawny back, pressed his wet curly hair and flattened his parka. He then took one deep breath and climbed up the stairs.

Four steps later, he met the door. He cleared his throat, took another breath and gently knocked on the mahogany door. Just two feeble knocks, just enough to call his prey.

'Who is it?' enquired a coarse voice from the inside, which was casually met with 'A friend of Veronica's'.

For Henry, for father Dillion reminded himself and pressed his rough skin against the cold metal.

'Just a second, I'll be right there,' said Mark and walked towards the door, clutching his coffee mug that said, "World's Best Daddy".

The Ox snorted once and waited. His heart pounding like a beast.

The latch clanked open and the Ox instantly punched Henry's saboteur's face, summoning every last dime of ferocity to his humongous fist. The impact of the metallic weapon against the fragile bones was massive. Mark's nose cracked, his cheekbone dented, his lips chipped and his glasses shattered.

Immediately after the punch, the Ox took a step forward, balanced himself on the frame of the door and gave a reckoning blow to Mark's abdomen.

'That's for hurting, Henry!' groaned Dillion and walked through the door. He looked outside for a brief second and then closed the door shut.

Mark was sprawled on the ceramic floor, his face covered with blood. Dillion looked at him triumphantly and extracted a roll of duct tape from an inner pocket of his parka. He took a few steps forward and kneeled beside his prey. He lifted Mark's head by the hair and made sure that he was out for the moment, but not dead.

Dillion shifted his gaze to the tape and rotated it in circles, round and round, trying hard to find the starting point of the tape.

After three turns, he was irked, irked by the fact that he was getting delayed. So he let out his frustration by kicking Mark's buttocks, kicking him with his humongous foot. After a couple of kicks, he thought better of it and walked towards the kitchen.

Once there, he picked up a knife off the stand and grated the tape with it. After that, he put the knife on the granite slab and blew the dust off the tape's surface.

'Ah! There it is,' said Dillion with innocent joy and pulled the tape off the surface. He held the tape neatly in his hands, the left holding the roll and the right holding the sticky part of the tape, and walked towards Mark. As he left the kitchen he figured that he needed something to cut the tape. So he marched back into the kitchen and picked up the knife off the slab. He held the knife along with the roll and walked back into the drawing room.

He once again knelt beside Mark, flipped him over, placed the knife next to his head and ran the tape around his legs. He bound him tight and then cut the tape with the knife. He then sealed the *vijand's* hands, and once he was done with it, he plastered the mouth along with the head.

The Ox then neatly folded the tape and placed it on the floor, before removing Mark's glasses and tossing them on the couch. He again picked up the tape, cut the folded bit off and wrapped it around Mark's eyes, extending towards the ears, the rear portion of the head and back to the forehead. The Ox made one final cut of the tape and dropped the roll back into his pocket. He slapped the forehead, the mouth and the ears and stood up.

He looked around for a brief moment and checked his watch. His eyes then landed on the floor, rather, the knife. *The ends justifies the means* ruminated Dillion and grabbed the knife. Like a man out of cuckoo's nest, he stretched out Mark's plastered hands, and with one ghastly blow, chopped off the walking-dead-man's middle finger from his right hand.

He threw the knife on the door and then picked up the severed finger. He placed it neatly on a table and like a maniacal psychopath, looked at the blood gushing out of Mark's finger and saw him squirm viciously. Mark experienced pain all over his body. He was in living hell right now, the sort of paradise to where he'd deliver people from the nooks and corners of Spain and France. But things seemed to have taken a U-turn in the Netherlands.

Once a killer always a killer. Try turning into a nice person and the world will be your purgatory!

'Suffer! You bastard! Suffer!' cursed Dillion and put his hands again in his inner pocket. He retrieved a small case containing Henry's anti-seizure shot and thrust the syringe into Mark's spinal cord.

Sleeping...beauty! As much as I'd like to see you struggle with excruciating pain, I'd have to wrap up things soon. I hate to be late for the party!

As Mark struggled with his pain and to keep his unconsciousness at bay, Dillion dipped the finger in the pool of blood and wrote, "If you want him whole, step outside and find my car. Dillion."

The Ox then picked up the landlines and dumped them in his many pockets. He then lifted Mark's broken body off the floor and walked out of the house, leaving the door unlocked.

Fuck Henry, right?

CHAPTER 52

October 20, 1978
Cour d'assises

Lorenzo: The defense can cross-examine the witnesses.

Sebastian: *Monsieur le President et Monsieur l'Assesseur,* I would like to examine the prosecution's witnesses from last to first.

Lorenzo: Proceed.

Sebastian: Thank you, *Monsieur.* Sub-Inspector Joseph, please.

Sub-Inspector Joseph walked back to the witness box, and was reminded that he was still under oath.

Sebastian: Mr. Joseph, during the prosecution's case-in-chief, you said that Mr. Achak denied leaving home, didn't you?

Joseph: Sure did, defense counsel. My *gendarme* testified the same and the security guard at *chateau de la Fermont* also provided proof to support the fact that Mr. Huritt was lying.

Sebastian: Very well. Now did you tell Mr. Huritt as to why he was being apprehended?

Joseph: Yes, Mr. Sebastian. It would be *illegal* otherwise.

Sebastian: Well, blessed are we to have a law-abiding police officer in this courtroom, sub-inspector Joseph. Now getting back to our case, do you remember what you said to him at the moment of arrest? The exact words I mean.

Joseph: "Mr. Huritt, you are being arrested on the charge of murder."

Sebastian: Period?

Joseph: Y-Yes.

Sebastian: Does the *gendarme* accept that these were the exact words the Sub-Inspector used?

The *gendarme* rose from the stands and confirmed it.

Sebastian: Thank you, *gendarme*. Respected jurors and the court, I repeat the sub-inspector's statement, "Mr. Huritt, you are being arrested on the charge of murder". Now if you analyse the report, you will observe that nowhere during the time of arrest was Ms. Bibiana's name mentioned.

Reyes: Learned counsel, what difference does it make?

Sebastian: Oh, it does make a difference. Trust me. I'll get there in a moment. Now, Mr. Joseph, was Mrs. Fermont present when you stated the reason for arrest?

Reyes: No.

Sebastian: All right. So what happened then? What did Mr. Huritt say *after* you arrested him?

Reyes: Well, I think he asked me who was murdered and I remember mentioning Ms. Bibiana's name.

Sebastian: You couldn't possibly know that she was "murdered". Anyway, was Huritt still alone when you told him that Ms. Bibiana was…dead?

Joseph: No, Mrs. Fermont had joined us.

Sebastian: Excellent! So I presume that you asked my client if he visited her residence that afternoon –

Joseph: Something along those lines.

Sebastian: – And he told you that he hadn't set his foot out and that he was at home the whole day.

Joseph: Yes, quite so.

Sebastian: Thank you, good officer. Court, I want you to note that Mrs. Fermont was by Mr. Huritt's side when Sub-Inspector Joseph told him that Ms. Bibiana was dead. Had the statement been, "Mr. Huritt, you are being arrested on the charge of murdering *Ms. Bibiana*", he would have confessed to you that he had visited the deceased's house that very afternoon.

Reyes: So you are trying to tell us that he lied because Mrs. Fermont was there?

Sebastian: Two bodies, one mind, prosecutor. One mind.

Reyes: *Monsieur le President et Monsieur l'Assesseur,* I would like you to consider this statement which Bayol said, "Of course he wouldn't have told Mrs. Fermont about Sarah. My sister probably tried to hint about his sadistic character, and Huritt, discovering this unpleasant act, wanted to shut her up before she could spill out all the beans."

Reyes read this out from a sheet of paper and added, 'Now this statement has gained more weight, considering the fact that Huritt confessed against going out because Mrs. Fermont was standing right next to him.'

Some jurors seemed impressed and made a note of this point, as did the President and the judges.

Sebastian: Well, I'll get to Mr. Bayol in a short while. But before that, learned counsel, let me tell you that your statement is not entirely valid. True that Mr. Huritt was lying. But he did so to keep a certain promise he had made to Mrs. Fermont... as a husband and as a man who believes in maintaining the divinity of a marriage.'

'Bullshit!' shouted Bayol from the stands.

'I agree!' yelled Cortez from his seat.

Sebastian: Mr. Bayol and Mr. Cortez, please be convinced of the fact that I shall prove the validity of my assertion. Now, *Monsieur le President et Monsieur l'Assesseur,* I would like to summon Mrs. Fermont to the stand.'

Lucy, who had just announced that she was pregnant, walked towards the witness box, looking afraid and concerned. She slowly walked the daunting pathway and climbed up on the box.

Sebastian: Mrs. Fermont, I don't like to beat around the bush. So allow me to get straight to the point. Were you aware that Mr. Huritt was living with another woman? Ms. Bibiana, to be precise?

Lucy: Yes, counsel, I did know about their relationship. I was well aware of it before our marriage.

Some people gawked, and the prosecutor was flushed.

Sebastian: Why then do you think Mr. Huritt lied when our good Sub-inspector questioned him?

Lucy: When Huritt first confessed to me that he had a fairly long relationship with Sarah, I asked him to promise me that he would never see her and never try to contact her again. Of course, every noble woman in this land would want her husband to be loyal to her, won't they?

The three women in the jury nodded their heads.

Sebastian: Of course, Mrs. Fermont. The women of this great country are noble indeed. Now did he keep his word?

Lucy: As far as I know, Yes.

Sebastian: Do you think that he would *lie* to you about not seeing her even though he were to see her…behind your back?

Lucy: It's possible…

Sebastian: Has he ever upset you in the past, Mrs. Achak? Did anything devastating ever happen between the two of you?

Lucy: No, Sir, I don't recall anything. He is the best husband anyone can possibly ask for.

Every question and every answer was so perfectly rehearsed. It was like they were staging a play. Although in her heart, the answers for Sebastian's questions were quite the opposite.

Sebastian: "The best husband anyone can possibly ask for." Thank you, Mrs. Fermont.

Lucy quietly walked back to the stands and took her seat right next to Eloy. She looked at Huritt once, cast a hateful glance, and then turned back to face the judge.

Sebastian: Respected prosecutor, could we now assert that Bayol's testimony was farce? For the benefit of the jurors, I want to restate Mr. Bayol's testimony. Ms. Linda, could you please read it out?

Linda: "Of course he wouldn't have told Mrs. Fermont about Sarah."

Sebastian: Not so obvious after all. Linda, proceed.

Linda: "My sister probably tried to hint about his sadistic character."

Sebastian: Probably, *Monsieur et Mesdames.* Probably. Castles in the air, I'd say. There is neither evidence nor record to support my client's so-called sadistic character. Mrs. Lucy, do you think that your *husband* is sadistic?

Lucy: No, Sir. I don't.

Sebastian: Why don't we ask Inspector Eloy about this?

Eloy: I-I can't say.

Sebastian: Sub-inspector Joseph?

Eloy: I agree on the "no previous record" part of your statement.

Sebastian: Very well. So, Mr. Prosecutor, can you prove the correctness of your witness' derogatory statement?

Reyes hastily retreated.

Sebastian: Ms. Linda.

Linda: " – and Huritt, discovering this unpleasant act, wanted to shut her up before she could spill the beans."

Sebastian: Now I don't know if Huritt "discovered" this. But let me tell you that there was nothing for Ms. Bibiana to spill. Mrs. Fermont already knew everything! Thank you, Linda.

Linda was asked to sit, and then Sebastian called Sub-inspector Joseph back for cross-examining.

Sebastian: Sub-inspector Joseph, can you tell us what happened after you arrested my client?

Joseph: We took him to the station and handed him over to inspector Felipe for questioning.

Sebastian: Did Mrs. Fermont accompany you to the station?

Joseph: No, Sir, she went to fetch the lawyer.

Sebastian: Right, that would be me. All right, so did he ask anything else before you handed him over to the inspector?

Joseph: No, Sir. He remained silent. He knew his rights.

Sebastian: That will do, thank you Sub-Inspector. Now it is evident that my client lied to Sub-Inspector Joseph and *gendarme*, telling them that he "was at home" for the simple reason that he didn't want his dear wife to be upset with him. Also, it was established that Mrs. Fermont knew everything about the relationship between my client and Ms. Bibiana. Do you agree with me so far, prosecutor?

Reyes: Please proceed, counsel.

Sebastian: I'll take that as a yes, prosecutor. Excellent. Now there is no need to cross-examine the security guard, I suppose. He is of course right. So once again, going by the chain of events, I would like to call Inspector Felipe.

Reyes looked at the jurors and they seemed to be impressed with the way Sebastian was executing his cross. He just wished that

Felipe would say something that would jeopardise the defense and something that would shift the burden off the prosecution.

Sebastian: Inspector Felipe, before questioning you, I would like to play this videotape. *Huissier*, could you please arrange for it?

The *Hussier*, with the approval of the judge, agreed and arranged a TV and a video player.

Sebastian: This is one of the many tapes recorded during the interrogation between inspector Felipe and Mr. Huritt.

Reyes: Objection! This tape wasn't in the disclosure. I ask you to treat this evidence as hostile.

Sebastian: *Monsieur*, I got this tape this very morning. I literally had to slog to get it. The Commissioner of Police gave me access to these tapes, and the manager at the archives can prove that I haven't tampered with it.

Lorenzo: The prosecution can file a motion and the matter shall be dealt with after the trail.

Reyes agreed and sat down. He angrily looked at Sebastian, ruminating on the prospect of getting out of the courtroom.

Sebastian: Would the prosecution reject its plea to treat this piece of evidence hostile if I were to provide additional proof to back this evidence?

Lorenzo: Prosecutor?

Reyes thought for a while and then said, 'I think so.'

Sebastian: Brilliant.

The *Hussier* then played the tape and the picture was in motion. The TV showed a room, at the center of which there was a table, two chairs and a couple of papers.

Felipe: Mr. Huritt, do you confess to the crime?

Huritt: No sir. I'm innocent.

Felipe: The arrest report says that you denied visiting the residence of Ms. Bibiana. Do you still validate the same?

Huritt: No, sir. I'd been there.

Felipe: Can you tell me why?

Huritt: No, Sir. I want to talk to my lawyer. I have the right to remain silent.

Felipe: Very well, Mr. Huritt. I thought of bringing out a confession and dusting this case off without much ado. Looks like you want to go on trial. So be it.

Huritt: So be it.

The tape stopped and the TV buzzed with numerous grains.

Sebastian: As you can see, gentlemen, Mr. Huritt has confessed the fact that he wasn't at home. Do you agree with me, Inspector?

Felipe: I do.

Sebastian: Why didn't the prosecution submit this evidence of the interrogation? Why was this *not* in the disclosure?

Reyes: There wasn't any confession or any discussion in it. I mean, you heard the accused say that he wanted to remain silent and that he wanted the case to go on trial. So I felt that this evidence was too trivial to be produced as evidence.

Sebastian: Did you hear that jurors? "Too trivial." Just a few moments ago he was broaching the topic of Joseph's testimony and feasting on the fact that Huritt lied. But Mr. Huritt's confession on the tape, clearly spelling out that he went to her house that very afternoon, is "too trivial". What do you have to say about this, Mr. Prosecutor? Trivial?

Huritt looked at Sebastian with renewed respect. During their "rehearsal talk" before the trial, Sebastian had narrated the importance of the tape, which he had procured from the archives without the knowledge of the inspector. *Had I not picked up the tape, Huritt, there would have been no proof to show that you confessed about your visit when Lucy wasn't near you. The prosecution would have nailed you by asking, "Why couldn't you confess during the interrogation? Your wife wasn't there then."*

Sebastian: Inspector Felipe, do you back the credibility of this videotape?

Felipe: I can't deny it.

Sebastian: *Monsieur,* he upholds the credibility of this evidence. So this video footage is as strong and valid as any other.

Lorenzo nodded his head and asked Sebastian to proceed.

Sebastian: Mr. Felipe, let us break away from the case for a bit. Let me just ask you this: are you married?

Felipe: Yes, Sir, I am.

Sebastian: Brilliant. Have you taken any pictures with your wife?

Felipe: Uh, yeah…I mean, definitely.

Sebastian: So please pardon me for what I'm about to say. Consider a case hypothetically, you go home today and discover your wife in the same state as that of Ms. Bibiana, you know, dead and clutching a picture of you. Does it mean that she is pointing out to you as her murderer?

Reyes sat there, not knowing what to do. Not being able to raise any objections.

Felipe hesitated for a moment and said, 'No.'

Sebastian: Can it mean that she was thinking about how much she is going to miss you?

Felipe: I-It can, yes.

Sebastian: Do you agree with me that the pictorial evidence is purely circumstantial?

Felipe: I-I do.

Sebastian: Now if I establish that she liked him, as much as your wife likes you, would you be convinced to waive this piece of evidence?

Felipe: I don't know. I mean…

Sebastian: What do you think, prosecutor?

Reyes: Well, I...

Sebastian: I need an answer, counsel.

Reyes: That is up for the court to decide.

Sebastian: Very well then. I shall do just that, *Monsieur et mesdames.*

The jurors and the judge had heard enough for a day. So the court was adjourned and the defense was asked to continue the next morning at half past nine.

The ushers cleared up the court, gathered leftover items and lost property, and finally locked the courtroom before they left.

* * *

Reyes and his associates had a tough time preparing for counter-arguments and gathering more evidence. But in spite of their many efforts, no credible evidence popped up.

Reyes had just one credible shred of evidence and he was comfortably depending on it. He believed that that evidence might be able to pin down Huritt.

On the other hand, Sebastian had a casual evening. He spoke to Huritt, went for drinks at the sports clubs and went to his condo. He didn't find it necessary to prepare for further defense. The trial was more like he playing chess with himself. He had purposely left all the evidence at the scene. In fact, he wanted the prosecution's case to present itself in the way it presently had. So well, he was like a cool breeze on a warm summer day.

CHAPTER 53

Stock number:	LA0165775
Price:	$51,493
Price per carat:	$10,266
Carat weight:	5.02
Cut:	Very Good
Color:	J
Clarity:	SI2
Depth %:	66.2%
Table %:	69%
Polish:	Excellent
Symmetry:	Good
Girdle:	Thin to Slightly Thick
Culet:	Pointed
Fluorescence:	None
Measurements:	9.88 x 9.37 x 6.20 mm
Length/width ratio:	1.05

Chapter 54

June 20, 1979

9:50 AM
Mark's garage

'Felix, give her another shot of that sedative. I don't want to leave her alone with you. She is a highly smart woman. Cunning. If given the chance, she *will* manipulate you. She might even persuade you to run off with her.'

'I informed Oscar. He'll be at the restroom by 10:15,' interjected Ricardo and then lit himself a cigarette.

'No, Sir Huritt. My loyalty is for you and you alone,' said Felix, as he removed a spectacle case from the inner pocket of his windbreaker. He extracted a syringe from it and walked towards the pregnant woman saying, '*Capitaine Porc,* we almost got caught today. Phew! *Le Chien* was so close.'

'What happened? Did he suspect – ?'

' – suspect? That is his sole job. Fucking Fermont commissioned that bloody hound to suspect my every move and to keep a close watch on how I fuck my wife. This bloody piece of crap,' said Huritt angrily and slapped Lucy's face.

Felix tapped Lucy's palm and tried to find a vein, as he said '*Le Chien* peeped inside the car and asked me where Huritt was. I said he was at the Triathlon. He then asked me what I was doing there and I told him that I was there to pick up the supplements. The bastard then opened the door and sat inside!'

'Holy fuck!' said Ricardo and looked at Huritt.

'Yeah, and then – '

'Oh! Give me that,' said Huritt and snatched the syringe from Felix's hand. He clasped it tight in his right hand and thrust it on her forearm. 'That's how it's done. Why the fuck do you worry if it pains her? Let her feel pain. Let her feel fear.'

Felix looked at Huritt with widened eyes and gulped once before saying, 'Y-yes, yes, *Patron.*'

'Good. Now finish your story,' said Huritt and unzipped the supplementary bag. He extracted a power bar and tore its cover open as he listened to Felix say, in a lower tone now, 'He asked me to drop him off at the City Hall. I told him that I had to reach the restroom before the commencement of the Inner Loop, and if I went all the way to the City Hall, I couldn't deliver these to Huritt on time.'

'Did that son-of-a-bitch buy it?'

'No!'

'So?'

'He asked me to go to the restroom. I had no other option. I said yes.'

'And Huritt was below him all the while?'

'Me and this bitch,' said Huritt and pinched her nipple as he crunched his power bar.

'Wow! Okay. So you dropped him all the way?'

'No. *Le Chien* asked me to stop the car at the corner of the road. He asked me show him the truck and then he asked me to take him back to the *chateau*.'

'Weird.'

'It's not weird if it is in one's character to be paranoid,' said Huritt and finished up his power bar.

'I hope that is it,' said Ricardo and tied up his hair.

'Yeah, pretty much. He looked at me intently for a few seconds and then asked me to leave.'

'Bloody hound!'

'Hope he didn't smell the stench of my filthy wife.'

'Yeah, that's the hope.'

'Okay, it's late. Let's get going. I have a world record to set,' said Huritt and took his face close to Lucy. 'Honey, have a safe ride. Daddy won't be seeing you again,' he said and kissed her goodbye.

I'm going to miss her ass. The juicy little treat.

10:25 AM
Lac Daumesnil to Hotel de Ville
Paris, France

Someone was here before me! Mark thought and walked closer to the door. *Out of order*. 'That's Oscar's handwriting,' whispered Mark as he studied the words on the sheet that was affixed to the second cubicle. *God bless him!*

'Reporting Black *fleur-de-lis*, from restroom 1, Route de ceinture du Lac Daumesnil, exit at ten hours, twenty-five minutes, fifty-seven seconds. Over.'

'Black, 10:25:57, affirm, black, 10:25:57.'

Ireland's biker was a bit suspicious about the French biker, because right from the commencement of the cycling event he had failed to talk to anyone, which wasn't like Huritt at all. Huritt was a chatterbox. He always bragged about himself and ridiculed others. But today, he had refrained from speaking. Completely. So the Irish biker peddled fast and came to Huritt's side, just as he had done during the previous lap, and extended his acknowledgement again. *If he doesn't respond this time, I'm going to have the coach talk to the officials and confirm his identity.* But that thought was rendered moot. This time, very much unlike the previous lap, the French rider looked up at him condescendingly and said, 'Yo fag! What are you lookin' at? Keep yo eyes on the road, man. I know I'm irresistible. But you see, a race is a race. You need to stay focused!'

The two competitors wished each other and then returned back to the race. Huritt slowly regained his pace, as he grew closer to UK and farther away from Ireland. He maintained his spot in between the two countries, as he headed towards the first destination on the inner loop, Notre Dame Cathedral.

Back in the eleventh century, Pope Alexander III had laid the foundation stone for the construction of this magnificent Cathedral in the fourth arrondissement, and since then this place has stood witness to umpteen number of historically acclaimed events like the coronation ceremony of Napoleon I, Henry VI of England's coronation as the King of France, Beatification and Canonization of Joan of Arc and the Requiem Mass of General Charles de Gaulle.

A good many number of people had assembled near Notre Dame and the roads connecting *Lac Daumesnil* to *Notre Dame Cathedral* were isolated from traffic and extensively crammed with the frantic crowd.

Time to rack them up! Huritt was now completely warmed up. *Hotel de Ville* was just a kilometre away and Huritt was very much eager to take the lead before reaching the City Hall. The delegates stood on a raised platform in front of the *Hotel* and waited for the participants to pass them by. Two choppers were circling overhead and the SWAT team was stationed on every high-rise building, with snipers and telescopes scanning the periphery. The DSPAP (Organisational management of security near the Paris area), DTPP (Organisational management of transport and public protection), Sub-Directorate of Public Order of the Paris agglomeration, Sub-Directorate for the protection of institutions, guards and transfers from the Paris agglomeration and sub-regional traffic management and road safety officers blended with the crowd in civilian apparel and searched for signs of danger.

Aid Station 3 was setup right in front of the City Hall, so that the delegates and the crowd would get to have a better look at the participants.

Huritt was the first to reach Aid Station 3, and the crowd couldn't have been more hysterical. He was completely energised and his muscles were fit, in contrast to the others who had cycled almost sixty kilometres more than Huritt. Huritt drained his drink in just half a minute and left the aid station.

He was in the lead and the British participant had absolutely no intention of continuing without rest. His right leg was a bit cramped and he needed to take care of it prior to exiting the aid station.

All the cameras swept along *Rue de Rivoli* as Huritt rocketed on his bike.

The French politicians on the dais stood up and clapped, while the citizens blasted their lungs out. The cheering fuelled more aggression and passion in Huritt, who was now more determined to set a new World Record.

CHAPTER 55

September 27, 1992

Henry's office

Veronica jolted off the burgundy carpet and screamed, 'Nahiossi! Wait! It's not what…wait!'

'Stay away from me! Stay…away!' yelled Nahiossi and banged the door shut. 'Bitch!' he moaned, and sprinted on the slushy terrain. He didn't want to go back into the factory. He didn't want to retrace the path from where he had come. He wanted to take the shorter route. He knew he couldn't face anyone now. He knew that the only thing he had to do, he could do, was break away from his mother.

Veronica grabbed her thick coat of fur, wrapped it around her naked body and pulled the door open. *Oh God! Oh God! What is he –*

'Mom? Did he call you…Nahiossi? He is…Albert,' blabbered Henry and looked down at his ebbing penis. He had ejaculated the very moment he'd entered her. He hadn't fucked anyone in nine months! His hand had been his only *compadre.*

Mom! Henry! Mom…mom…Henry, blabbered the voice in Nahiossi's head, as he yanked the mesh-gate open and ran out on the street dotted with puddles.

'Wait! Please, Nahiossi, wait, listen to your mother!' bawled the woman in the thick fur coat and darted out onto the pathway. Her loins were burning and aching. She fought the instinct to halt and kept her eyes fixed on Nahiossi's diminishing silhouette.

The Ox, slumped on the steering wheel, heard the screams and woke up. He looked at Nahiossi turn along the corner and then his eyes flicked to Veronica. He quickly retrieved the key from the glove compartment and fidgeted it into the keyhole.

Henry was all worn out. He was drained of energy and could barely stand up. He ruefully mustered the strength to pull himself up with the aid of the couch, and then wore his underpants. *Albert... Nahiossi. Why would he lie? Albert Nahiossi? God! Why is this happening to me!* Henry cried.

Veronica knew that she couldn't repair the damage she had unintentionally caused. She was convinced that chasing after her seventeen-year-old son was a lost cause. Nevertheless she fought to keep up with him.

She simply ran, her legs aching and her head spinning. *Hope he doesn't hurt himself. Hope he is safe!*

Nahiossi dashed into a proletariat bar located on a darkened alley and stopped at one of the booths. The bar reeked of crummy alcohol and the lighting was so dim that he could barely see the druggie easing his hands into his pocket. Nahiossi pushed himself away from the stranger and ran into the restroom. He shut the rickety door and fell on the floor. He pressed his head against the toilet floor and looked under the door, to see if the druggie had followed him into the restroom. He cautiously looked for a few seconds, his emotion of anguish being replaced by fear.

Meanwhile Dillion started the Cadillac and brought it closer to the gate. He nervously looked at the cabin to see if Henry was looking at what was happening.

Veronica's shoeless legs stuck in a puddle and pulled her down onto the ground. Her body lost balance and she collapsed on the filth. He ample breasts hit the ground hard and then her face met the same fate. The pain in her loins spread to her legs and she was rendered temporarily stunned.

The defenseless mother was cut off from all hope. Her chances of catching up with Nahiossi were extinguished and her chances of rescuing Mark from the Ox looked bleak at best. She kept her eyes fixed on the fine particles of gravel and breathed hard. *It's all over. It's all so terrible!* mulled the prostitute, stripped of every last atom of hope. She gave in to the hostility of the situation and let her tears meet with the dank ground.

'Fuck!' yelled Dillion and quickly jumped out of the Cadillac. He pushed his limits and ran through the gate, his saggy breasts jumping side to side, and his lungs thumping with every severe twinge. He came to a staggering stop beside the gorgeous-woman-turned-grotesque, and lifted her slender body with astonishing ease. *Henry, Henry, Henry* screamed a voice in his giant head, as his legs painstakingly carried three-hundred-and-sixty pounds.

*He said he wanted to talk about something important. He...he missed his choir practice. Did he want to talk to me about Veronica? Did...*Henry thought and slowly collapsed into a chair. *I can't go out now. I can't face them both. Everything just...just went out of hand. I lost...he doesn't respect me anymore. And, and she...she doesn't, she won't.*

Nahiossi lifted his face off the dingy floor and curled up in a corner. *Why would Mom be doing nasty things with Henry? Mom is bad. Mom doesn't like Papa. Poor Papa, I wonder what will happen to him when he...oh! Wait a minute, he can't know anything if I don't tell him. Mom surely won't. I won't tell him anything. No, I won't. I don't want to hurt Papa. But how can I be with Mother? I can't live with her, knowing that... Henry.*

Dillion dumped Veronica on the seat beside him and quickly drove away.

'It's over. It's all over. You ruined my family. You ruined everything. Henry should have let you rot in hell! You never lived with your parents. You have no fucking idea about how the parents feel when their child hates them. You filthy beast! Do you know what it is like to be with parents – '

The Ox took one deep breath and then whacked her face with his right hand. Veronica's bruised legs kicked the door and her scarred face hit the seatbelt buckle. Veronica's head reeled and her vision blurred. 'Nahio – ' she whispered, before shutting her eyes.

Chapter 56

June 20, 1979

12:00 PM
Restroom 1

Hotel de Ville to Centre Georges Pompidou, 2 minutes; Centre Georges Pompidou to the Louvre, 4 minutes; the Louvre to Place de la Concorde, 5 minutes; Place de la Concorde to Basilique du Sacre-coeur, 9 minutes; Basilique du Sacre-coeur to Avenue des champs Elysées, 10 minutes; Avenue des champs Elysées to Arc de Triomphe, 3 minutes; Arc de Triomphe to Place de l'Alma, 6 minutes; Place de l'Alma to Eiffel Tower, 5 minutes; Eiffel Tower to Palais Bourbon, 8 minutes; Palais Bourbon to Institut de France, 9 minutes; Institut de France to Saint-Sulpice Cathedral, 7 minutes; Saint-Sulpice Cathedral to Place d'Italie, 7 minutes; Place d'Italie to Lac Daumesnil, 9 minutes.

'Huritt finishes the inner loop in 95 minutes and 24 seconds,' announced Aimon excitedly. *'This is by far the best lap timings in the history of the Fermont Triathlon! Ladies and Gentlemen, brace yourselves, for today you might stand here and witness Monsieur Huritt Achak create a new world record!'*

Huritt didn't stop at any aid station for the entire loop. He straightaway dashed to the restroom, changed his gear and ecstatically dashed out.

Nearly 10 minutes after Huritt had left the restroom, Belgium's contender entered it, second in the line, followed by UK. Spain was the last to enter, 20 minutes after Huritt had left and 5 minutes after Ireland and West Germany had exited.

The delegates were now being escorted to Arc de Triomphe, where the nerve-racking event would come to a stupendous consummate.

The participants were supposed to run the last stretch on *Avenue des Champs-Élysées. "La plus belle avenue du monde"* (the most beautiful avenue in the world), was specifically chosen for the final leg in order to commemorate the historical significance associated with the Avenue and also to celebrate the eminence of Paris.

The *Champs-Élysées* forms a part of the *Axe Historique* (the Historical Axis). The axis represents a line of monuments, buildings and thoroughfares that extends from the center of Paris to the west. It is also known as the *Voie Triomphale* (triumphal way), owing light to the fact that throughout history, many triumphant armies marched on this very street. It was here that the German troops marched, celebrating the Fall of France on 14 June 1940, the French 2nd Armored Division (Free French) marched on 26 August 1944, commemorating the liberation of France, and subsequently, the US 28th Infantry Division marched on 29 August 1944, following the liberation of the city.

This is your last run, Huritt. Ace it.

CHAPTER 57

Dillion cleaned the blood off the floor, neatly washed the knife and replaced it in the stand. He undid the tape on Mark's hands, feet, mouth and eyes, put the serrated finger in his pocket, removed Veronica's coat and Mark's pajamas and then dumped them in the bath tub. He poured soap water on the drawing room floor and the kitchen, and turned the shower on, let the drain open and quickly walked out of the house.

The water hit Veronica's face and woke her up. She slowly opened her eyes and saw Mark right in front of her. The sheer sight of his ruptured face shocked her. Her instincts forced her to stand up and go to his aid, but she was so damaged that she could barely move an inch. She breathed heavily and looked at herself. *I'm naked! Who? God! My legs…they are…swollen.*

'Help…' she whispered. Her breasts had turned bluish and her face red. She pushed back her hair that was slightly blocking her vision and looked at Mark's right hand. 'Mark, Mark!' She managed with all her strength and tried to reach him with her hands. But she couldn't. She simply pushed herself along the wall of the bathtub and let the shower hit her chest. 'Nahiossi, safe. Nahiossi!' she cried, and closed her eyes again.

I'm sorry.

CHAPTER 58

June 20, 1979
Avenue des Champs-Élysées
Paris, France

1:13 PM

Huritt ran on the Triumphant Way like a bolt of lightning, fuelled with inexplicable excitement and passion. *In a couple of months, you'll be in par with the sixth richest man in the land of France! Come on, Huritt, come on! La Patron* transformed all his instigation, felicity, trepidation and zeal into vigour and ran with all his might.

Lean forward, look straight, focus on the horizon, constrain your path, don't move sideways, straighten your torso, straighten your hips, flex your ankles... he said to himself and staunched to maintain the right posture. This posture helped him to maintain the desired center of gravity and hence the center of mass. Furthermore, it facilitated perfect spring mechanism, giving him the right speed with minimal loss of energy.

The Avenue was stacked with fans and enthusiasts on either side, flaunting the National flags and cheering the contenders. The French ministry was informed that their contender was sure to slam the Triathlon, and more importantly, the hope of Huritt Achak setting a new world record was formidable. So the ministers of various departments were chauffeured and choppered to *Arc de Triomphe* to witness the magnificent consummation of this promise.

Cops (uniformed and non-uniformed), snipers, SWAT teams and armored vehicles secured the area. *Arc de Triomphe* was given a reminiscence of its glorious days.

'Fuck!' shouted Huritt, with a loud overwhelming cry of aggression, and ran, clenching his jaw and hampering every sinew. It is often conceived that when one necessitates to augment his adrenaline rush, for any fragment of aggressive pursuit, he not seldom indulges in heaving out swear words.

The audience was exhibiting their anxiety and nervousness. Some spectators stared at the track without the blink of an eye, some fittingly jumped, shouting the name 'Huritt', the young children ran for some distance along the track, the oldies stood wherever there was stalls, munching on whatever eats they had in store, the teenagers formed a file and jumped unanimously. Patriots erected the flags high up in the air, couples held hands, every other shopkeeper came out to the streets and the delegates couldn't help but stand. Every other person assembled there was having a blissful time.

'Huritt is in the final mile! Mesdames et Messieurs, Can he do it?'

'Yes!' shouted the multitude, almost unanimously.

The video correspondents pressed their cameras against their eye and focused on the ribbon at the finish line, as the track assistants held the timers and reporters pressed their pens against their jotting pads.

Huritt's eyes began watering as he rocketed through the blanket of air. He was biting his teeth and screaming like a banshee. His nerves were protruding out of his skin and his limbs were now out of control.

The EUN was furiously cackling, *'As you can see the Fermont Triathlon is coming to a spectacular end with Huritt, the French competitor, thriving hard to beat Farren Leroy, the current world record holder who completed all three-circuits in a total time of five hours, twenty minutes and thirty nine seconds..."*

'The last one hundred metres, Mesdames et Messieurs!'

The medics had already predicted the landing and were prepared with their medical equipment. The security, nearly 350 in number, held hands and stood on both sides for a hundred metres and acted as human barricades.

Huritt roared and sprinted towards the finish line. With his legs pushing the ground at around twenty-two miles per hour, he pushed the satin tape at the finish line, as the cameras flashed and the timers clanked. The official timer standing right next to the track pressed the stop button at the precise moment Huritt touched the tape, 05:18:14 (five hours, eighteen minutes and fourteen seconds). Reporters tried to force their way through to get the official result, as the security resisted them.

'We have a new world record...' informed Aimon, but he couldn't finish what he had intended to say.

The spectators began clapping and singing the anthem, while the medical personnel ran with a stretcher towards the track.

'Huritt is hurt. He is terribly injured!'

More than half the crowd watched in agony as Huritt failed to slow down. He slipped and hysterically crashed on the track, head first, with his hands opposing the inertia by pushing the ground involuntarily, just a few microseconds after his head had hit the ground. His hands pushed the ground in forward direction, as he rolled twice prior to being completely decelerated, and he finally landed on his torso. The fine particles of gravel scarred his face, arms and legs. His dress was in shards, his mouth bleeding. A thin stream of blood disembogued from his salt and pepper hair, as did the blood from his elbows, ankles, knees and palm. He seemed to have conceived multiple injuries, supported by the fact that he could not move as much as an inch. He laid there, with his arms stretched, ten metres off the finish line. He could feel his heart roaring like a lion. He was shivering with pain and fighting for breath as his eyes began to mist.

CHAPTER 59

September 27, 1992
Mark's and Veronica's residence

Vincent, a team of doctors and their allies in the police department entered the unlocked house on Tunistraat, discreetly. They didn't have their uniforms on and they didn't make their entrance in a fancy car owned by the department. They were there as friends, as well-wishers.

'In the bathroom! In the bathroom!' yelled Vincent and ushered them inside. *Stay calm, stay calm!* He swiftly led them down a dim-lit corridor, his neck scarred and bleeding, and finally came to a halt in front of the brown door. Not that he had to lead them. They all knew the house inside out. They weren't new to the place. But then, Vincent had wigged out. He really didn't have any grasp over the situation.

At the end of the corridor, he caught his breath, looked at the *Inspecteur* and said, 'Bram, it isn't...both of them...in here. Even... even the...even Nahiossi.'

'I'll look into it. Whatever happened to your neck?' asked *Inspecteur* Bram.

'Nahiossi. I tried to get him out of there. But he didn't move. He resisted. I then tried to carry him…this happened.'

As Bram and Vincent spoke, Dr. Martha, Dr. Roel, Dr. Lowie and two *Hoofdagents* entered the bathroom and processed the scene.

'Okay, you go and clean yourself up at the kitchen. I'll take a look at – '

As Bram was about to enter the bathroom, Piet pushed himself out of the threshold and threw up on the wall that was adjacent to Vincent. 'I'm - I'm sorry. It's just…terrible!'

CHAPTER 60

June 20, 1979
The Fermont Hospital

1:30 PM

'Keep your eyes open, Huritt. Look, look over there. You made it. Don't close your eyes,' repeated Kramer, time and again, as the siren slowly died down...

...The red light over the OT was lit up for an hour, after which the World Record holder was transferred to the ICU, owing not only to the issue of injuries, but also to the security concerns.

'Is there anything I should be worried of?' asked Sebastian, as he met with Dr. Martin immediately after the operation.

'No. Absolutely nothing. He'll recover soon enough. You need not worry about the fractures and bruises...it's pretty common these days. The prime matter of concern was the concussion.'

'Why? What about it?'

'If it was a stage III concussion, he would have succumbed to memory loss, headaches, intense confusion, light sensitivity, double vision, and on prognosis, the conditions could have grown worse.'

'Oh God!'

'But luckily, he is in stage I. The impact didn't last for long. He managed to push himself and roll over. The deceleration prevented serious injuries.'

'What about the prognosis?'

'The concussion might cause headaches for a few months. That is all. His fractured bones may take some time to recover. He would eventually have to take up physiotherapy and he has to be bedridden for at least three months. I'll mention everything in the report.'

'T-thank you, Dr. Martin.'

'Anytime sir, nothing to worry.'

'Can I talk to him now?'

'I've given him a sedative. Um, you can talk to him in the evening, I suppose.'

'Sure, Dr. Martin. Thanks again'. *Please help him God, please be kind to him as You are to me.*

CHAPTER 61

On a lukewarm Friday evening in February, Henry returned from the hospital with a one-way ticket to heaven.

Clutching the tenuous ticket in his hand, he drove straightaway to his cabin, the only place where he had docketed his cherished memories, and placed a call to the only person on the top of his mind...Veronica. He called her up and told her that he needed to talk to her and promised her that this was the last time he was going to annoy her...the last time ever.

Almost five years into the past, in 1984, when Nahiossi was 5 years old, Henry got his divorce and that very night Veronica had been to his condo. Henry Diederik Douglas, the billionaire airliner and the face of the Dutch business conglomerate, spent the night with the boss of *Verlangen*.

It was given that Henry was the least attractive of men, with his bulging belly, misshapen head, unkempt beard and besmirched teeth. But back in those days, *Verlangen's* workers would have fucked even a corpse if it meant good money. So after Henry's stunning night and Veronica's day of phony pleasure, Henry asked her to desert her family and move in with him. Veronica considered it a joke and quite simply said, "Keep fucking me well and keep that thing flowing. Money, I mean."

But Henry wasn't kidding when he asked her to move in with him. He took her "keep fucking me well" way too seriously. Had she known Henry's clingy attitude, she would have fended him off at the first chance of his unreasonable advances. To Veronica, Henry was a consumer, but to Henry, she was more than just a provider. She was his woman and he wanted nothing but to be with her…to fuck her, without paying, and to live with her, without her faking.

As time progressed, after she offered her service to him for over six times, she became tired of him. The sixth time after they had done it, she felt as though she were being held captive. He seized her by the arm and forced a ring on her finger. Veronica slapped the persistent fool and threw the ring on his face. She spit right on his bald head as he kneeled, and she stormed out of his cabin. She then had Mark give him an ultimatum and believed that a bizarre chapter in her life of outlandish escapades had come to an end.

For the purposes of preserving the integrity of the industry and to keep their shares from depreciating, his diagnosis was kept from the public. The Board of Directors of Roulette Airlines retained all broadcasting rights and they asked Henry to take a holiday and make himself unseen at the industry.

The media had it that Henry was back with his family and was now holidaying in the Caribbean. But in reality, Henry was in a sequestered mansion in London, where his wife sucked every last dime out of him. He was given chemotherapy, and three doctors tended to him. But then they were asked to do nothing to prolong his life, let alone save it. They were paid heftily, all hugely benefited by their lack of service.

Having not heard from Henry, Veronica moved on with her life. As Nahiossi turned seven, Veronica stopped working for good... or so she thought. With Tracy gone, she alone was responsible for Nahiossi. She started the business for Nahiossi and had to end it for the same reason. So she handed over *La Roja* to Vincent and kept herself busy with the cassette stores. With the money they had earned over the years, they bought a decent house in *Jordaan* and made it their humble abode. But then, soon enough, her cancer came back. Henry was back in town!

The Baron had signed the Final Will and Testament, and was soon literally thrown out of London. Dillion backed him, all through the journey, and had him stay at the cabin. The factory was more than happy to have their visionary slump in the backyard and offer them free services, and the Board of Directors was more than happy to have the prick off the table. He was vulnerable and he was beat. So casting him out wasn't that tough a task.

But the people loved Henry. They admired his arrogance, his marketing and his vision. So for the betterment of the industry's income, the BOE still had to have Henry near them. He was near all right, but not involved. He was like a supermodel attracting the crowd with her stacked teats and raunchy buttocks. Nothing more. "Just keep the cash coming in and we'll take care of the rest" best painted Henry's state of melancholy.

Even though Henry dreaded living with his wife and being robbed of his empire, he couldn't do anything about it. He had to keep his calm for the betterment of his son, who would be the next Baron of the industry. William was intelligent, and with proper training, he would rise to take charge of the industry. So in view of the future prospects of the industry, he sold his honour.

Henry had Dillion pursue Veronica. He had her go down to her residence and he had him follow her wherever she went, begging her to visit the cabin. So one unforgiving morning, when Nahiossi saw Dillion fall on her knees and beg her to go with him, Veronica gave in and agreed to go to the cabin that evening. She wanted to put an end to all of this before Mark learnt of Henry's frivolous tantrums. She would warn him once, then if things went south, she would have a job for Mark. A job of yore!

Henry Douglas waited at the entrance of his office, timidly clutching a bouquet of lilies. *She loves lilies. She had given me that look of hers when I gave them to her the last time.*

CHAPTER 62

26th July 1979.

3:30 PM
Ryk Douglas, SA

A few minutes after 82BJJ8462 had bid *adios* to Nathan, he went to the Femhörnig New York and called the Ryk Douglas in Northern Cape. 'Good morning. I need to speak to Kato. Tell him it's Nathan.'

The operator immediately transferred the call to Kato, and then upon Kato's approval, switched it to a private secure line. A few clicks and beeps followed, and then a deep grim voice said, *'Hael Verlossers!'*

'Tomorrow.'

'The Kimberly Hanger.'

The phone went dead.

* * *

4:35 PM
Femhörnig, London

'Welcome to Femhörnig.'

'My day just became lovelier.'

'How may I help you today?'

'The same way you did last weekend.'

'Shhh, shut up!' whispered the dark-haired, wrinkle-faced receptionist, as the black private phone on her desk jingled.

'Krista, you two can have your cheesy talks later. Okay? Now if it not too much trouble, could you patch him through?' asked Morgan roughly and rammed the phone down.

'Mr. Morgan wants to see you now, Sir,' said Krista gravely and put down the phone. She didn't even lift her head until she heard the door behind her open and close.

'Good...good morning boss...Sir. Morning.'

'What?' asked Morgan sternly.

'Nathan gave the green signal. 82BJJ8462. Tomorrow.'

'Pick them both at the Kimberly Hanger.'

'I will, Sir.'

'Good.'

'Hael Verlossers.'

Morgan had his secretary cancel all his appointments for the day. He called up Frälsare and then walked to his private elevator on the lobby just outside his room and pressed the only other button on the pad. Nineteen seconds later, he stepped out of the elevator towards his Rolls Royce and casually drove out of the Femhörnig.

Chapter 63

June 20, 1979
Mark's garage

11:00 AM

Ricardo picked up Mark from Restroom 1 on *route de ceinture du Lac Daumesnil* and dropped him off at the garage. Mark had fared commendably at the Triathlon and his fatiguing efforts had paid off. He was now not just an assassin, but an athlete who had managed to gain the affection and admiration of Huritt.

'*Le faux patron*! You were...boo-yah! Funkadelic!' said Felix excitedly as he saw Mark entering the room.

'I fucked them just right,' replied Mark and walked into the living room as he stripped off his sweaty garments. 'Where is she? Madame Lucy Francois Benoit Achak.'

'Right th – '

'She is right here!' said Mark and pulled down his underpants.

Lucy saw Mark's naked body and tried to shout in shock. The tape stuck across her mouth muffled the sound and she couldn't be heard anywhere outside the building. Her tears wetted the tape and she closed her eyes, hoping that in reality too, Mark would be shut off.

'Felix! What's wrong with you? Give me the cutter,' said Mark and kneeled in front of her. Felix had taped most part of Lucy's legs to a steel chair that was tightly bolted to the ground. She was in perpetual pain and didn't know if the kid inside her was alive or dead.

As Lucy listened to Mark, she stopped clenching her teeth and opened her eyes, perplexed.

'This must be so hard. How can anyone do such a thing?' quizzed Mark and cut the tape around her thighs.

She closed her eyes and breathed a sigh of relief.

'She needs air supply not just for her. There is another life growing inside her!' he said, and cut the tape across her mouth.

She took in huge amounts of air and breathed sporadically.

'Thank you,' whispered Lucy.

'Felix! I asked you a question. What's wrong with you?'

'Huritt told me to – '

'No, of course he didn't. You're just making that up. I can sense your intentions,' said Mark, moving closer to Felix.

He then stared at him for some time, after which he turned around and asked Lucy, with apparent heap of concern, 'I hope you are alright!'

Lucy simply stared at the ground, crying.

'I can't believe this! Felix, what's wrong with you?'

'He is a savage, a demonic savage! He has lived under my roof for almost a year now and he – '

' – and he still doesn't know to fuck! He is hiding the truth, he isn't telling you just how unattractive you are!' yelled Mark and gave a braying laugh.

Both Felix and Lucy were dumbfounded. They didn't follow a word of whatever Mark was saying. Felix looked at Mark, confused, and then looked at a perplexed and horrified Lucy.

'What?' asked Lucy, in dismay.

'About what happened earlier today.'

'What?' asked Lucy, her fear rising.

'Felix, didn't you tell her about the – '

'*Miroir,* no! Just-just don't – '

' – Tell her that you tried to fuck her?'

'I did it only because Huritt ordered me to do so! I didn't want to – ' protested Felix.

'You what! I was fu –' cried Lucy.

'– fucked? No. Not really. But it appears so in the pictures.'

'Pictures! But why wo – '

'Exactly! Why won't his dick stand up? Something is terribly wrong with him. I mean, I don't know why he doesn't find you attractive. Look at me!' said Mark and looked at his partially erect penis. 'If I happened to,' continued Mark and walked closer to little Lucy. 'Put this back on your mouth,' he said, pasting the tape back to the place from where he had removed it. 'And if I happened to place my hand over…look! Look how it is shooting up!'

'Lucy, my dear, let me ask you the question again. What's wrong with him? How did he expect me to fuck you with your thighs joined together?' asked Mark with a grin, and pushed her thighs apart. 'You see, Huritt needed something to threaten you,' said Mark and put his finger in her navel. 'With the pictures out, your uncle would go all Stalin. He won't give you even a penny from your father's fortune. He will vouch against your credibility and you will be stripped of the right to inherit Sir Benoit's empire. Then on it will go down the chain of inheritance and Huritt would get a fine share from your noble relative. So you see its significance, don't you?' he added, slowly bringing his finger down from the navel and finally putting it into her vagina.

'Lucy my dear, why the fuck couldn't he fuck you?' asked Mark, and pushed his finger further inside.

I've got to do something!

CHAPTER 64

September 14, 1978

Alexis Hospital

'The sooner you open this fucking door, the sooner you get to fuck me,' said Veronica in a fizzy tone, appearing in the same way as she had during her previous visit, except for the fact that she was now wearing a strapless cotton top and she had gotten rid of her stockings. She now appeared more appealing and more turned on.

As Denver excitedly opened the Records Room, she pushed him inside and pulled down his pants, even as she desperately tore off her cotton top and threw it on the floor. She then removed her skirt, pushed her buttocks towards his face, and puckered her glittering lips as she moaned sensually. They then had raunchy intercourse for the next 15 minutes.

'Yours was the best I've ever had. You are really the man. I love your big fat junk,' she said, kissing it before he zipped it and tucked in his shirt with the name "Alexis" printed on it.

'What was the need for you to tear your dress? You can't walk inside the hospital displaying these,' said he and lifted her breasts.

'People will get a panic attack,' he said, squeezing them both. He so wished that he could hold them forever.

'I'm sorry. It's just that you know... you were so irresistible,' she said, and put a sad dramatic face.

'Don't be sad, Steph. I'm so sorry, I wasn't complaining or anything. In fact, I loved the way you ripped it apart. Don't worry. I'm going to set things straight.'

'Definitely not better than me,' she said, touching his crotch.

'Oh Steph, my dick ain't tired yet. He wants to go inside you again,' he said, spanking her twice, as he removed his pants and plunged it inside Veronica's wet pussy.

Veronica was amazed by his stamina and she really did orgasm. She enjoyed being fucked. Another twenty minutes later, she tucked his penis inside his pants and got down to business. Huritt's business.'

'Oh! And I have the case files right here, in my bag,' said Veronica and opened it, drawing out three files from a compartment. 'You give me the keys. I'll stack them properly.'

'It's okay, I can put them back, no problem.'

'You seriously think I can't stack properly?' she asked, pushing her breasts up and down.

'You definitely can, woman,' he said, kissing each of her breasts before handing her the keys.

'There are just two keys to enter this room. One is with me and the other one is with Mr. Edgard, the owner of this hospital. He is unlikely to visit today, for he is in London. So right now, I am the only person possessing the key to enter this room,' he said, and paused to stare at her circling her finger around her nipples. 'Stephanie, will you please stop playing with your tits and listen to what I say?' he said, unintentionally.

'I'm sorry, honey,' she said, and asked him to continue, folding her arms around her breasts and making herself appear bustier.

Denver managed to shift a smile and said, 'You stay here, quietly, and put those case files back in the right place, while I go to the cloak room and fetch a uniform.'

'Great thinking. You are such a darling, Denver,' she said, hugging him, her breasts pressing against his chest.

Almost a minute after, he cleared his throat and pushed her aside, not heartily intending to do so.

'Dr. Leroy's on the left, Dr. Christine and Dr. Edwige's on the right. I'm sure that you can find the right spots.'

'Oh, I'm good with spots and positions. I'm good...'

He smiled and closed the door, and then he locked it from the outside. Once she heard the clicking sound, she ran to the door, bolted it from the inside as well and stuffed a piece of torn cloth inside the key hole in such a way that it wasn't protruding from the other side.

She ran across a series of cupboards storing Dr. Martin Leroy's case files. She opened the second cupboard - with the year 1978 written on it in white paint - with the aid of the keys handed over to her by Denver. She then opened the drawer concerning the month of July with another key and found the folder with the number 6, indicating the 6th of July. She ran to her bag and drew the folder containing a report of Huritt, reporting that Dr. Leroy had diagnosed him with "Erectile Dysfunction". She immediately put it back in between file 5 and file 7 and moved on to replace the three other files, after which she ran to the door and removed the cloth, unbolted the door and sat at the far corner of the room.

You are so smart, bitch.

CHAPTER 65

October 19, 1978

The weather was cool, but the prosecutor's temperament seemed to purport the contrary. There were many media personnel gathered outside the courtroom, interviewing the jurors, judges, lawyers and everyone else associated with the case.

The mundane formalities were completed smoothly and the fiery cross-examination was back on high.

Sebastian: Dr. Denis, congratulations! Your analysis that Mr. Huritt was at the scene that afternoon was spot on!

Dr. Denis: I'm in the field for two decades. I can't be wrong.

Sebastian: Does the prosecution agree with Dr. Denis's assertion, "I can't be wrong"?

Reyes: Yes, I do. In fact, he is the best forensic expert in town.

Dr. Denis: M.Sc., C.Chem., F.R.S.C., F.S.Soc. Dip., F.A.E, R.F.P. I have also served for our army for a decade. I was discharged honourably from the Military's Research and Development Corps in 1956.

Sebastian: That is indeed highly commendable, Sir. Now let me ask you something that doesn't really require your prowess. It's plain simple. Did you find my client's fingerprint on the bottle of Midaxolac?

Dr. Denis: No.

Sebastian: Whose prints did you find on the bottle?

Dr. Denis: Ms. Bibiana's.

Sebastian: Were the fingerprints in such a way so as to suggest that she herself could have opened the bottle and administered the tablets herself? If you think it is possible, could you please care to explain the reason to the court?

Dr. Denis: We found Ms. Bibiana's left hand fingerprint on the body of the bottle and the right hand print on the cap. We also retrieved her right hand print from the glass with which the poison was administered. I think it is possible. But in this case, I don't think it makes sense.

Sebastian: We'll get to that, Dr. Denis. Now my next question, is Midaxolac available in the medical shops?

Dr. Denis: Yes, Sir, it is. The bottle from which she had consumed the tablets offers reinforcement to your question.

Sebastian: Thank you, good doctor. So this drug is available for sale at *any* medical store. I repeat, *any* medical store. Now for you to believe that there is less than 50% probability for Mr. Huritt to have murdered Ms. Bibiana, I'll have to account for the fingerprints on Ms. Bibiana's cheek, the inundations on Mr. Huritt's face and the cause and reason for the fight. Is that right?

Dr. Denis: I'm inclined to answer in the affirmative. But let us not be presumptuous.

Sebastian: Well said, Dr. Denis. Well indeed. Now let me just give the synopsis. Huritt's fingerprints weren't found on the bottle of Midaxolac. Midaxolac is available at "any" medical store and Dr. Denis will, as a reasonable man, hopefully give leverage to my client if I happened to prove three, let me repeat, *three* prime points.

Dr. Denis: Probably.

Sebastian: Thank you, Doctor. You can be seated now.

Monsieur et Mesdames, before the break, I would like you to find Mr. Bayol biased and I adjure the court to impeach him.

Bayol: You filthy son-of-a-bitch! How dare you impeach me… motherfucker! You come outside now…I'll break your bones.

The judges frowned, as did the jurors.

Sebastian: *Monsieur et Mesdames,* based on Mr. Bayol's testimony, we can clearly see that he is biased. I have no other option but to use those heinous words again in this serene courtroom. Now with your permission, I will, with utmost grief, repeat the daunting aspects of Mr. Bayol's testimony.

Lorenzo, the two judges, and the jurors didn't object. They asked him to proceed. Sebastian thanked them and began extracting pieces of statements from Bayol's testimony.

Sebastian: "Fucking bastard", "This sociopath should be punished. He should be hanged and…" and just now he shouted, "You filthy son-of-a-bitch. How dare you impeach me motherfucker. You come outside now. I'll break your bones".

Monsieur et Mesdames, evidently this isn't healthy behaviour. We can't entertain people like Mr. Bayol to act as credible witnesses in a murder trial. Without probing further into Mr. Bayol's lack of tenability, I humbly request you to consider my motion to dismiss.

Lorenzo: The jury will deliberate this during the break and give us the verdict in the next session.

Sebastian: Thank you, *Monsieur.* I would also like to point out some serious mistakes in Bayol's testimony.

Lorenzo: Proceed.

The jurors were now thoroughly impressed and keen on listening to what Sebastian had in store.

Sebastian: I have already proved that his testimony, "Of course he wouldn't have told Mrs. Fermont about Sarah. My sister probably tried to hint her about his sadistic character and Huritt, discovering this unpleasant act, wanted to shut her up before she could spill the beans", is farce.

Also, people brought up in orphanages aren't sociopaths! They are the best, cultured and most obedient of citizens. Mr. Bayol is not just hurting the sentiments of my client, but is also fiddling with the sentiments of every orphan who has been an integral part in the growth of this great country! This statement of his must be discredited.

Huritt's character has nothing to do with his parents. Agreed that his parents were felons. There is no denying it. But that shouldn't influence Huritt to murder a woman! Yes, he had a tough childhood. But isn't it too convenient for Mr. Bayol to accuse Mr. Huritt on grounds of his parents' incapability and upon the fact that he grew up in an orphanage? These have no binding on this case. If he were a sociopath, he wouldn't be sitting here in front of you without any criminal record.

Bayol: Learned counsel, it does have a binding and I ain't gonna fall for your petty ploy!

Sebastian: If I prove to you that he isn't a sociopath and he truly values relationships, would you be convinced?

Bayol: No.

Sebastian: If I prove to you that he didn't send away your sister, would you be convinced?

Bayol: Fuck no!

Sebastian: If I prove to you that Achille is her child and not Huritt's, would you believe me?

Bayol didn't reply.

Sebastian: If I prove to you that Huritt valued his friendship with Mr. Cortez, had the compassion to give a stable future to your sister, had the desire to consider Achille as his own child, intended to pave way for him to lead a better and a decent life, and wanted to make you, Mr. Bayol, content and relieved by the fact that your sister was cradled in the capable hands of a well-educated man with a decent job and a commendable family background, would you believe that Mr. Huritt isn't a sociopath?

Silence.

Sebastian: If I prove to you that your sister loved Huritt until her last breath, would you believe in Mr. Huritt's innocence?

Bayol: I-I don't know. It-it is left for the court to decide.

Sebastian: Excellent! Now respected members of the jury, I shall prove all these points during my defense-in-chief and I'm sure that in the end, you will have nothing but one simple decision to make; finding my client innocent.

The court broke for tea and was scheduled to convene after a half hour.

The sworn usher escorted the jurors to the deliberation room and was handed over a copy of the documents concerning Mr. Bayol's conversations at the courthouse.

The court gathered again after tea and the jury had a decision regarding Bayol's impeachment. Everybody resorted to their respective tasks, after which the President asked the jury to give their verdict concerning the impeachment.

Juror #1 (Teacher): We have unanimously decided to impeach witness #7, Mr. Bayol.

Sebastian: Thank you, *Monsieur et Mesdames.*

Reyes frowned and was afraid that the jury was more inclined towards Sebastian. Bayol and Cortez looked dejected. Huritt remained passive. Sebastian was enjoying the chaotic tune and Lucy was feeling drowsy.

Sebastian: I would now like to *speak* to Mr. Montego Cortez.

As Cortez slowly stood off the bench and walked towards the box, he glanced at Huritt. Huritt gave him a warm smile, but Cortez didn't acknowledge it. Soon he was at the box and was made aware of his oath.

Sebastian: Mr. Cortez, your testimony in a nutshell is that Ms. Bibiana was mentally disturbed, but she refused to take the necessary treatment and her condition worsened when Achille became sick. Am I right?

Cortez: In a way.

Sebastian: In a way that is considered normally right. Yes, now, do you know why she was disturbed?

Cortez: Because of this man! Huritt!

Sebastian: Well quite frankly, you don't "know" that. You just "think" that Huritt is responsible for her mental…illness, if I may call it so.

Cortez: Considering the chain of events, I think that that is the only possible explanation.

Sebastian: Be rest assured, Mr. Cortez. I shall account for everything when I present my witnesses. Now I just need to know if she was under any medication?

Cortez: Can you be specific?

Sebastian: I don't want to go into the loop now and I don't want the prosecutor jumping up and yelling that I'm leading the witness. It is to simple save time for the court. So here is my question, Mr. Cortez, was she prescribed Midaxolac?

Cortez remained silent. He looked at the prosecutor and stood there quietly.

Sebastian: Mr. Cortez, I know that you hate to think that she committed suicide. But I also want you to know that our job and your responsibility is to see to it that truth and justice is brought to the fore. We can't just live on junk science. We need positive, believable and sustainable evidence and testimonies. Now keeping that in mind, could you please answer my question? Truthfully and without any reservations.

Cortez: Well, yes. She was taking that drug. She was deprived of sleep and was always anxious. So almost six months ago, when we consulted our physician, he prescribed Midaxolac and asked her to take it once every alternate day. But with regards to our case, I believe that she was forcefully fed an excessive amount of tablets. She didn't voluntarily kill herself. Huritt forced it on her. She might have resented his advance and so Huritt might have slapped her and then he might have forced the tablets down her throat. Somewhere during this chaos, Sarah might have succumbed to fear and tried to harm Huritt, as a result of which she would have tried to strangle him, which is supported by the presence of the inundations on his neck. He might have then thrown her on the bed and left. Then once the murderer had vacated the scene, my poor Sarah might have struggled toward the cupboard, taken a photograph of the wretched man and clutched it in her hand before she finally collapsed. Well that was the least she could do. She wouldn't have had the capacity to alert the authorities! She didn't even have the...she didn't even call me. I didn't get to...

Sebastian: Hurray for the Bard! Wow, Mr. Cortez. Wow! Great story. A fine piece of fiction. I'd like to hear more of it, but then you see, we have to live in a world called reality. So please bear with me for a few more seconds and come back to this world...the real world. Now assuming that your "fiction" was true, if Mr. Huritt had in fact forcefully drugged her, there would have been prints on the bottle and on the glass? But Dr. Denis, M.Sc., C.Chem., F.R.S.C., F.S.Soc. Dip., F.A.E, R.F.P, who has served for our army for a decade and has been discharged honourably from the Military's Research and Development Corps in 1956...and the person "who cannot be wrong" asserted the fact that Huritt's fingerprints weren't found on the glass. What have you to say about that, Mr. Cortez?

Cortez: Well, he must have been wearing gloves.

Sebastian: And he was stupid enough to not wear them when he slapped her?

Cortez: I…I don't know why he didn't. You must be asking him. He is the one with a demented mind. God knows what transpires in his wretched head!

Sebastian: Mr. Cortez, why are you so adamant? Just open up to the possibility that she might have committed suicide.

Cortez: No! No she didn't. Mr. Sebastian, two people have testified that they saw them both fighting –

Sebastian: Let me interrupt you there. The two people, Linda –

Linda: – Mrs. Absolon and Mr. Dominique.

Sebastian collected a couple of sheets from Linda, wore his horn-rimmed spectacles and said, 'Mr. Dominique said, "On the 14th of August, Tuesday, I saw this man…" and Mrs. Absolon said "I was watering my plants when I saw this man, getting out of a taxi and banging on Ms. Bibiana's door. There appeared to be a fight between the two, after which they entered inside. That is all I saw". Now, both the testifiers "saw" Huritt go to her and they "saw" them fight. Mrs. Absolon says that it "appeared" like a fight. Anyway, I'll get to that later. Now I would like to ask the two witnesses if they "heard" what Mr. Huritt and Mrs. Bibiana were talking about, or in your terms, Mr. Cortez, "fighting" about.

The two rose from the stands and said that they didn't hear anything.

Sebastian: Mr. Cortez, nobody heard them. So, we don't know what they were talking about. Or if it was a fight, what was it about. Who started the fight...

Cortez: It is quite evident that he started the fight.

Sebastian: Inspector Felipe, what does your wife do when you promise to take her to dinner and it turns out that you are held up at work, you know, on cases such as this one, as a result of which you are forced to cancel the dinner plan?

Felipe: Well, she'd be quite mad at me.

Sebastian: And then you'd fight, won't you?

Felipe: I suppose.

Sebastian: But?

Felipe: But we'd be fine the next morning. All it takes is a good night's sleep.

Sebastian: Sleep? Well, a good wife you have, Inspector. A good one indeed. Thank you, Inspector. Now what about you, *Madame*?

Juror #6 (The housewife): Almost the same as what Mr. Felipe said.

Sebastian: Will you "fight" with him? Be "mad" at him for some time?

Juror #6: Yes, Mr. Sebastian. It's a common trait. Women get upset when their men fail to live up to their expectations.

A few of them chuckled, but Sebastian moved on. He wanted to be done with this line of boring questioning.

Sebastian: Thank you, *Madame,* Juror #1, do you agree with Juror #6?

Juror #1: Yes, I do.

Sebastian: Mr. Prosecutor, you are married, aren't you? How would your wife react? I'm sure you can't lie to this question…

Reyes: We get your point, counsel.

Sebastian: Please answer me. Do you people fight?

Reyes: *Monsieur,* the defense is –

Sebastian: What do you say, Mr. Cortez?

Cortez: You are talking about a husband/wife relationship.

Reyes: – ruining the court's precious time.

Sebastian: Do you think a boyfriend/girlfriend relationship has less fights? Seriously?

The people laughed again and Lorenzo hammered again. 'Order in the court!'

Sebastian: Sorry, *Monsieur.*

Reyes: My apologies.

Lorenzo: If the order is disturbed again, I'll hold both the parties in contempt of the court. Am I clear?

Sebastian: Yes, *Monsieur.*

Reyes: Yes, *Monsieur.*

Lorenzo: Proceed.

Cortez: But Mr. Sebastian, they weren't in a relationship!

Sebastian: If I prove that both of them still loved each other, would it be sufficient to make you change your opinion?

Cortez: What about the fight inside the house, the shoeprint scattering and all the scars and slaps and...

Sebastian: You mean, your opinion depends entirely on Dr. Denis's testimony? If I make him believe that there is "less than 50% probability", would you buy that?

Cortez: I would if my attorney would.

Sebastian: Thank you, Mr. Cortez. I shall not disappoint you.

Cortez walked back to the stands and took his seat right next to Reyes.

Sebastian: I shall get back to Mr. Dominique and Mrs. Absolon after I present my witnesses, only if the jury and the judges are fine with it.

The three judges and the juror agreed to the same, after which they asked if Reyes wanted to redirect. He resented and said, 'the prosecution rests.'

Lorenzo: The defense shall present its case-in-chief after the lunch. The court is adjourned.

CHAPTER 66

Nahiossi heard kissing noises. He heard a women giggle and a man asking her if she'd like to go inside the restroom.

The scared boy again pressed his face against the floor and looked under the door. He saw four feet, two booted and two heeled. He then heard the man banging on the door and saying, 'We are waiting here! How long you've been there? Are ya alone? D'ya have company?'

Nahiossi remained quiet for a bit. He then thought that it would be better if he said, 'Yes. I have company.' But it wasn't.

'Hey! There's a kid in there. Yo kid, get out now, go home and play with your handy. This ain't the place for you to be shaggin'. I have a pretty lady out here who wants to...play with me. So why don't you let me in before I break the door open?'

'Go away!'

'I ain't goin' nowhere. Put your dick back inside ya pants and get out o' there!'

'Leave me alone!'

'You little beast! This is the last time I'm asking. Open the goddamn door and get lost!' said the man who already had a boner because the pretty lady was hugging him from behind and nibbling at his neck.

'No!'

'Son-of-a-bitch!' yelled the man in the shiny boots, and asked the pretty lady to step aside. He took a few steps backwards and then kicked the tacky door open. Nahiossi immediately jumped out of the cubicle and swiftly ran back into the bar. He made his way out and ran as fast as he could. He ran until his heart came to his mouth and then he stopped. *Papa, help me! Papa! I need to go to my papa. I have to go home! He is alone. I have to…I'm…I'm scared.*

Nahiossi silently cried. He let his mind settle and his lungs breathe. He then decided to go home to his dad and walked towards the bus stand. He fixated his mind on his hero, his dad, and boarded the bus to Voorburgwal.

'Tickets, Sir?' asked the conductor the moment Nahiossi stepped inside. The scared boy put his hands in his pockets and searched for the money. The conductor, after a long day of standing and screaming, appeared stern. He looked at the boy and again asked, 'Tickets, Sir?'

The man in the bar! 'I-I…someone picked my pocket. I don't…I lost my money.'

'Then get off the bus! We ain't runnin' free service!' yelled the stern-looking man.

'Sir, please, I've had a bad day – '

'Jolly good to hear that. But my day hasn't been any better. Don't make it worse, kid, get off now!'

Nahiossi bowed his head and looked at his wrist. He quickly removed his watch, his favorite Superman watch, and pushed it towards the conductor. 'My papa bought me this watch last year. He bought it from the United States. Mr. Bob Hastings has signed it. Look, look here,' said Nahiossi and showed the signature of the man who portrayed Clark Kent in "The New Adventures of Superman".

'You can keep it, instead of money…or you can give it to your son. I'm sure he'll like it. He'll like you too. I love my dad. Please Sir, I need to go to my papa. I'm…scared. I've never been…'

'Alright, alright! Gimme that thing,' said the conductor and snatched his watch away. 'Where do you want to go?'

'To my papa.'

'Where do you want the bus to go?'

'Voorburgwal.'

CHAPTER 67

June 20, 1979
Mark's garage

11:30 AM

'Lucy, my dear, why the fuck couldn't he fuck you?' asked Mark and pushed his finger further inside.

I've got to do something!

Felix quickly walked out of the room, leaving poor Lucy with the demonic hound, as Mark quickened the pace of his finger going in and out of her vagina.

'Do you like it, Lucy's cunt? Do you want to feel something bigger inside you?' asked Mark as the telephone in the drawing room buzzed.

'Mark, Sebastian is on the phone. He wants to talk to you... urgently.'

CHAPTER 68

July 26, 1979
Harvard University
Boston, the USA

8:45 AM.

'Cortez?'

'Speaking.'

'Sebastian.'

'I'm listening.'

'I'm calling from Charles de Gaulle. It's time for you to fly.'

Cortez was muted for quite some time. Sebastian, who was six hours away from the Greenwich Meridian, contemplated the fact that Cortez was having an avalanche of excitement, fear, happiness and eagerness. They had waited long enough for this pivotal moment… for the time that would change the dynamism of everything they held dear.

The Almonte Research lab.

'I'm on my way.'

Cortez thought of chipping in a few more words, but the indication that Sebastian had hung up the call made him do nothing more than just gasp.

The Almonte Research lab!

A month after the trial in Paris, Sebastian had Cortez acquainted with the Femhörnig *Vennotte* at Boston. That very day, Cortez was abducted by the troopers of Morgan's syndicate and taken to their Dispatch Centre. The Chemistry Professor was impregnated with a tracking device and then made familiar with the standing orders of their troupe, with prime emphasis on the precedent of smuggling and money laundering.

Cortez was primed in aspects of security, secrecy and seclusion, and was ordered to abide by their rules until the desired transaction was made possible. He had lived by the rules for quite some time, but he didn't have to anymore.

Only Kato, an official at Kimberly was allowed to contact the "Hotline" on Krista's (Morgan's secretary) desk. Upon confirmation of a unique passcode, the call would be transferred to Morgan directly; no business deals were to be spoken on the phone. The official had to fly down to London, where he would be allowed an incognito meet with Morgan; in case any Vennotte wanted to contact Morgan, they had to go to the respective official at the store, and with his permission, contact Kato, who would later pass on the message to Morgan.

Sebastian didn't want to go to the diamond store at Paris. He didn't want to be directly associated with the deal. Hence he transferred the burden to Cortez.

Cortez put down the phone and paced up and down the room, smoking his Marlboro Lights. He went through the complex web of plans that had to be executed with the utmost precision in the coming days. The days of the final battle that would transform everything.

After puffing half a dozen Marlboros, the grey-haired professor figured that he couldn't wait anymore. He gave himself a quick shave and shower, got neatly dressed in his tailored jacket and stormed out of his apartment.

Prof. Cortez walked under the shy sun, with occasional smoke tailing him. He walked on the stone pathway, passing the Electronics Engineering and Chemical Engineering blocks, as biting cold wind whistled through his ears and provoked him to shield them with the hood of his jacket. He timidly fought the instinct to go back into his apartment and get his overcoat, as he walked towards the department of Chemistry, with his will trumping the instinct.

Huritt's apparent best friend, Prof. Montego Cortez, issued leave of absence at the office of his department and then exited the college premises. He lit himself another cigarette and began walking down the narrow road. He passed four blocks and came in front of a small bar that was isolated, save a bunch of oldies.

The man whose financé, Sarah, died only a few weeks before their wedding, walked inside the bar and sat alone on a comfortable chair by the window. He ordered a hot cup of coffee and a few nuts, and then he lit himself another Marlboro.

Patience…crimson…82BJJ8462…MC…

Patience…crimson…82BJJ8462…MC…

Cortez thought about the future of the Almonte Research Lab and drained two cups of coffee. He then walked to the counter and placed a call to the Boston Vennotte.

The phone rang for a few ticks and then, once the Vennotte answered, Cortez composed his voice and said, 'Patience.'

'Colour?' asked the Vennotte in his unforgiving tone.

'Crimson.'

'Number?'

'82BJJ8462.'

'Name?'

'MC.'

'Begin the procedures for tomorrow.'

'Any amendments to the previously discussed plan?'

'No.'

'Good day.'

'Adios.'

The nervous yet ecstatic entrepreneur gulped another cup of coffee and marched back to the travel agency.

Diamonds are forever.

CHAPTER 69

June 20, 1979
Mark's garage

'I never expected this from you, Felix. Why in God's name did you betray my trust? Did Huritt offer you a fortune? Did he throw women in your filthy arms? What did he do to buy your trust? Felix, let me get out of here. I'll give you more than what has been promised to you. You can buy whatever you want. Anything. Fame, money, power. But please, let me go!' said Lucy in despair, a few minutes after Mark had pulled his finger out of Lucy's vagina and walked out of the garage.

'No, you can't give me what he has promised. You can never,' said Felix, staring at Lucy's perturbed face. He was awfully composed and the childish elements seemed to have evaporated.

'Of course I can. I can give you lots of money. Lots and lots of it. Tomorrow is my wedding anniversary and as per the conditions laid out by my father in his final will, I'm going to be the rightful heir of the Fermont family's fortunes. So if you let me escape from this place, I can go to uncle Eloy and claim what is rightfully mine. I'll then give you 40% of the entire...80% of the entire property, up front.'

'That is very generous and tempting, Madam Lucy. But I can't let you escape. I cannot as much as let you get off that chair!' said Felix and punched his thighs.

'What in God's name has he promised to you, Felix? I'll give you anything you want. You name it! Anything! Felix, please talk to me. Please, talk to...to the baby.'

'My parents, brother and sister,' said Felix and walked towards Lucy. He held his tears at the threshold of his eyes and slid her panty back up.

Lucy remained quiet. Her mind was addled. 'I...I'm sorry. I was of the opinion that you didn't have a family.'

'I lied!' said Felix furiously.

'But...but why?'

'Because Huritt asked me to! He told me that you had a soft corner towards the orphans. He said that was one of the reasons why you chose him to be your husband. He desperately wanted you to hire me.'

'But – '

'If I lose you, Lucy... I'll lose my family as well.'

'Oh God! What wrong have I done to deserve your wrath!' cried Lucy.

Felix silently walked to the door, then turned back to look at her and said, 'I didn't do it because I respect you.'

'I... I'm...My mind is blank. I feel like the world is collapsing on me. I just don't know whom to trust.'

'Trust me. Do as I say. I'll try to get you out of this mess.'

Lucy waited for some time and then wryly smiled.

12:30 PM

'Honey! I'm back,' said Mark as he came in front of Lucy and undressed.

'Mark, you can't,' said Felix and held Mark's hand firmly.

'Fuck you!' said Mark and pushed Felix away. 'Son-of-a-bitch!'

'Mark, please. Listen. Huritt wants her at the Registrar's office tomorrow and he doesn't want her to…to look injured. He so much as doesn't want anyone to see the tape marks on her hands! Now if you happened to rape her – '

'It's not called rape if she enjoys it,' said Mark arrogantly and walked closer to Lucy.

'I won't!' yelled Lucy, looking at Mark straight in the eye. She believed that she now had Felix on her side. She wasn't as afraid as she had been only a few moments ago. She believed that Felix wouldn't let Mark harm her. She knew she could count on him, or so she thought.

'You cunt!'

'Mark, please, just one more day. You can have her tomorrow, once all this is done. Huritt won't need her after that. But now, he needs her to stay…to stay undefiled. Please, don't do it, Marky. You don't want to anger Huritt, You don't want to betray him.'

Mark angrily started at both Felix and Lucy. He knew that Felix was right. He knew that he couldn't afford to ruin Huritt's plans. He didn't want to upset his *Patron.* He just stood where he was, looked at Lucy, and ran his hands up and down his penis.

1:00 PM
Arc de Triomphe

That morning after Felix had dropped Huritt at Lac Daumesnil, he had driven down to Mark's garage and swapped Huritt's Jaguar with a similar Jaguar, which Mark had tailored to suit the *Patron*'s needs. He had then escorted Huritt to Chateau de Fermont in the modified Jaguar and had thence returned to the garage in the same vehicle. Now after settling the sexual tension inside the garage, he swapped the modified car with Huritt's authentic Jaguar and went to pick him up at *Arc de Triomphe.*

CHAPTER 70

September 27, 1992

'Pa, where are you? I need to talk to you. Pa!' *The door is open. He should be...* 'Pa! Is Mama home yet?' screamed Nahiossi as he looked around the house. He went to the kitchen, the dining room, the master bedroom and then to the bathroom. 'Pa! Are you in the shower?'

Nahiossi pressed his ear against the brown door and listened to the familiar sound of the water-squirt. He knocked the door once and then called out to his father yet again. But there wasn't any response.

'I'm coming in!' said Nahiossi and waited for a 'Wait up, I'll be right there'. But nothing like that happened. *The sound is... unvarying. If Papa is showering then there has to be...*Nahiossi unlocked the door and slowly entered inside. 'Pa? Are you all right?' he asked nervously and inched closer to the curtain. *He isn't standing. He is... sitting? Why is he not answering?*

'Pa?' said Nahiossi and drew the curtain open. He timidly looked at his injured father and screamed. He then looked on the other side and found his mama, naked, just like he had seen her a few minutes ago, only now she was with his papa and she looked badly hurt. But Nahiossi didn't care about her. He just wanted his papa to be okay. He wanted to talk to his father, to tell him that he was scared and that he needed a hug, a warm embrace that would make his worries and fears go away.

Nahiossi shut the shower off and kneeled on the floor. 'Pa! Wake up! It's me, Nahiossi, wake up, Papa, open your eyes. Look at me!' blabbed Nahiossi as he slapped him and tried to bring him back to a state of consciousness.

Veronica couldn't feel the shower banging against her chest. She felt easier to breath and her legs felt less painful. Her head still ached, but her vision was back. The images weren't distorted and she didn't feel her head weighing her down. She opened her eyes slowly and fixed them on Nahiossi. She looked at her son with remorse and said, 'Nahiossi? Are you all right? Is...is Mark – '

'Shut up! Shut up! Shut up! Shut up! Bitch!' yelled Nahiossi and stood up. He faced his mother with disgust and said, 'you don't love my papa. You don't love me. You are a...a bloody whore! You ruined everything! Look what you did to my papa! You ruined my relationship with Henry! You aren't my mama anymore. You are a disease! You disgust me! I hate you! I don't want to be with you! I don't want to see you...ever! Get out! Get...out! Leave me and my papa alone. Please!'

'I didn't do it volun – '

'I want you to get out. Nothing you say will change my mind. You hurt my papa and that will always remain a fact. Nothing will change it. Now please, just let me be with my papa,' said Nahiossi and wrapped his coat around Mark's bare chest. 'Go out now!' yelled the kid who was experiencing immense mental trauma, and hugged his papa.

Veronica simply stood up, all the while looking at her darling son, and struggled out of the bathtub. She quietly walked towards the door and then she stopped and said, 'I didn't – '

Nahiossi stood up and savagely walked towards his crying mother. He clutched her hands, his nails piercing her warm skin, and he pushed her out. He looked at her in the eye for a brief second, infuriated, and then slammed the door on her face.

The mother who had just lost her sanctity stood alone in the corridor and gazed at the brown door. Her mind went blank. She simply stood there, unable to comprehend the debacle of her fate, and simply stared at the door.

Meanwhile Nahiossi walked towards the cupboard, retrieved the first-aid kit and walked towards his papa.

A few moments later, Veronica absent-mindedly shifted her gaze off the door and walked in to the drawing room. She headed straight towards the telephone and dialed Vincent.

'Hel – '

'I'm not a whore. I'm not a bitch. Tell that to my baby. Take care of my love,' said the despised mother, her voice strong and confident. She didn't listen to whatever Vincent said. She simply dropped the phone on the cradle. She looked at the phone for a couple of seconds and saw the three-year-old Nahiossi holding the teak wood telephone stand and struggling to stand up, as the poop in his diaper weighed him down. *Yucky, Mama, yucky.*

Veronica then lifted her head and saw the five-year-old Nahiossi, gracefully sleeping on Mark's stomach, as she cradled her dear husband's head on her lap. The three of them were watching a video of Nahiossi's first words. She was running her fingers through Mark's hair and was eating ice cream. Chocolate ice cream. She remembered it vividly. She saw herself and Mark laughing like crazy, looking at the one-year-old Nahiossi crying each and every time Mark picked him up. She smiled at the merry illusion and turned her gaze towards the entrance, the door through which the school-going Nahiossi would enter the house, every evening, Monday through Thursday, shouting 'Mama! I'm home and I'm very hungry!' *He was always hungry! Fatty pie!*

She tied her hair in a knot, just like the Veronica on the couch, and walked into her bedroom. She saw scented candles and a bottle of champagne on the table that Mark had built himself, and then saw a steamy Veronica and a passionate Mark making love to each other. It was the very night they moved into #34 Voorburwal. The plastering on the ceiling kept falling, every now and then, and their old cot was making the loudest squeaks ever. Loud enough to wake baby Nahiossi in the adjoining room.

She brushed her hand against the satin bed cover and then put on a dress that Mark had gifted her on the day before they'd married. She got dressed in it and looked at herself in the mirror. *'Veronica, my love. Now that we are here together, there is not one regret in my life. You cannot imagine how much I love you…how much I want to be with you. We will build a family. We will raise Nahiossi to be the person we aren't. We are going to be great together. I promise.'*

She looked at the clock and realised that she had only a few minutes before Vincent would show up at their doorstep. So she quickly looked at her reflection in the mirror for one last time and walked out of the room.

She then turned right and walked towards the adjoining room. Once there, she stood at the threshold and saw Nahiossi telling her, 'Mom, I'm not a kid anymore. I need some privacy. Don't enter my room without knocking!' *My baby is such a grownup! He'll do fine. He can take care of himself.*

She then turned around and walked to the kitchen. She saw herself burning her hands while cooking *Slavink,* her favorite dish…

As Nahiossi applied iodine tincture on his father's face, Veronica entered the bathroom. She looked at Nahiossi tending to his father and she smiled at the sight of having seen the two most important men in her life.

The iodine reacted with the wound and caused a burning sensation. Mark's face twitched and his lips split. 'Papa! Papa! Papa is waking up! Papa is fine!'

'Ver – Veronica,' whispered Mark and stretched his hands towards his dear wife. He didn't hear what Nahiossi had to say. He just opened his eyes and saw a haze of Veronica, standing with a knife in her hand.

'Baby, Mama loves Papa. Mama loves you too. Take care of my sweetie pie. Be safe, fatty pie,' said Veronica, her voice undaunted, and slit her throat in one clean sweep.

CHAPTER 71

1:15 PM
Mark's garage

Mark and Ricardo grievingly watched the tragic news of Huritt's accident on Mark's timeworn television, as Lucy started blankly at the faded wallpapers.

God, please help me. Please forgive my sins and protect me. Keep my child alive, thought the woman who was shocked and mentally disrupted by Mark's profanity and barbaric behaviour.

Ricardo had been considerably good to her. He had picked up a bedspread off Mark's dusty cabinet and had put it over her shoulders. *Women deserve to be treated with respect.*

'Well, what – '

'– I'm going to the hospital, Marky. I have to go. Now while I am gone, should there be any problem, I repeat, any problem to that little girl, I will have you killed right here, in this very room. Do you get it?'

1:30 PM
The Fermont Hospital

'Keep your eyes open, Huritt. Look, look over there. You made it. Don't close your eyes,' repeated Kramer, time and again...

'Hello, Mark?' asked Sebastian from the hospital phone after his talk with Dr. Martin.

'Yes. I-uh, I just saw the news, its-it's terrible. Is he alright?'

'Well, Dr. Martin says that Huritt will be fine by the evening. So I'm just waiting for him to regain his consciousness.'

'Oh! Okay, good. That's good. So what are we to do now?' asked a fidgety Mark, as he was sitting by the phone in the drawing room and watching the news on EUN.

'Um, I don't know. You and Ricardo just watch over *her*. Don't let her out of sight. Okay?'

'Well, Ricardo went right away to the hospital right after we saw the news. I-I'm alone with Lucy now.'

'What! Why is he coming here? Shit! She is afraid of you and if you don't...she might be suspicious. Damn! I'll ask Oscar to be at your garage in fifteen minutes. Don't stay inside the house. Stay outside until Oscar comes over.'

'Uh-okay.'

Sebastian hung up on Mark and immediately called Oscar at his residence.

CHAPTER 72

Being an international attorney, Sebastian travelled to many countries and trialed in many courts. An old couple had once asked him to prosecute against Mark on the charge of accessory to murder. It so happened that the old couple's bachelor son, aged 40, was killed in a car accident. The person driving the car claimed that there was a malfunction in the braking system and claimed that it was the mechanic's fault for not fixing it. Thus a suit was filed against Mark (mechanic) and Rosario (driver) on the charge of accessory to murder and murder respectively. Mark claimed that he wasn't liable as he had properly fixed it, and he blamed the driver for applying more than the required pressure. Upon investigation, Sebastian arrived at the conclusion that Mark had intentionally cut the brake wire. He then went to Mark and asked for a confession. Mark initially resisted. Sebastian then explained to him that he had sufficient evidence to prove his guilt and assured him that he could guarantee a prison sentence for a minimum period of twenty years. But Sebastian also offered to get Mark off the hook if he agreed to help him with an ordeal in France.

CHAPTER 73

June 20, 1979
Oscar's residence

1:40 PM

'What? I'm busy right now!'

'Listen, I need you to go down – '

'I'm already down at the – '

' – to Mark's. Listen!'

'No, you listen! I need to be with my breathtaking wife for some time. She is leaving for London this evening.'

'So you two were...'

'Yes! We are still. So could you please stop calling me? I'll call you when I'm done.'

'Okay, make it quick.'

'Well my wife says otherwise.'

CHAPTER 74

Mr. Walter Isak had made an oral (nuncupative will) and a conditional will in the presence of Roger Drake, the condition being that 25 years from the day of his death, his heir, Philip Isak, would be entitled to claim his right over 600 million pounds.

Once the money would land up in Philip's pocket, his lawyers would claim that the wealth amassed by Walter was not self-earned, but humbly given to him as a gift, by the Jews and the then-government, recognising and honouring his services in extending food and shelter to the endangered Jews and the Allies, in aiding the Allies to establish communication links, in providing a safe transport across borders, in harbouring the undercover agents and in extending support with supplying food, ammunition and other such war commodities.

On 27 February 1944, when the Jews bombed the British income tax offices, the records pertaining to the exemption of taxes from Walter Isak's gift fund were destroyed. Following his death in 1954, the money was transferred to a Testamentary Trust, which is a trust established under a Will, but it does not come into effect until after the death of the person making the Will or the Testator. The Trust was supposed to be secretive about the money and was required to safeguard the money until it was passed on to the rightful heir.

Of the two witnesses, one had very recently passed away and the other one was an advocate. The money was now transferred to the Bank of England and the Will, was executed legally at the registrar's office. Death and Attorney/Client privilege kept the government from asking too many unwelcoming questions.

And so the witness and the testator transferred the money from the trust to Mr. Philip Isak.

Six hundred million pounds in black money was elegantly being converted into foul white money.

Philip would eventually establish two hotels by spending a part of the money. Then Philip and Morgan would marry, and the entire would again go to Morgan.

The witness and testator would never say anything about the fraud, thanks to the attorney/client relationship, and the government wouldn't comment much until the money was inside the country.

Again, mischief managed.

CHAPTER 75

The Fermont Hospital

Ricardo walked past Sebastian and entered the ICU. He stood in front of Huritt's bed, in despair and shock, staring at the *Patron*.

The man from *Banshee* had always liked Huritt, and the two of them were extremely close to each other. They brought to the fore a fine example of the fact that in true friendship, richness doesn't really matter. Sebastian knew that Ricardo had walked past him and yet he remained seated. He simply wanted to give him a few alone minutes with Huritt.

Meanwhile inside the room, Ricardo undid his mask and walked closer to Huritt. He lightly brushed his hand on the *Patron's* scarred face, as tears began to well up in his puffy eyes.

Three minutes after the man with the surgeon's costume had entered the room, Sebastian stood up from the black fixed metallic chair in the lobby. He slowly walked inside the ICU, and put his hands on the gluttony maintenance truck driver. 'The doctor said that he'd be fine soon. There is nothing for us to worry about.'

'But this was...this was unexpected. This, this wasn't a part of our plan. Wh-What do we do now? What about tomorrow's plans? What about the Registrar's office, what about –'

'Well, Ricardo – '

'Australia, Eloy – '

'Ricardo, just – '

'Lucy and the money – '

'Just listen to me!' yelled Sebastian madly and added, 'I know this is bad, Ricardo. But Huritt wouldn't want us standing here and talking whether or not we can go ahead with the plan. We need to act, Ricardo. We have a plan. An elaborate plan. One which we have practiced so extensively. We can't afford to see our plan crumble in front of our very eyes. Buck up now! Don't be an emotional wreck!'

'Emotional wre – you are out of your fucking mind!'

'Ricardo, Huritt isn't dead. Not yet. He is badly hurt, terribly hurt, I agree. But that doesn't mean we shouldn't move ahead with our plans…his plans. We still are a team. We need to work together and we have to keep the ball rolling. We can't just let it stop!'

'What do you want me to do now?'

'I want you to return to the garage. At all times, I want two people to stay with Lucy. She is highly intelligent and cunningly manipulative. She can't manipulate two of us at a time. But one, she definitely can manage.'

Ricardo stayed muted for a while. He slowly comprehended the situation and then said, 'Fuck! Mark is alone with … '

'It's okay; I've asked him to step out of the garage.'

'Okay. I-I'm sorry. I just wanted to...'

'I understand. I really do. But I want you to go back – '

' – Yes, I'm leaving now. Just, um, just keep me upda…take care.'

'And Ricardo, before you leave, I just want to make clear that I trust all four of you. Equally. It's just that I –'

'You think in the best interests of Huritt. I get it.'

'Yes. Okay so Felix and I will stay here at the hospital. He'll keep an eye on Huritt, and I on him. You, Mark and Oscar stay at the garage till dawn. Adjust your sleeping pattern so that at all times, at least two of you are with Lucy. Is that clear?'

'Perfectly!'

7:00 PM

'Lucy, is that you?'

'Uncle Eloy – '

' – Where are you? Where...how did you disappear? I have an entire team looking for you!'

'Don't worry, Uncle Eloy, I'm safe. Now I want you to call off the investigators and to make no attempts to trace this call. Father had bestowed upon me a very important ordeal that *had* to be executed on the day before my anniversary. I really can't and shouldn't disclose the details to you. So, I'm sorry. I'll explain everything at the Registrar's office tomorrow.'

'How do you know about tomorrow?'

'I found my way out of the room through a secret door,' said Lucy and hung up.

Mark again escorted Lucy back inside, as Oscar drove the car to *Gare de Lyon.* He abandoned the timeworn car with the phone at the station's parking lot and then hailed a cab to *Avenue de Gravelle.*

CHAPTER 76

June 21, 1979
The Registrar's office
Paris, France

9:30 PM

Eloy, Sebastian, Justice Franklin, Adrian, Ethan, Robert Gustav and three other "disinterested" witnesses were assembled at the Registrar's office to see through the transition of the prodigious Fermont conglomerate.

At 9:15 AM, Felix escorted Lucy to the registrar's office. The news that Lucy had mysteriously vanished from *Château de la Fermont* was made aware only to a select few members and clear instructions were given to the investigators that the media should not be informed about the peculiar act.

The doors and windows were bolted from the inside, there were no signs of breaks or patches on the walls, the ceiling and on the ground, there were grilled windows in the bathroom, no one saw Lucy exiting the mansion, there appear to be no signs of struggle and no attempt was made by Lucy or anyone to alert the security. We sure have a lot of leads!

'Lucy…what-how did you…how did the ordeal – ' asked Eloy, perplexed, as he met his niece at the doorstep.

'Later, Uncle Eloy. After the registration,' she said, walking briskly into the office.

Sluggish-faced, silver-haired and rough-voiced Justice Franklin, her father's childhood friend and the testator of the Will, had stood by Sir Fermont throughout his career, even when he was assassinated on the 15th of May 1979. Sir Fermont had always trusted him more than any of his colleagues, and so had entrusted him with the responsibility of the execution of his final will and testament.

'What happened to you yesterday?' asked Franklin as she entered the office.

'Well…nothing, actually. Just…magic.'

'Lucy! Come, my dear. I'm so glad to see you! I was so worried!' said Sebastian and hugged her. He didn't want her to chat with Franklin for long.

Bastard. Cheater. Traitor! Lucy thought as she forcefully hugged the cunning lawman.

Lucy then looked at Felix, who was standing at the doorstep in Sebastian's line of sight. A few meters away from Felix, Mark was seated in his car, with his hands on the phone. Upon Sebastian's and hence Felix's signal, Mark was to call Oscar, who in turn was ordered to murder Camila. Lucy looked at her pawn for seven seconds and slightly nodded her head.

'Why the hell did you kidnap Camila?'

'We needed a "fail-safe". You know, I've heard you are quite intelligent and…manipulative. So for us to control you, we need some leverage.'

'You already do! My baby, the photos!'

'The more the merrier, wouldn't you say?'

'How can I trust you?'

'Do you have any other choice? My dear, you are at the receiving end. I have nothing to lose. So just do as you have been told. Don't try to act smart.'

'I've scrutinised the entire document in the presence of Sebastian and Robert. I am convinced that this will is authentic and the provisions mentioned by Sebastian's client are legally valid. As you are well aware, Mr. Eloy, Sir Edgar Fermont's nephew was the benefactor of the will, and he has suitable evidence to show that all the demands mentioned by Sir Fermont in his will has been thoroughly satisfied to the very last sentence. So I would request you all to verify the clauses and amendments, and stand as witnesses to this execution,' said the registrar in his usual well-rehearsed style.

'Sure, sir. Definitely,' said the two witnesses from the registrar's office, in addition to those who had come with Eloy.

Lucy remained muted. She was asked not to speak unless and until it was necessary and she followed the instructions. She had to. There were far too many lives at stake.

One of the witnesses scrutinised the papers concerning the attestation on the will, making Lucy the sole inheritor of nearly one billion American dollars. The second witness verified the power of attorney given to Huritt. The third surveyed the amendments made by Lucy to Sir Fermont's will and the fourth witness reviewed the validity of the aforementioned conditions listed in the will.

1. The couple, Huritt Achak and Lucy Fermont Achak shall live in harmony for one full year, with effect from the 20th of June 1978.
2. With regards to the above-mentioned condition, I accredit Eloy Dufort ...

Forty-five minutes after the meeting had commenced, the auditing was concluded and the concerned parties were asked to step forward and sign the necessary documents, thereby transferring everything therein to Lucy Fermont Achak.

'Justice Franklin Gaubert,' called the usher.

Justice Franklin stepped forward and sat in front of the registrar.

'Is this Sir Edgar Fermont's final will?'

'Yes,' replied Justice Franklin, loud enough for all the five witnesses to hear. Of those five witnesses, Ethan, Adrian and Arthur had stood witness on the day after Labour Day, a year before, when Sir Fermont signed his final will & testament. They knew the will inside out and they knew that Lucy was the rightful heir in all respects.

'I, Ethan Margot, testify the validity of Justice Franklin's statement.'

'I, Adrian Pierrick, testify the validity and authenticity of Sir Edgar Fermont's will.'

'Mr. Franklin, have you read the will in its entirety and do you understand everything therein?'

'Yes sir, I do,' replied Gaubert, as Doriane, one of the five witnesses, recorded the proceedings with a dictaphone, and Candice jotted down the verbalised statements on the registrar's official pad.

'Does it dispose of Sir Edgar Fermont's client's property in accordance with his wishes?'

'Yes, Sir, it does.'

'Do you request Adrian Pierrick, Ethan Margot, Doriane Yann, Cadice Gagnon and Arthur Herriot to witness the signing and execution of the will?'

'Yes sir, I do.'

'Ladies and gentlemen, I now ask the testator, as mentioned by Sir Edgar Fermont, to sign the will.'

The registrar turned the thick stack of the papers towards Franklin, who signed the will and fulfilled the promise he had made to Sir Fermont.

Rest in peace, Eddie.

'On the second day of May in 1978, the preceding document was signed in sound mind by Sir Edgar Margaux Fermont, and he requested us, Adrian Pierrick, Ethan Margot & Franklin Johan Gaubert, to act as witnesses to it and to his signature therein. He then signed the will in our presence, with Franklin Johan Gaubert being officiated as the testator. We now, as per his request and in the presence of each other, hereunto subscribe our names as witnesses, and each of us declare that in his opinion this testator is of sound mind,' read out the notary, Adrian, while Ethan nodded in agreement to the same. 'In addition to Adrian Pierrick, Ethan Margot and Franklin Gaubert, we have called upon the public notary, Arthur Herriot, assistant DA, Doriane Yann and Candice Gagnon, a medical practitioner, to be present as supplementary witnesses.'

Once the announcement was done, Lucy, Eloy, Sebastian and a few other invitees from the Fermont family who had the opportunity to contest were asked to do so by stepping forward and stating their case. But no one came forward to contest. It was quite frankly impossible for anyone to claim or contest against the validity of Sir Fermont's will and its provisions.

So upon the usher's summons, each witness stepped forward, signed and wrote their addresses next to their signatures. The registrar, Serge, authenticated the same and as per the court order, he was ready to execute Sir Fermont's final will and testament.

'Thank you, Justice Franklin,' said the registrar and adjourned him. 'Please, take your seats, ladies and gentlemen,' he continued, directing the usher to call the benefactors.

The two benefactors, Eloy and Sebastian, produced the documents to support the fact that Huritt and Lucy, as per the statutory conditions, had lived in harmony together as a congenial couple for the stipulated period.

'Franklin, you will keep the Will with you, wherever you think it is safe, until the 21st of June 1979. Eloy, you give this affidavit to Sebastian and tell him to draft a deed. Franklin, assist Sebastian with the draft and once that is done, I don't want you to linger around the Chateau or any other enterprise of the Fermont conglomerate. No one should know about the Will or about the provisions mentioned in the Will until and unless each and every condition is met...

The true identity of a person can be known only when he is alone. Make that bastard believe that, but never stop spying on him. Franklin, see to it that Eloy is promoted to detective inspector, it will be easier for him to do the same job both on and off official duty. Covey whatever I've told you to Adrian and Ethan. Bind them by an oath...

Eloy, you and Sebastian are responsible for keeping Frank updated. I want the two of you to send him your reports on every weekend...

Eloy, convey whatever I've told you to Sebastian.'

'Uncle Edgar, I see that you don't trust Huritt. So why not just stop them from getting married?'

'Love.'

Eloy and Sebastian signed mechanically on innumerable pages. The signatures were cross-referenced by the witnesses, after which Justice Franklin and the other witnesses duly attested it.

The registrar, as a general custom, asked for Robert Gustav's word on the authenticity of the will. Robert, M.Sc., C.Chem., F.R.S.C., F.S.Soc. Dip., F.A.E, R.F.P. was the chief forensic handwriting expert and document examiner for *Préfecture de Police de Paris*. He quickly sifted through the documents and unequivocally verified the authenticity.

Finally Lucy Fermont Achak was called forward and asked to sign the will, bestowing her the entire property therein.

'Madame, it is not the question of your life alone. It is the question of eight innocent lives. Yours, your baby's, Camila's, mine, my father's, my mother's, my sister's and my brother's. Well, not just lives, it is also a question of the name and regards of the Fermont family. The photographs I mean.'

'Yes, I understand, Felix. But I don't know what I'm supposed to do!'

'Well, just do as he says. We'll prove that we were being threatened once he sets us all free.'

'What can we possibly prove? I don't get it. Tomorrow, I'll be getting 85% of the property. He wants me to give him the Chateau, and the rest of the property to our close associates. Well, that would have happened anyway. Why abduct me? Why threaten me? Why torture me? I mean, you know what I mean.'

'I do. But he has the reputation of being a complicated spook.'

Almost two hours after they had arrived at the court, Lucy signed on the final page and she was now the legal heir of the Fermont family.

'Congratulations, my dear,' said her uncle and brushed her hair.

'God bless you, doll,' said her aunt and hugged her.

'Way to go, sis!' babbled her cousin. 'Wanna party tonight?'

'Sorry for *spying* on you, Lucy, I just did what your father asked me to,' said Eloy.

'Your father will be proud of you,' said Franklin.

'All the best for your future endeavours, Dame Lucy,' conveyed Ethan.

'I hope you'll raise the family banner to a far greater height,' offered Adrian.

'At your service, my Dame,' deposed Arthur.

'Sir Fermont was a great man, make him prouder,' advised Serge.

'Hope the baby will grow up to be just as charming,' wished Doriane, while Candice smiled and shook hands with Lucy.

The usher, security guards and all other workers at the registrar's office greeted her, and at the end, Sebastian walked towards Lucy and said, 'Quick, let's get this over with!'

A minute later, two photocopies of the executed will were taken and duly signed and sealed, with the word "COPY" running across each page. One was handed over to Lucy and the other one was submitted to the archives. A couple of affidavits were signed and the will was again handed over to Justice Franklin.

Finally Lucy signed affidavits, giving Huritt the power of attorney and the right to buy/sell the Fermont establishments. Even though the affidavit attracted the frowns of many, nobody could do anything about it. Dame Lucy was the new Fermont and they had to accept her decisions. There was no other option.

12:00 PM.

'Felix, we made it!' shouted Lucy and sprinted towards him as soon as she walked out of the registrar's office. She fell into his arms, and they kissed each other briefly.

'Lucy...Felix!' shouted Sebastian, running towards them, as the rest of the family members stood on the pavement and stared at the couple incredulously.

The Dame and the Driver quickly ushered a taxi and whizzed away towards *Charles de Gaulle*. Sebastian tried to stop the taxi, but in vain. He quickly ushered another taxi and followed them. A second later, Mark joined the chain.

'She manipulated him!'

CHAPTER 77

'This drug will stop the blood flow through the veins of both of your hands for a short duration of time. Now don't ask me how it works cause I ain't no doctor,' said Felix, placing the vial in her hand. 'I picked it up from a friend at the hospital. They manufacture all sorts of things in there...Well again, it all just boils down to this, trust. If you – '

'How is he going to believe you? I mean, you can just tell him that you murdered me. How would he know? He'll be all the way over in Paris!'

'Well, he obviously doesn't trust me. He'll send someone to verify.'

'So – '

'So I'll have to kill you.'

'I do...I-I trust you, Felix,' said Lucy, and gulped the sedative.

* * *

8:30 PM

The Fermont Hospital

'221 B-wing,' said Ricardo and handed over the surgeon's apparel.

'Thank you, Ricardo,' said Mark prior to disguising himself again. He then walked out of the car, marched towards the B-wing and climbed a long flight of stairs leading to the twenty-first room on the second floor.

Mark loitered for a while, and then the moment he placed his foot inside the ward, Huritt said in a coarse voice, 'Come in, Marky.'

'How did you...how did you know it was me?' asked Mark with awe.

'Well firstly, I heard a minute squeaking noise of the hinge as you tried to open the door. But then it abruptly died and that was when I saw someone shying away from the nurse who was just about to enter the ward. I hence deduced that the person wearing the surgeon's mask wasn't a real surgeon. Now soon after the nurse left, I took the knife from the tray and waited for that intruder to reappear. Half a minute later, I saw the same person scanning the surroundings and making sure of the fact that no one was around. You then scrutinised the ward through the transparent circular glass on the translucent door, an act that no doctor would ever perform, and again you opened the door hesitantly. In addition, the fact that doctors would never wet their masks, unlike you, made me one hundred percent sure of the fact that you were not a doctor. I then saw the scar on your left hand and the MJ pendant, and thus confidently deduced that the disguised person was none other than...than my apparent self, Marky!'

'But your head was turned away from the door.'

'The mirror, of course.'

'God bless you!' said Mark, smiling at him.

'So? How is everything going? How is our "plan" working?'

'Well – ' said Mark, taking a chair by the window. He brushed the itchy corner of his eye. He then let out a deep breath and said, 'Frasco just told me that Felix and Oscar betrayed us!'

'Sadly so...'

'How did you get to know that? He sent me here to tell you the devastating news!'

'I'd sent one of my men to spy on Felix. He eavesdropped on them and heard all their plans.'

'Plans?'

'They plan on returning to Paris and regrouping at Oscar's farmhouse.'

'Oscar's farmhouse? Why there?'

'Well, with me in the picture, their share would be less than one sixth of the total. But with her, it's almost one third!'

'So she bought them off?'

'I told you. She is highly manipulative.'

'So what do they intend to do at Oscar's?'

'Recuperate. They'll stay there overnight, and then they'll go down to the police station and meet with Eloy!'

'What! Wait, one of our informers had to verify Lucy's death, right? Well, what happened there?'

'He said she is dead. But then again, I'm not able to establish contact with him since yesterday.'

'Which means that – '

' – The answer, is pretty obvious, Mark.'

'Damn! Don't you worry, Huritt. I'll kill him before he meets that bastard. I'll chop his head right off!' yelled Mark.

'No, Mark. You will do no such thing. We don't want to attract unwanted attention from law enforcement. Felix's death will – '

' – No, it won't. The police won't find his body. I'll make sure of that.'

'Are you sure? I mean, they helped us with all the – '

' – It doesn't matter what they helped us with. They betrayed us…they betrayed you. That is what matters.'

'You sure you can do this, Mark?'

'It's what I do, *Padrino*. I can take care of it.'

'I want Oscar's death to look natural. Do whatever you want to the other two.'

'Even Lucy?'

'…Even Lucy.'

CHAPTER 78

June 20, 1979
The Fermont Hospital

12:30 PM

'Huritt, we have bad news.'

Eloy stood beside Huritt's bed and rotated the shaft, propelling the backrest to incline. He then leaned forward and whispered, 'I'm sorry.'

Eloy and Huritt rarely spoke, for he was utterly biased by his uncle's thoughts. His hatred had taken a massive leap when Huritt was accused of Sarah's murder. His hatred didn't fade even when Huritt was found not guilty. The blind belief that Huritt was not a trustworthy and honourable man had made him tyrannical.

'Wh-What's wrong? Is-is Lucy back? Is she hurt? Is she – ' said Huritt, as he struggled to sit.

'You need to calm down, Huritt. The situation demands us to put our brains together…and you are very crucial for us,' chipped in Eloy, placing his hand on Huritt's chest.

Huritt let out a heavy gasp and flexed. 'Okay. The bad news. What is it?'

'Um...' started Eloy and cleared his throat. 'Well…'

'Soon after the will was signed, Lucy and Felix kissed in front the Registrar's office!' said Sebastian sternly.

'Oh!' said Huritt calmly.

Sebastian and Eloy stared at each other.

'"Oh?"'

'I already knew it.'

'What!' exclaimed Franklin, rising from a plastic chair.

'Justice Franklin! I'm sorry, I didn't see you there,' said Huritt and tried to push himself forward, but Franklin stood up and said, 'It's fine, Huritt. No need for any customs here.'

'If you say so, Sir.'

'What did you say about Lucy and Felix?'

'I knew that Lucy and Felix…liked each other.'

'No! That-that can't be true. I-I was played. Tricked. No!' said an agitated Eloy, punching the wall. 'I've let down Uncle Fermont. The two of you weren't…Justice Franklin, they have breached the conditions. You…you'll have to revoke it.'

'I'm afraid that can't be done, Eloy.'

'Why not! Fuck!'

'Huritt, why the hell did you stay with her? You could have told me about…you could have moved out. Why did you choose to stay with a woman who loved someone else?' enquired Sebastian angrily.

'I loved her beyond reason. I never wanted to leave her and also...never mind.'

'What? Tell us Huritt! And also? And also what?' asked Sebastian, as Eloy stood on the other side of the bed, with a poker face, and pondered if Huritt was telling the truth or simply lying. Eloy's qualms were beyond reason.

'Nothing, that's it. I loved her.'

'Huritt?' said Sebastian and put his hand on the *Parton's* shoulder.

'She...she-uh, she used Cortez's name.'

'Used?' asked Eloy suspiciously. *Cortez v. Huritt. Sarah's death.*

'Well you know what I'm saying. She used it against me. She... she used him as a bait to keep me from taking about her to anyone. To keep me chained...'

'You could have told that to me!' yelled Eloy, feeling abashed.

'Really? You hated me! As a matter of fact, you still hate me! Even if I happened to tell you something about her affair with Felix, I'm sure you wouldn't have believed me. Well, no one in all of Paris would have believed me. Hell, I don't know if you people believe me even now!'

'What about the kid she is carrying?' probed Justice Franklin.

'...His,' said Huritt and closed his eyes. 'Eloy, do you know what happened in the court during my trial? When we were summoned to the chambers?'

'No. Of course n –'

' – I asked Justice Lorenzo to permit me to answer the question "Why did you leave her *after* she was pregnant?" at his chambers. Sebastian, do you remember me objecting to take the medical tests suggested by Lorenzo?'

'Yes, I do. I remember.'

'Well the reason for it is...is because I had erectile dysfunction. I was on severe medication. Last month, my doctor told me that my condition has improved, but anyway, if I had revealed that information to the public, suspicions would have been aroused. People would have questioned her pregnancy and God knows what she would have done!'

'No, it can't...Lucy can't...'

'That is what even Sir Fermont thought,' said Frank, scratching his face.

'Should I dispatch a search operation? We can block their passports and alert the security at all exit points. We can have plainclothes – ' rambled Eloy.

'Is she a fugitive, Eloy? Has she done something illegal, something which concerns the security of the nation? Or is she a suspect with the French Police? No! They are in love and she did what she had to do to make their love work. I don't think you can arrest your own niece for falling in love.'

'She-she threatened you. She gave you ultimatums. You can file a complaint. We-we'll ask for a trial. Yes, a trial. That way she has to come back and face us. Yes, that is totally possible. Huritt?'

'For God's sakes, Eloy! Have you gone haywire? That is your niece you are talking about,' interrupted Justice Franklin. 'She is Sir Edgar's daughter! She is Dame Lucy now. She is the heir of the Fermont family!'

'I've let down Sir Fermont. I've been so irresponsible. I completely let him down! I-I'm not fit to be an investigator...I've let...I've not been responsible...I've...'

'And you think that it can all be undone if Lucy were to come back?' asked Sebastian, walking towards Eloy. 'If nothing, it will spoil the name of the family...publicly. And that would upset your Uncle Fermont the most. The situation is now contained. It can be sealed within these walls. Eloy, we weren't assigned the task of dragging this family to the ground...I think Justice Franklin agrees with me.'

Justice Franklin remained quiet. He didn't want to take a stand. He didn't want to commit perjury.

'Let us not brood over the past. What should we do now?' asked Sebastian.

'Just wait. She will try to contact you. She didn't give us a...a proper goodbye.'

* * *

June 22, 1979
Paris

It was 9:00 PM in Australia, when Felix and Lucy finally settled into a small inexpensive hotel room on the outskirts of Canberra, Australia.

Unlike European countries, the Australian hotels didn't demand passports to lodge their customers, so they really didn't have to worry. They gave some proxy details and booked the room for one day.

'I'm sorry, Madam. Th-this is all I could afford,' said Felix wryly, as the bellboy opened the door and let them into a small room on the first floor.

'Felix, you saved my life! I owe you, big time. And, I have been to such rooms. I used to go and stay with Camila during vacations... and um, I really loved my vacations.'

'Thank you, Madam, thank you very much.'

'Lucy, call me Lucy.'

'I-I can't. It'll take a lifetime for me to get used to it.'

'We have all the time, Felix.'

'Speaking of time, I think it's time for you to call your uncle.'

'Okay. Yeah...sure, yeah.'

'I-I'll go get the...kit,' said Felix and walked towards the cupboard. He brought a vial containing a certain liquid, and then handed over the telephone receiver to Lucy.

At 9:15 PM, local time, Lucy placed a call to *Chateau de la Fermont*. Eloy immediately picked up the call and expectantly said, 'Yes?'

'Hello, Uncle Eloy.'

'Don't-don't you dare call me that. How can you – '

' – I'm sorry, Uncle. Please listen to what I have to say…Please!'

'Where the hell are you?'

'We… we are in Australia,' said Lucy confidently.

' – In Australia!'

'I'm really sorry for deceiving you, Uncle Eloy. But…I had no other choice. I love him, as I love you. I couldn't just give up on you. I need you to trust me. I just didn't do it just for the money. I did it for the family. My family. I wasn't tricking you or in any way trying to hurt you. I was just planning on securing my future.'

'Bullshit! You want to reason with me? Okay, here goes. Why did you marry Huritt? He was just as scanty and just as underprivileged. Why this, this unpleasant relationship hoopla?'

'Avril.'

'What!'

'Felix Delacroix Avril.'

'Oh my God!'

'Uncle Eloy, I don't want you to do anything about it. The Avril family believes that he is dead…so likewise, you make the people of our family believe that I'm dead. I'll talk to Huritt about this. He'll do as I ask him to. Now all I want you to do is to find a way to get Huritt and me off the records. Declare that we are dead!'

'Avril! Are you even remotely aware of how Uncle Fermont and – '

' – Were enemies? Yes. I do. But I really can't help it. My *father* was a great logician. Probably the best in France. And as the *daughter* of a great logician, I believe that he would have exempted love from the logical bounds. He would have understood what I wanted…he would have understood my love.'

'Why the fuc- why the hell didn't you tell him then? Why did you hide it from him?'

'Because logic wouldn't allow him to publicise it. If my father wasn't the Great Fermont, if he wasn't *La Meneur homme d'affaires,* if he wasn't the visionary, if he wasn't the People's politician, if he were just another man, just another father, he would have approved my love.'

Eloy didn't answer. He didn't have an answer.

'This will be the last time I'll be talking to you, Uncle Eloy. Please discuss the matter with Huritt and Sebastian. I want you to see to it that the entire conglomerate is sold and I want the monetary equivalent of my property, the property that is rightfully mine, to be electronically transferred to the Commonwealth Bank in Sydney.

I followed every syllable that was stated in my father's will and I'm not at fault. He just stated that none of you should tell the provisions of the will to Huritt or me. He said nothing about what happens if I happened to eavesdrop.'

'Take care, Lucy, goodbye.'

'Have it transferred to Mr. Diego Gonzalez's account.'

'No such thing will happen, Lucy. I'm going to report it all to Justice Franklin tomorrow.'

'I love you, Uncle Eloy. Goodbye.'

CHAPTER 79

Henry read the newspaper on his bed and found out that Veronica had committed suicide. He jumped off his bed and walked out of his room. He wore a robe with shaky hands and he asked the Ox to drive him to Veronica's.

As he reached OZ Voorburgwal, the inspector came forward and greeted him, as did many other people. Most of her customers and employees were standing outside the house and the police were just leaving. No one was allowed to enter the premises, but Henry was an exception. He was immediately let in.

'Are you sure that this was a suicide?' asked Henry to the detective-inspector.

'Well on the face of it, it looks pretty much like it. But we'll have to investigate it anyway.'

'Did she leave any message or note?'

'No, Sir. Her husband says that she slit her throat in the bathroom,' said the detective-inspector and handed over the report to Henry. Nahiossi slowly lifted his face and looked at the person who was responsible for his mother's death. Nahiossi brushed the sergeant's hand away and ran towards Henry.

'Asshole! You bloody bastard!' yelled Nahiossi and ran towards Henry.

'Nahiossi...listen...wait,' said Henry, as Nahiossi ran to him and then bit him.

'You are responsible for her death! Bastard! You...' screamed Nahiossi, holding on to Henry's legs.

Henry's eyes moistened. *Nahiossi...I didn't. How can I explain!*

The inspector pulled Nahiossi away and took him to a room.

'I'm...The kid is devastated by his mother's suicide...'

Henry turned around and dashed out of the house. 'The Magistrate!' directed Henry to his driver and angrily hopped into his car.

'I killed her! I fucking killed her!' yelled Henry and coughed.

'No. You didn't. You weren't responsi – ' said Dillion and looked at Henry through the rearview mirror.

'– I was! I was fucking responsible for ev – ' screamed Henry, in between coughs and spit out blood.

'Are you? *Pa?* Fuck!' yelled Dillion and stepped on the pedal.

CHAPTER 80

October 19, 1978

Sebastian: During my cross-examination, I had agreed and successfully satisfied Mr. Joseph, the security, and the gendarme, to change their opinions regarding Huritt's lies. Witness #1 and #2 were right about seeing my client enter the house, but they didn't hear anything. They have neither doubts nor any confusion. Witness #7 was impeached; nevertheless, I have to clear his suspicions. Out of the other four, satisfying inspector Felipe would imply the satisfaction of Jean. Satisfying Cortez would imply satisfying Dr. Denis. So I am answerable to Mr. Cortez, Inspector Felipe and Mr. Bayol. All of this would obvious satisfy the prosecutor and hence the honorable court.

Every juror and every judge agreed to the same, as Reyes grew hot under his collar.

Sebastian: I would like to call the accused, Mr. Huritt Achak.

The crowd began their jibber-jabber as Huritt walked towards the witness box, assisted by an armed police officer. Huritt smiled and bowed at the jurors and the judge, introduced himself, and was then confronted by Sebastian.

Sebastian: Honorable court, Mr. Huritt –

Huritt: – before we begin, I would like to confess a few topics of interest to my dear friend, Cortez, and thereby to all the honorable people present here. I humbly request the learned court to kindly listen to what I have to say, so that I can try to wavier the false, if I may say so, accusation impeached on me by my dear friend.

Lorenzo glanced the courtroom once and granted him the green signal.

Huritt took a deep breath and began his well-rehearsed speech.

'Well, this is so difficult. My wife, Lucy Fermont Achak,' he said, giving emphasis to the name "Fermont", 'knows that I love her now and that she means the world to me. But back then, during my college days, I loved Sarah. We both lived together, as lovers, for almost a year. Eleven months and nine days to be precise. We lived so happily,' he said, closing his eyes and smiling at the prospect. He then continued, 'we met each other at the Imperial College in 1974. I, Sarah and Cortez were batch mates…Sarah lived with her brother, Bayol, I stayed at the hostel and Cortez stayed at his own apartment.'

'…Anyway, we fell in love with each other in the very first week of college - which we discovered later – yet, we didn't disclose it to each other for almost half of the college term. I never knew what love at first sight meant. I would laugh at people who believed in that concept and criticise the authors who would say something, like "their eyes met and then at the next instant, without their knowledge, they were in love". Well on the third day of college, her beauty and her attitude insanely drew me, and as time progressed, not even a single moment ticked by without me thinking about her. I made a pact with myself that I wouldn't tell her how I felt about her, as I was scared of losing her. I didn't want to lose her. I wanted to see her, talk to her, go out with her and live with her forever, admiring her every move, which had left me dumbstruck from the moment I saw her!' he said as tears filled his eyes.

'I shall have to skip some part of the story, for it delays the court schedule,' said Huritt, emphasising the last two words.

'It is quite all right, Mr. Achak, you can proceed,' said Justice Lorenzo immediately.

'Thank you for being so considerate, *Monsieur*, but I have to admit that I'm becoming too cumbersome. Anyway, the moment that I had longed for arrived at last. After three long years of dreadful withdrawal, in our final year of college, she boldly approached me and asked me out, saying, "You still don't have the guts to ask me out, do you?" I said, "I guess." We then immediately kissed each other, which explains everything therein. After that, we were seeing each other for almost a year, and once we were done with our exams, we moved in to our new home,' said Huritt and saw Bayol.

'That was when Sarah fought with Bayol and left their house. I wanted to talk to him and make him believe in me. But Sarah always resisted it. She would say, "He hates orphans! And also, since your parents were felons, he thinks that you too are a felon. So it would be better for you to stay away from him for the time being. We can live together for a few days and confess the truth when you become the father of my child. He will definitely accept us then. Rather than asking for his blessings now, we can just apologise later." What was I supposed to do, Bayol? Go against her wishes and talk to you? Please be honest for the sake of Sarah, weren't you angry and prejudiced? Would you have accepted me? Speak the truth, Bayol...you owe it to Sarah!'

'Yes.'

Sebastian: Mr. Bayol, Mr. Huritt asked many questions there. For which question is the answer "Yes"?

Bayol: I agree to what Sarah said. I was angry and prejudiced. She was right.

That was quick! I thought he might drag on. The "owe it to Sarah" worked. Stupid humans with stupid emotional attachments.

Sebastian: Thank you.

Bayol: If you really loved her and agreed to abide by what she said, why didn't you come to me once you knew that she was carrying your child? Why did you ditch her instead?

Sebastian: *Monsieur et mesdames,* this witness has been declared hostile. He can't participate –

Huritt: – It's fine, Sebastian. I would like to answer his questions.

Sebastian reluctantly sat down as Huritt continued, 'I would ask the judge to permit us to discuss this particular matter in his chamber.'

Reyes: I object.

Sebastian: Would it be okay if we allow Mr. Cortez and Mr. Bayol to accompany us in addition to Mrs. Fermont and the juror #3?

Reyes just nodded his head in agreement with Sebastian.

Lorenzo: Motion granted. Bailiff, escort them to my chamber. The court breaks for a short recess.

The usher announced the departure of the President and the associate judges and asked the members in the courtroom to rise. The Juror #3 followed the judges, tailed by Cortez, Bayol, Reyes, Huritt and Sebastian.

CHAPTER 81

June 20, 1979

9:00 PM
Oscar's residence, *Rue Jules-Chaplain*
Paris, France

Rue Jules-Chaplain is a street located in the 14th arrondissement of Paris. It is situated to the left bank of River Seine and is home to a number of landmark locations like *Paris Catacombs* museum, *Cimetière du Montparnasse, Gare Montparnasse, Musée Lenine, Musée Jean Moulin, La Santé Prison* and *Tour Montparnasse.*

'Oscar.'

'Sebastian?'

'Yes. Listen, Felix has left Brussels. He'll be here in three hours. It's time for you to leave.'

'Okay. That's great! Yeah. I'll leave in five. So what's the status?'

'Everything looks all right, so plan A.'

'The one where I pick up Mark and then go to the farmhouse?'

'Yes. The same. Remember, contact no one.'

'Affirmative.'

* * *

9:15 PM
Mark's garage

'Mark!' called out Sebastian, banging on Mark's trailer.

'What's wrong? What are you doing here?' asked a half-asleep Mark.

'Shhh. Now listen to me. I've asked Oscar to pick you up and go to the farmhouse. I told him that Huritt asked him to do so. Now he doesn't know that we know. Okay? So try to keep it that way.'

'Okay! But I haven't thought about how I'm going to make it look "natural".'

Since all of this was planned months ago, Sebastian knew exactly how he would go about making Oscar's death look natural. His lawyerly skills gave him a profound understanding of facial expressions and timing. So he just wore a not-so-sure face and said, 'Well, I guess, I hope that this plan works. I have given some thought to it and here is an idea. So – '

'Not here! Come on, let's go inside.'

'Right. So once he picks you up, avoid talking to him. Remember, he is going to try and pull you onto their side, now that the money is in Lucy's hands – '

'It's never going to happen. He'd have to kill me if he wanted to pluck me from Huritt's side.'

'Good to hear that, Marky. Now turn a deaf ear to whatever he claims. Then on entering the farmhouse, go to the kitchen and offer him a drink mixed with this,' Sebastian said, while he pulled out a vial from his pocket and passed it on to Mark.

'What is this?' enquired Mark, intrigued.

'Valium, a Benzodiazepine that is usually used to treat anxiety and insomnia. Doses of these could cause severe drowsiness in the presence of alcohol, increasing the risk of household and car accidents, and in the right combination, it can result in depressed heart and breathing functions. Doctors usually prescribe 2mg – 10mg of Valium taken twice a day. Each time, the drug hits the peak blood concentration at around an hour after the consumption and induces drowsiness, tiredness, dizziness and weakness. When taken in excess quantity or with alcohol, the reaction time is quicker and the effects can be more severe. It can knock down the CNS and cause adverse effects…

10:00 PM

Oscar's farmhouse, Bondy

'Here you go, Oscar,' said Mark and offered him a glass of bourbon.

'Oh! Thank you,' replied Oscar, resting comfortably on his couch and scanning the TV channels. He took the drink from Mark and drained it, as he watched the reviews of the Clint Eastwood starrer, *Escape from Alcatraz.*

'Mark, can you fix another drink for me, please?' asked Oscar.

'Sure,' said Mark and took the glass from him. He went into the kitchen and mixed 100mg of Valium with the drink and offered the same to Oscar.

Just a couple of minutes, Marke. Stay calm, thought Mark and handed over the glass to Oscar.

'I so wanted to watch this movie. Damn!'

'Who is he?' asked Mark.

'Clint Eastwood! You don't know Clint Eastwood?' exclaimed Oscar, sipping his drink.

'Uh-no.'

'The Good, the Bad and the Ugly, A Fistful of Dollars, For a Few Dollars more, Joe Kid? Come on man! Oh-oh, *Dirty Harry*. *Dirty Harry*?'

'Don't know.'

'Man! How can you not watch his movies?'

'No believe in movies. Thrill and excitement forced, not real... no fun' replied Mark sternly.

Oscar showed first signs of drowsiness. His head wobbled, and he rubbed his eyes.

Mark appeared to have not noticed Oscar's strife. He just sipped bourbon from his glass and asked, 'What did you tell your wife before coming here?'

'Mr. Sebastian asked me to tell her that I'm going to the farmhouse and then to Bruda. Told her I couldn't contact her for a week's time.'

Bruda was a village near Lille, located at around 250km from Paris. The village was sparsely populated and the communication systems were still ancient. It had a post office and a telegraph office and the residents hadn't seen a lot of telephones. In case of emergencies, the villagers would go to the government offices and request for their permission to place a call through the in-house telephones.

'Arras?' asked Mark, surprised.

'Yes. We are taking Lucy to Arras. Sebastian and Huritt are going to join us there. Sebastian said that the chances of anyone noticing us are minimal. Mr. Sebastian is going to make her sign some stuff and then I'm going to get my citizenship, as I was promised,' said Oscar, gleefully.

Too bad you believed in this shit. How can Sebastian grant you the citizenship?

'To the Smoke? Yes, of course.'

Just a few more minutes.

The two discussed a few trivial matters for some time, even as Oscar's condition steeply deteriorated.

'How is Ada?' asked Mark, half an hour after he had administered the drug to Oscar.

'Ada? Ada is good. He is good. What do you mean how? He is of course good. Ada is good. Good.'

'Okay…okay.'

'So – '

'Hey, Marky, I-I…I don't feel so good. I…' said Oscar and collapsed.

'Movies fake. Crime in real life good,' said Mark and downed his drink. He then wore Ricardo's surgeon's apparel and put Oscar in a customised coffin.

The rectangular shaped coffin was 9 inches thick, 5.8 feet long and 2 feet wide. It had cushions on all the inner sides and two handles on the shorter side of the coffin.

Mark carried Oscar to one of the rooms and put him inside the coffin in such a way that his head was on the side opposite to that of the side on which the handles were affixed. Then he shut the coffin tightly and carefully locked it. He swiveled a rope passing through the two handles and then lifted the coffin, so that it rested on the face opposite to that of the side on which the handles were adhered. Now inside the box, Oscar was standing in an upside-down position, having the blood gravitate to his head. Mark manoeuvred both ends of the rope on a horizontal wooden beam and hoisted the coffin. Then he tied the ends of the rope to the grills of one of the windows. Now the coffin was suspended in air and the blood began to gush in and saturate his brain.

Mark looked at coffin with a deep sense of pride and in his gibberish English said, 'Oscar, most people put in coffin after die. You die after put inside coffin!'

CHAPTER 82

June 20, 1979

9:20 PM
Mark's garage

'Hanging upside-down for a long time leads to blood clots, particularly in the brain. The clots and swelling in the brain will eventually lead to a stroke. Since the brain lacks the muscles that pumps blood back to the heart, other muscles of the body won't receive adequate amount of blood. Progressively the blood accumulates in the lungs, resulting in a disorder called "Pulmonary Oedema". This leads to impaired gas exchange and causes respiratory failure and cardiac arrest due to hypoxia – a pathological condition in which the body as a whole or a region of the body is deprived of adequate oxygen supply – and ultimately death,' read Sebastian from a torn sheet of paper. Once Mark had heard everything, Sebastian burnt it.

'How long is "long time", exactly?'

'I can't be precise. But it won't take more than two hours. In any case, don't open the coffin until tomorrow. Wait for me to come.'

'So what do we do when Felix and Lucy show up?'

'First things first. We'll think about them both tomorrow.'

'Okay. And, what about the smell? You know, Oscar's dead body.'

'Well, he is plenty filthy as it is.'

* * *

June 23, 1979

10:00 AM (2 AM in Paris)
Dickson, Canberra

'Excuse me, Sir, we'd like to check out.'

'Sure, mate, here's your bill,' said an old man behind the reception desk.

Felix paid the bill in cash, put a fake signature, and then walked out of the hotel.

'Thank you for staying at the Opera Lights. Please do visit us again.'

Never again, Snow White Grandpa!

The duo walked to a local restaurant around the corner and tried some country cuisine. They then hailed a cab to Canberra International Airport. Once there, they boarded the 12 o'clock flight to Brussels, Belgium.

On reaching Brussels, they would board a train to Bondy, a commune in the northeastern suburbs of Paris, where a farmhouse was registered in the name of Oscar O'Donnell.

The farmhouse, which was located at a convenient distance of eleven kilometres from Mark's garage on *Rue de Confians,* served as a prime hub for sensual meetings and as a retreat for the "Stupendous Six". Not once during the many meetings that convened at the farmhouse had Oscar thought that the place would be his grave...the place where his life would meet with the sweet embrace of death.

***

June 24, 1979

5:00 AM
Oscar's farmhouse, Bondy

Lucy and Felix landed at the Brussels International Airport at 0200 hours and then boarded a three-hour train to Bondy. At 0500 hours, the duo reached Bondy and sped towards Oscar's farmhouse in Oscar's car, which was waiting for them at the station, and to which Felix had the key.

Fifteen minutes after, Felix and Lucy were at the doorstep of Oscar's farmhouse. Felix pressed the doorbell and Lucy waited for Oscar to show up, but Felix knew that he wouldn't. Sebastian had told Felix that Oscar wouldn't be at his farmhouse as his son, Ada, had met with a fatal accident and it was utterly necessary for Oscar to leave Paris and head to London.

'I suppose he isn't at home,' said Lucy worriedly.

'Well, let's hope you are wrong!' said Felix and knocked on the door. And as he did, the door flung open.

'I guess he is in the backyard. Well, come on in, come on. This place is my second home,' said Felix, and walked her to her death. 'You are perfectly safe now. You need not worry. Sorry for keeping you from contacting your family members. You do realise why I did that, don't you?'

'Yes, I do. Don't worry, I trust you. And...and please do not use question tags. It reminds me of that asshole!'

'I'm sorry. Um, make yourself comfortable. I'll get us something to drink,' he said, walking to the kitchen. *Why does she trust me so much?*

As Felix entered the kitchen, he walked toward the fridge and he opened it. Sebastian immediately came at him from behind, flung a metal wire around his neck and pulled him away from the fridge.

Meanwhile Mark stealthily went into the drawing room, put a hand on her mouth and neatly cut her neck in one go.

CHAPTER 83

September 28, 1992

When Henry woke up, he was at the hospital with a hundred wires stuck to numerous parts on his frail, bony body. His voice was very faint and he couldn't sit, but he mustered the strength to push the lamp on the table next to his bed. The crashing sound drew the nurse's attention and she immediately entered his ward.

'Call Magistrate Mohammed and ask him to come with the witnesses and everything relating to my will. Quick. Five minutes,' whispered Henry in her ear.

'I'll call him right away,' she said, running out of the ward to fetch the chief doctor.

Once she had informed the doctor, she flipped through the telephone directory and called Magistrate Mohammed. Within fifteen minutes, the two witnesses, a notary and Mohammed were at the hospital...but they weren't on time. Henry had asked them to be there in five.

'He was refusing to cooperate with us, and also, the blood pressure went down. So I had to sedate him and bring his heart rate back to normal. You can wait in the lobby. The nurse will call you when he wakes up,' said the nurse and had them seated in the waiting room.

After an hour of impatient waiting, the nurse came and informed that Henry was conscious.

Soon after Henry saw Mohammed, he waved him to come near him, gathered every ounce of energy and said 'Mohammed. Don't ask me any questions. Just…just do as I ask. I want to make a new will. I want you to arrange for a camera and I also want a press reporter to be here as soon as possible.'

Mohammed sent one of the witnesses to call the chief doctor and the other to call the media personnel.

The chief doctor came in, gave him some medication and made him eat a little something. Just then, the media personnel arrived as well as the camera that he had asked for.

'I want everything that I say to be taped,' said Henry and asked the doctor to help him sit. The camera rolled and the reporter was all ready with his scribe. 'I am Henry Douglas, Chairman of the Roulette Airlines. I am in a sane state of mind and I am under no external pressure. The chief doctor of this reputable hospital can testify the same,' said Henry and pointed at the doctor, who confirmed that he was perfectly sound and free from the undesired effects of drugs.

'On the 11th of January this year, I had drafted a will in the presence of Mohammed, Geert, Anthony and Koopman. I had bestowed all my holdings in the airlines to my only son, William Douglas. Since this is a self-earned enterprise, my lawyer tells me that I can redraft the will and exclude William from the benefits. So now I have decided to leave all my assets, movable and immovable, to Mr. Nahiossi Griffiths, son of Mr. John Griffiths and late Veronica Griffiths, #34, Tuinstraat, Jordaan. At the moment he is seventeen and until he reaches the right age, his father, John Griffiths, would take a place on the board and my company's vice chairman, Benedict, is to assist him wholeheartedly and with no reservation. I thus wish to cancel all the provisions of my previous will, signed on the 11th of

January this year, and wish to bestow everything therein to Nahiossi Griffiths,' he said, as his heartbeat dropped slightly.

The nurse tended to him, while Koopman, the notary, wrote down everything on a bond paper. The reporter read the content out loud, as the cameramen recorded. Once everything was as Henry wanted, the witnesses signed, after which Henry signed and added 'In case my son, William, contests for the property, I ask the court to reject the plea, for it is my property and I intend to give it only to Mr. Nahiossi Griffiths.'

The media personnel agreed to send a copy of the same to every news channel and newspaper. He thanked everyone who had taken time off their busy schedules and met him at such short notice. Once everyone left, the nurse replaced the drips, gave him some painkillers and went off to run some usual errands. The doctor checked on him again and was satisfied for the moment. Just before the doctor left, Henry held the doctor's arm and asked him to send in Dillion.

CHAPTER 84

26th June 1979

9:30 AM
Justice Franklin's residence, Xe arrondissement

Magistrate Franklin greeted each one of trio accordingly and ushered them into his study. The room was centrally air conditioned and it adorned numerous paintings by acclaimed Spanish painters like Mariano Benlliure, Vasco de la Zarza, Juan Bautista Monegro and French painters like William Adolphe Bouguereau, Pierre-Auguste Renoir, Claude Monet and Paul Cezanne.

'Gentlemen, what can I get for you?' enquired Franklin's butler.

'A cup of Irish coffee would do, thank you,' said Franklin.

The trio agreed to the same and a minute later, they sat facing each other on an oval oak table, which could seat 10 people at a time. The table harboured a Faroudja line doubler camera and projector equipment, and five telephones. The table had numerous sheets, reports and precedents sprawled on its surface. Franklin pushed aside all the reports in one clean sweep. Both Huritt and Eloy placed numerous stacks of papers on the table as his ONO fixed line buzzed.

'Sir, Mr. Adrian Pierrick and Mr. Ethan Margot are here,' said the security.

'Let them in.'

Similar calls for permission followed, and by 10:00 AM, everyone who was present at the registrar's office on the day the will was signed, with the exception of family members and Dr. Robert, were assembled at Justice Franklin's residence.

Adrian Pierrick, Ethan Margot, Franklin Gaubert, Arthur Herriot, Doriane Yann, Cadice Gagnon, Huritt Achak, Theodore Sebastian, Eloy Dufort and Serge took their seats around the table and organised their papers and jotting pads.

Franklin replaced the phone on its cradle after ordering the security to not let anyone in.

'Good morning everyone, it is emphatically known that Mr. Huritt has been given the power of attorney to sell the entire of Fermont family's property, which amounts to..." said Frank and glanced down the document to make sure of the figure, 'approximately 7.7 billion francs, and we are here to discuss the terms and conditions concerning the same. So to begin with, let us go through the documents pertaining to the Benoit conglomerate.'

Frank and the others scrutinised all the documents pertaining to the Fermont Empire. The Fermont Constructions, the Fermont Hospitals, the Fermont group of hotels, the estates, villas, bank accounts and all other movable and immovable assets amounting to about 9.2 billion GBP.

Almost an hour after they'd begun the meeting, Franklin collected all the documents back and said, 'Everything looks neat.'

CHAPTER 85

5:00 PM

The Fermont Hospital

'She wants us to give her portable cash amounting to seven billion francs! How are we to do that? And what does she mean by portable?' said an exasperated Huritt, as he, Sebastian and Eloy sat hunched at the ICU.

They decided that it was a nice place to talk. Huritt's medical condition was stable, the room was isolated, secure and "bug" proof.

'Gold, platinum, pearls, diamonds...'

'Diamonds? I think Eloy can lay hands on some diamonds,' interjected Huritt.

'Some? We aren't talking about *some,* Huritt. We are talking about seven billion francs!'

'Well, deducting the taxes and the 15% share to the members of the family, you will have to buy approximately...five-and-a-half-thousand diamonds, each of ten-carat and the best diamond on the market!' said Sebastian.

'Probably even more than that. We can't buy the best available diamonds. Rather we can't get rid of them easily. It is like leaving a trail,' said Eloy.

'10,000 diamonds!' exclaimed Huritt.

'Eloy, how much can you manage?' asked Sebastian.

'Well, definitely not 10,000. I mean, no one in Paris can deliver so many diamonds. I can manage a few hundred. That's all.'

'But before we do that, we have to get the money out of the country.'

'And may I ask why?' put in Huritt.

'Well, no company in France is capable of catering our need of 10,000 diamonds... legally. So we have to buy it in some other country,' said Eloy.

'And the government won't allow so much cash to flow out of the country. It affects the national economy, per capita income and tens of other doltish regulations,' added Sebastian.

'So can either of you arrange for the money to be moved out of Paris, rather France?'

'I have no idea. I've come across many money laundering cases, Huritt, but nothing of this magnitude. This is huge. Preposterous. Seven billion francs!'

'So let me get my facts straight. We can't directly transfer the money to Australia.'

'No. The government won't permit it.'

'We can't just ship the money or steal it by any other means.'

'One, it is risky, and two, you can't exchange seven billion francs to Australian dollars.'

'We can't buy a property there.'

'You can't pay the seller in francs. Plus it can't be done without government intervention.'

'We can't buy diamonds here.'

'We can, but it won't cater to our need.'

'How about we quantify the seven billion into…'

'Can't be done. We cannot afford to illegally buy diamonds or gold from multiple sellers. What if someone blows the whistle on us?'

'Wow! It looks quite simple, doesn't it?'

CHAPTER 86

Bibliothèque de sciences humaines et sociales Descartes (CNRS - The Human and Social Sciences Library Paris Descartes)

Sebastian was sitting on a huge mahogany table, with books piled up in front of him. He searched the contents consisting of various research papers, journals and textbooks, and made a note of the key facts on his jotting pad.

The European Economic Community (EEC) was established with the idea of bringing about economic integration, including common market, among its members (Belgium, France, Germany, Italy, Luxembourg, the Netherlands…

…safeguarding and realizing the ideals and principles that are their common heritage and facilitating their economic and social progress…

He then moved on to another pile and got a few law books. He briefed himself with the contracts, ownership deeds; transfer of shares, establishment of foreign-based companies, tax evasion, money transfer, partnerships and so on and so forth.

It was in this temple of knowledge that Sebastian conducted his research and studies. He frequented the place more than he frequented his office. He always used to say, "The solution to every problem is in our history. You just need to know where and how to look."'

8:00 PM.
Sebastian's condo, La rue Joseph-Kessel.

'Good evening, Sebastian.'

'Good evening, Frank.'

'I called you to inform that every government has acceded to the soft law proposal. They are going to probate it for now, and it won't have a complete legal binding. But nevertheless no one can overrule the provisions of the OECD. The news and provisions are going to be published and aired in every other newspaper and electronic media, starting tonight.'

'Wow! That is, that is great news Frank. Really good, thanks for the info.'

'Yes, it really is. Huh, isn't it nice to see our world coming together?'

'You bet. Well, I-I'll spread the word, alright?'

'Excellent. So…let's have a meeting at my residence tomorrow, say at around 10? We'll discuss and analyse the provisions.'

'Sure, Frank. Um, thank you. I'll be there.'

CHAPTER 87

June 25, 1979

4:00 PM
The Fermont Hospital

'Evening!'

'Did you go through the transcript?' asked Sebastian.

'Yes. But before that, I have something to say. I contacted my... my agent, and I can arrange for about 500 diamonds. No more. Just 500.'

'Sounds good, Eloy. But we'll get back to that later. Now did you go through the transcript?'

'Yes, I did. So...what are you suggesting?' asked Huritt.

'I am suggesting that we sell the assets of the Fermont group to UK based companies, buy diamonds from Femhörnig illegally, and then take them with us to Australia.'

'Femhörnig smuggles diamonds?!' asked Eloy, his eyes bulging out of shock.

'Well, yes, they do. And the expression on your damn face is a conclusive proof of the fact that they smuggle *real* well. Now I want you to keep that information to yourself, all right?'

'Well, I'll see what I can do.'

'Even if you choose against it, you can prove nothing. They are too damn good with maintaining their books and you'll be gone before you realise what hit you. Anyway now Huritt, are you aware of the term "Soft law"?'

'No. I haven't heard about it.'

'Well I heard that that was the prime agenda of the incognito meet at *Chateau de la Muette* on the day of the Triathlon,' said Eloy.

'Yes, that's right. So, basically…'

Sebastian took the next hour to explain the concept in detail. As Sebastian began unveiling the provisions of the law, their faces gleamed with happiness.

'…So now, you can easily sell the Fermont Hotels, Fermont Constructions and this Hospital to UK based companies and sell the other assets like villas and estates to the local rich,' said Sebastian and concluded.

'And use the money earned from local buyers for paying off the taxes and other fees,' added Eloy.

'Now you also have to buy a decent apartment in London. You have to declare to the French government that you wish to move out of France and reside in London. I don't know how, but you will have to frame a genuine reason and convince them of its validity.'

'Well I think we can say that the business companies in London are offering a fair price for our industries, and as you said earlier, we are anyway selling the other assets to the local rich. So we are doing this just for the purpose of earning a few extra pounds,' said Eloy.

'And, I'm not going to sell the *Chateau*. I'll tell the government that I want to start a manufacturing industry in London and so I'll obviously have a lot of work prior to the inception of the industry. Therefore I'm going to have an apartment in London,' told Huritt.

'It will hence be easier for you if you get the money in London,' continued Eloy.

'You can then apply for citizenship in London and eventually be a citizen of both countries. I can arrange for that,' followed Sebastian.

'So is everything done?'

'It's just the beginning.'

'For Lucy.'

'And the end.'

'For you.'

* * *

June 25, 1979

7:00 PM
The Fermont Hospital

'Ever heard about Femhörnig?'

'Yeah. I read an article about it in the *Paris Match*,' replied Huritt.

'So?' asked Huritt, as Sebastian showed no signs of continuing.

'What do you think about it?'

'Well, I-I think that it was…it was…interesting!'

'You haven't read it. Have you?'

'Okay, fine! I haven't read it. Now stop beating around the bush, Sebastian. Get to the point, won't you?'

'Femhörnig is owned by Fredrick Morgan. He is one of the biggest diamond merchants in the world. I am almost sure that whoever Eloy contacts will in turn contact Femhörnig.'

'How come you are so sure about it?'

'Have you heard about the case, State v. Gale? The diamond smuggling case?'

'I remember reading about it the newspaper.'

'I can bet a million francs against it.'

'Fine! Guilty as charged. I don't know. I don't read magazines or newspapers. I hate reading. After all, I'll always have people like you to keep me informed, won't I?'

'Well actually, I don't read them either. Anyway, coming back to the discussion. State of Paris v. Gale was the only case that didn't go in my favour. I was the public prosecutor back then and I was quite convinced about nailing him. I had almost sent the defendant, Gale, to his grave when all of a sudden the judge dismissed the case and waved off all the charges on him.'

'And?'

'And guess who bailed him out?' asked Sebastian, spreading out his hands.

'Morgan?' replied Huritt, laughingly.

'Yes! Morgan's nth silent agent!'

A few seconds later, Sebastian regained his composure and said, 'Well, I obviously wondered why Morgan bailed him out.'

'And?'

'And I figured after a year of through spying and research, that Morgan was the conman. He was the head of the world's top diamond syndicate.'

'How exactly did you do that? I mean, if you could do it, even the police could have done it. They obviously won't let someone just steal the wealth away, would they?'

'Thank God, you are at last asking sensible questions. Well I put my life at stake, which the police wouldn't, and I am intelligent, cunning, smart, rich...'

'Get to the point!'

'I worked for Morgan for over a year. I worked at their head office as a legal advisor and I also had a chance to meet him personally.'

'Well, how did he trust you with the company's secrets and then let you quit? I'd never let you leave me.'

'He didn't let me quit.'

'So how come you are in France?'

'Well, why can't I be? I still work for him. I am his French *Vennote*. Morgan wouldn't want to lose an international attorney, would he? He would never let me go. He loves me, literally.'

Literally?'

'Yes. He's gay.'

'Oh wow! Go-good for you.'

'Much appreciated. Anyway, Eloy's agent works under me. So now we can even frame him. We never had anything against him, Huritt. I can prove that he is involved with the smuggling business. We can make him lose that uniform he holds so dear. We can frame this entire conspiracy on Eloy and we can do away with our wealth!'

CHAPTER 88

July 27, 1979

9:00 AM (Boston)
2:00 PM (Cape Town and Paris)
3:00 PM (London)

Ricardo handed over an envelope to Cortez before he boarded his flight back to London, where he would join Huritt and Sebastian at the Trellick Tower.

Ricardo passed the immigration check at the Kimberly Airport and called up Philip's chamber at Frälsare. Philip answered the call and passed it on to Huritt, followed by Sebastian, who in turn passed it on to Morgan.

Morgan called up his South African *Vennote* and asked him if Nathan was present with his client. The South African *Vennote* confirmed Nathan's sighting and signaled Kato, who was savoring a cappuccino at a café just on the other side of the airport, to lead them to an alley, just two blocks away from the Kimberly Hanger.

Nathan, soon after seeing Kato walk past him, ushered his client, Cortez, to move a few paces behind Kato.

Two blocks away, the two entered an alley, where an armoured metal truck was waiting for them. Kato showed Cortez inside the truck, where two heavily-built men were waiting for the professor. Nathan took an oath on their sacred *rooi modder,* stating that Cortez wasn't involved with the police or any other anti-Verlosser agent. Cortez was then thoroughly checked for electronic gadgets, recording devices and weapons, and when found clean, the bodyguards asked for a few papers, following the confirmation of which he was blindfolded and injected with Sodium Thiopental.

The truck went round the city until Cortez was completely knocked out, and then, once Cortez was out cold, it headed towards the mine...to Nkosi's jurisdiction.

CHAPTER 89

July 20, 1979

10:00 AM
Sebastian's office

Huritt, Sebastian, Ricardo and Mark sat in the plush and cozy office that was situated just adjacent to Sebastian's condo, drinking vodka and discussing a few trivial financial matters.

'...As you all know, Lucy is giving me 10%,, that is approximately 500 million francs.'

Ricardo grinned, Sebastian let out a gasp and Mark whistled.

'I've decided to give Sebastian, the highest share...250 million. Who is with me on this?' asked Huritt and raised his hand.

Mark and Ricardo raised their hands high up in the air.

'Thank you, *amigos*,' said Sebastian and smiled.

Sebastian had been the key conman. He was the one who cajoled Huritt to plunder Sir Fermont's wealth. He was the one who educated him regarding the provisions of the will and the provisions that he must omit while telling Lucy about the will. Clause (4), "Further, if the benefactors/court finds/proves Huritt Achak as liable/guilty of any misdeed/crime, then the trustees have the authority to transfer the property back to Lucy. Should it be the other way around, Huritt Achak shall be given 20% as compensation. He shall in no way be entitled to the property" had been omitted when Huritt told Lucy regarding the terms of the will, and Sebastian had validated the same. This minor omission, proved to be fatal to Lucy, and became the key to their enthralling success.

Five years after Sebastian had started practicing law at Paris, he was given Pro Hac Vice in order to participate in a case pertaining to a multimillion-dollar French Liqueur Company's copyright infringement case. He nailed the case and eventually he was given the Pro Hac Vice for almost 60% of the jurisdictions in the USA. The US government, heeding to the request from the French Fermont Family, had allowed him to take up the bar exam. Sebastian cleared it easily and subsequently he was licensed to practice law in France, Sweden, Michigan, New York, England and Wales.

In 1978, when Sebastian was in London on a case involving the death of an American who was allegedly suffocated to death by a stripper's breasts, he came across Oscar. Oscar was drowning his worries in alcohol and was blabbering about the "barbarism" of the London government, which was forcing him and family to leave the country. Sebastian, who pricked up his ears at the sound of guilty and sorrowful cries of people, walked up to Oscar and started talking. A half hour later Sebastian offered him a place in the Fermont Construction industry and also promised to "buy" him the citizenship if he agreed, for the time being, to move to Paris.

After the move he bought Oscar a farmhouse "on behalf of the company" and helped him secure the position of the Project Manager for the Fermont Triathlon.

Ricardo and Felix were with Huritt in the orphanage. So there was no trouble in finding them. But it was Sebastian who managed to make them agree to help Huritt. Most of the planning too was accredited to Sebastian. So everyone agreed that it was fair to give most of the share to him.

'Now, let's come to Mark. I have decided to give him 100 million.'

Mark was more than happy for that. He would have never earned so much if he were in Spain. Not with all his crimes and all the "repairs" at the garage.

'Thanks you so much Huritt… and Sebastian.'

'Now, Ricardo. I'll give you 50 million. Okay?'

'Aye aye.'

'And the rest, for personal use,' said Huritt and asked Sebastian to pay Mark and Ricardo.

'Now, Sebastian, get rid of all the evidence you have against Mark,' said Huritt.

'Sure. I'll go get it.'

'Great…so, Ricardo, what are going to do with the money?' asked Mark.

'Well, first, I'm going to quit my job and go to a far-off place, maybe the Caribbean. Then I'm going to start some business of my own. I'm going marry some woman and live with her until death parts us…who am I kidding, I'm gonna bang every hot piece of ass on the Carribean!'

'I don't mean to bring your enthusiasm down, but just be careful to not attract unwanted suspicion. Believe me, women talk. Word of a rich foreigner going around banging women travels fast and you will come under the radar of people who might con you or investigate you. So try to keep your head low and do your business with caution.'

Just then, Sebastian entered the room with a file full of evidence. He showed it to Mark and then he burnt it. 'Our part of the deal.'

'Yes. Thank you so much,' said Mark and shook hands with Sebastian.

'Now, Mark. Don't be offended, but do you have any material evidence against us? You know what I mean, don't you?'

'I do. Well, it's in Valencia. I'll have to go and get it.'

If Mark's answer was "No", Ricardo, Huritt and Sebastian would have murdered him then and there. Huritt wanted Mark to be alive until the time he was off to London. He needed him to take care of people in case any trouble arose. Now that everything was almost done, Huritt decided that he didn't need him anymore. The payment was just a method to lure him to Sebastian's office, which was totally against Mark's principles. He always wanted meetings to take place at the places of his choice or somewhere in public. He trusted no one. But today money trumped his principle.

'What evidence do you have?' probed Sebastian, shifting his gaze from Huritt.

'Audio recordings, a few video recordings and a couple of other "classified" information.'

'Well, we are leaving to London on the day after. So why don't you leave it at Ricardo's locker at the post office?' asked Huritt.

'Sure. I'll leave it there. I'll give him a call,' said Mark and took the key from Ricardo.

'It's just that I don't want us to…to meet again,' said Huritt and gave a wry smile.

'Okay. But, before I leave, I want 1.5 million in cash, two traveller's cheques, each at its maximum limit and the rest of the money to be wired to this bank,' said Mark, and handed over a list furnishing the details regarding the bank and the account number.

'Thanks for everything, Marky.'

'See you never.'

Now as per the records, Huritt would give 450 million dollars to Sebastian and the *chateau* to Eloy. The apparent reason being that he didn't want any benefits from the Fermont family, and also as a token of appreciation for the two benefactors who had so efficiently maintained the entire holdings of the family for one full year, without reaping any benefits and with no involvement of fraudulence.

Upon Mark's insistence, Huritt signed a bond, bringing to the fore a list of the gifts Huritt had bestowed upon the two benefactors. Mark took a copy of the same and left.

A few hours later, Mark had 1.5 million francs in his suitcase in addition to two traveller's cheques, and also, his bank at Valencia confirmed that the transfer was on its way. Once the money was in Valencia, he would take the money from that particular account and deposit it in a new account at the same bank under the name of John Griffiths.

CHAPTER 90

July 26, 1979
Morgan's diamond mine, Nkosi's jurisdiction.
Kimberly, South Africa

3:00 PM

'Welcome, Mr. Cortez. Good to have to here.'

'Thank you, Mr. Nkosi.'

'So how do you like my jurisdiction?'

'It's certainly better than DC!'

'Did you hear that people? Nkosi's jurisdiction is better than DC!' shouted Nkosi and gave Cortez a powerful pat.

'Come. This way,' said the two-hundred-and-fifty pound powerhouse and directed Cortez to his chamber. The man-who-reeked-of-sweat's chamber had nothing but a table and a few chairs. It didn't give any information whatsoever. No photos, no artifacts, no papers and no phone.

Cortez handed over the briefcase to Nkosi, who studied the contents in detail and then excused himself for a couple of minutes.

He went to his personal chamber and called Frälsare. He ran a background check on Cortez and had his team test the authenticity of the documents. He then walked back into the chamber and escorted Cortez to the tech room, where diamonds vs. simulants test, the transparency test, the fog test, the U.V. test and under the loop tests were being performed to check for the correctness and consistency of the mined diamonds.

Cortez and Nkosi chatted and smoked for a few hours, while the technicians tested for the authenticity of the diamonds.

Nkosi's soldier, as he preferred to call them, returned an hour and a half later, and handed over a sheet of paper to the General.

Stock number:	**LA0165775**
Price:	**$51,493**
Price per carat:	**$10,266**
...	

'Excellent!' said General Nkosi and handed over the paper to Cortez.

'It sure is impressive,' said Cortez and smiled at the sweaty-shirtless-forty-year-old-African-General.

'I shall have the consignment moved as soon as possible.'

'I hope so.'

Three weeks later, the diamonds would be smuggled to fifteen different countries. The USA, China, UK, Germany, India, Australia, Japan, Canada, Italy, Sweden, Brazil, Russia, France, South Korea and Iraq. The *Vennotes* would then sell it to their clients. The remaining diamonds, if any, would be exchanged for gold, paintings, jewellery and any other artifact which dated somewhere behind 1960. These would then be transferred to various bank lockers sprawled across each country.

The *Vennotes* would access the assets in the locker and the exchanged goods would be sold to prospective clients at auctions. The money derived from both the agents and the sale of artifacts would be quantified and distributed among the subordinate agents, who then would wire a fairly decent yet unsusceptible portion of the money to "The Almonte Research Lab" and to twenty proxy accounts in the eight most corrupt states, Michigan, the Dakotas, South Carolina, Maine, Virginia, Georgia, & Wyoming.

The *Vennotes* were citizens with a neat track record. They were men and women from various precincts of society. They worked at major IT companies, or they ran businesses of their own, or worked as professors at universities, as managers at banks, as doctors or nurses at hospitals, as managing partners at legal firms and/or all or some or none of all these professions. There were no records on paper as to where the diamonds came from. The mine at Kimberly wasn't registered and there were no signs of standardisation on them. In case of an enquiry, the fact that the diamonds were smuggled would be revealed. But in no way it would be traced back to Femhörnig. The dealers, at the most, could trace the *Vennotes,* but there was no written testimony or affidavit to prove that there was a sale. The *Vennote* could in no way be convicted and proved to be guilty beyond a reasonable doubt. But the dealer would have to face serious criminal charges. A few of them took the risk, but were never once put under the scanner. Everything was smooth so far and with Morgan's backing, it would be the same for ages.

The *Vennotes* would then visit the different states at irregular intervals of time, withdraw quantified amounts of money and close the account. They would then hand-deposit the money in a long term fixed deposit in the name of Vaughn Fletcher at the McIntosh and Barney's, New York, USA.

The Internal Revenue Service Department is always keen on nosing out the income tax fraud and enforcing the Internal Revenue Code. The revenue department, and many such organisations, are involved in investigating and probing every person, whosoever it may be, concerned with laundering and evading taxes.

If the IRS or the financial crimes enforcement networks or the financial intelligence unit was to investigate the funds received by the Almonte Research Lab during the fundraiser, the donations would be traced back to the *Vennotes,* who would direct them to the source of money. The *Vennotes* would show the legal document concerning the sale of jewels, gold, paintings and so on. The investigation would then lead to the auctions and then to the strangers who bought the artifacts. The auctioneer would then point at benevolent donors who would point at their dead ancestors. And with that, the digging would end.

CHAPTER 91

November 22, 1978

The President sat behind his desk as usual, in between the two associate judges. Juror #3 sat to the right of the associate judge on the right-hand side of Lorenzo. Reyes sat on the smaller side of the rectangular desk, facing Sebastian seated on the other side. Cortez, Bayol and Huritt sat on the other side of the desk, facing the three judges and the juror.

The usher gave them water bottles, a few sheets of papers and other necessary stationery before he left the room to stand guard with a police officer and stop the people from walking in on the discussion.

Huritt: Thank you so much for giving me this opportunity –

Reyes: – I'm sorry to interrupt. But could you please cut to the chase and tell us why you wanted to have a secret conversation in here?

Huritt: – Thank you so much for giving me this opportunity. I didn't want to talk about it in the courtroom because what I'm about to say is a matter of grave sensitivity. Do I have your confidence that this matter won't ever cross these walls?

All agreed. They were all required to keep it a secret. The law required them to do so.

Huritt: Bayol asked me why I didn't meet him once I knew that Sarah was carrying my child. Well the straightforward answer to this question is that Sarah wasn't carrying my child.

Reyes: What does that mean?

Huritt: I was…impotent! I-I had ED. Erectile Dysfunction.

Sebastian: I hope that the juror is aware of this problem.

Juror #3: I do. Erectile dysfunction is sexual dysfunction characterised by the inability to develop or maintain an erection during sexual performance.

Reyes: That is just a truckload of …

Cortez: Do you have any proof to support that assertion?

Sebastian: Yes, we do. A photocopy of Dr. Martin Leroy's medical report from the Alexis Hospital.

Sebastian unbuttoned his folder and extracted the photocopies of documents concerning the same and distributed it. Everyone studied it intently and Cortez seemed to have bought it. Bayol looked a bit confused, one of the two associate judges looked convinced and the President remained passive, just like the juror and Reyes.

Huritt: If anyone here is not satisfied with the copy, you are welcome to call the Alexis and speak to the doctor.

Reyes: I'm on it, if the Court permits, of course.

Lorenzo granted him the permission and he had Reyes call the Alexis. Reyes put the phone on speaker and everyone heard the usual mechanical monotonous tapped voice, after which an official picked up the receiver.

'Good afternoon, I am President Lorenzo calling from *Cour d'assises*. I would like to speak to Dr. Martin Leroy.'

'I'm sorry, Sir, but that isn't possible.'

'We have to speak to him now. If he doesn't answer the phone right now, I'll have to subpoena him,' said Reyes hotly.

'Dr. Leroy isn't with us anyone. It has been almost two weeks since he passed away.'

'Passed away!'

'We are sorry for your loss, *Madame*. I am sending down a few men now. Have your supervisor informed.'

'Sure, Sir.'

Lorenzo issued warrants for searching the records section, bringing the chief doctor for questioning, in addition to the receptionist.

A half hour later, they returned. In the meantime, Lorenzo adjourned the court and postponed the hearing for the day after tomorrow.

'*Monsieur*, we retrieved the documents from the records section and examined it. Here are the reports,' said Juror #3 and passed the original documents to the judges, who later passed them on to the prosecutor's clients.

Sebastian: This is Dr. Bertin, chief doctor at Alexis.

Lorenzo: Mr. Reyes, do you accept the credibility of Dr. Bertin?

Reyes: Yes *Monsieur*, I do.

Sebastian: And this is the receptionist.

Lorenzo: Mr. Reyes?

Reyes: No problem, *Monsieur*.

Lorenzo: Dr. Bertin, could you briefly explain to us the credibility of Dr. Leroy?

Dr. Bertin: Definitely, *Monsieur*. Dr. Martin was a physician at Alexis for over 20 years. He was the editor in chief of *the ED* and a well-respected philanthropist. Here are the official records concerning his employment. He was a doctor of high calibre and his patients loved him. Unfortunately, he passed away on the first of this month. Massive cardiac arrest. It's all in this file.

Lorenzo and his comrades went through the documents and were convinced with its authenticity. They all agreed that Dr. Bertin was a doctor in good standing and that Leroy's cause of death was cardiac arrest.

Lorenzo: Thank you, Dr. Bertin. Does the receptionist agree with Dr. Bertin?

Receptionist: Yes, Sir. I do. He was a really good doctor.

Lorenzo: What do you think, Mr. Reyes? Do you agree with Mr. Huritt?

Reyes: Can't the court have him checked?

Dr. Bertin: Sorry for speaking out of turn. I just want to say is that ED is curable by medicines. Dr. Martin's analysis clearly shows that it was completely cured two months ago, in August. The report says that it took fifteen months for Mr. Huritt to regain the girth and make it functional. So we just have to go with Dr. Martin's report.

Juror #3: I agree with Dr. Bertin. There is no point in having him tested now. The results will be redundant.

Sebastian: If the parental test reports are presented in front of the court and if it turns out that Mr. Huritt isn't the father, would the prosecutor be convinced?

Reyes: I would like to be present during the testing and I would like it if Dr. Bertin conducts the tests.

Sebastian: No objection, *Monsieur.*

Dr. Bertin: As the court deems fit.

CHAPTER 92

July 20, 1979

12:00 PM
La Poste, 15th arrondissement
Paris

Mark had partly lied at Sebastian's office. He had the recordings and other "classified" information at his garage. Not in Valencia, but at his garage.

Soon after the slimy Spaniard left Sebastian's office, he went to a money exchange and exchanged a few of his francs to pesetas. Mark then drove to his garage, collected all the tapes and stacked it all in the truck of a defunct car. He cleaned his garage completely, packed all his personal belongings and bid *adios* to his beloved garage.

The hazelnut-haired man walked out of his garage and hired a taxi to the post office. Once there, he met with the office supervisor and took a new locker. He deposited the tapes in it and handed over the key to the office supervisor.

'Sir, my brother is not in town today and I won't be in town for the next week. But he forgot something really important at our residence. So I've kept the key to our residence in a locker here and I was wondering if you could please keep my locker key with you and give it to my brother?'

'Sure, Sir. I'll keep it where we keep the duplicates. But...but how do I recognize your brother?'

'His name is Ricardo and I'll ask him to show this letter to you,' he said, easing an envelope out of his pocket. 'Could you please sign here?'

'Sure sir, that a good idea.'

1:30 PM
John's quarters
Barcelona

'My dear brother!'

'Hello Mark, what a pleasant surprise! I-I wasn't...wasn't expecting you to show up today. You...you've reduced a lot of weight, kiddo. Come on, I'll buy you lunch.'

'No, no, no... I'll buy you lunch today. I have lots of great news,' said Mark as he hugged his twin brother.

John was Mark's only known living blood relative. When their ages were counted in mere terms of minutes, their mother had passed away and their irresponsible father passed them off to the streets. When their ages were counted in terms of days, they were taken by the beggars and were used to beg money from people by instigating pitiful emotions. When they reached five years of age, a group of four children were allotted certain streets, where they interned prior to being promoted to beg in the trains, buses, local restaurants and theatres. As they turned nine, they were trained in pick-pocketing and stealing and were deputed to the posh localities. Then they were sent to work in factories, restaurants, bars and construction sites. By the time they reached 14, their supervisors couldn't keep an eye on them as they used to do before, and so they eventually lost control over them. Thus they were out on the streets, with no proper food, insufficient money and improper shelter. They finally came to a safe harbour, the Church of Eternal Light, and submitted themselves to the service of God. Reverend Saunders took them in and named them Mark and John. John attended the classes with special permission from the father and stole books for knowledge, while Mark went to work in a garage and stole money for greed. As time elapsed, John was given a job at the post office, while Mark became a mechanic. The former was happy with his job, while the latter liked the job, but wanted to live lavishly. Mark thus began assisting rich people to forge their documents, give false evidence as witness in courts and in transporting weapons across borders. He then ascended to bank robberies, kidnapping and prostitution, and ultimately he reached the top step on the criminal hierarchy. He became a contract killer.

Mark always ensured that his dear brother John never got to know anything about his criminal activities. John worked very hard for the welfare of his brother and he loved no one else in the world. Mark knew he couldn't afford to let him down. And so, he was always a poor mechanic to John…not *contracto de assasino.*

The two brothers were separated from each other in the year 1962, when John was deputed to the Barcelona post office. That was when Mark began killing for money.

All these images entered and exited his mind in quick succession, as tears of the past rolled down his cheeks.

'Those memories, John, they…they always haunt me. The days when we passed out starving, and shivered and struggled in the night, lived in the slum beaten up by those bastards, roamed around the city with torn clothes, scaring everyone around us. I… I dread those days, John. I really do.'

'I know, Mark, even I get those nightmares, and I wake up in the middle of the night, trying to find you and to protect you. But then I think of the days we spent in the church. Father Saunders was so grateful to us. If not for him, I don't know what would have happened to us,' whispered John and wiped his eyes.

'I love you, Johnny,' said Mark.

'I love you too, Mark,' replied John and the two walked towards a classic Spanish restaurant.

'Mouton Rothschild, rosemary-and-thyme-and-olive oil basted, grilled rib lamb chops, roasted chicken breasts with sherry, *chorizo* and two *flan de fresas,*' said Mark, as John stared at him in amazement.

'Mark? What are you doing?'

'Don't worry. I-uh, I made a fortune.'

'What? A fortune?'

'I did a few classified jobs for a French billionaire and he rewarded me well.'

'Classified?'

'I...I-uh, I forged a document.'

'Forged a...what in God's name were you doing in Paris? You've just been there for a year and look at what you've become! This was the last thing I expected of you, Mark! Jesus have mercy,' said John angrily.

'I'm sorry, John. I really am. I did it all for...for a kid.'

'A kid?'

'I am in love with an amazing woman, Veronica, her name is. Her husband got her pregnant and ditched her. I offered to help her look after the baby. If not for me, the baby would have suffered like us and I didn't want that. I want to create a good future for Nahiossi. I committed a felony just once and was rewarded real well. It was for family. It was for us. Please forgive me, John, please,' said Mark, weeping.

'You can't commit crimes under the cover of "family". Mafias fight for family. That doesn't make them good people!' sternly replied John.

'Come on, John,' said Mark, as the waiter interrupted and served them the delicacies.

'If what you say about that woman and child is true, I can forgive you...but only if you confess everything to Father Saunders and pay the penance for your sins.'

'Okay, yes, I will. I promise. First thing tomorrow.'

Both of them remained muted for a few minutes. Each drained his drink and then John ventured shyly, 'I would like to meet them sometime.'

'I would love that, Johnny! I'm going to Valencia today. Why don't you come with me? You can get to meet them.' *Please say you are busy.*

'Well, I am a bit busy around here. I'll come down by next weekend.'

John had asked for a transfer to Paris and the authorities had agreed. At the moment he was being under scrutiny and was shortlisted for the position of assistant post-master. Evidently he could not afford to submit a leave of absence and he could not go back to Valencia with Mark.

'Oh! You are always busy, John! Right from the time we hit the streets! Anyway, what are you busy with?'

'Well, something official. I can't talk about it'. *I'll surprise you when I come to Paris.*

'Okay. But we won't be in Valencia next week. We are going to Rome.'

'Oh! Okay. Great. That is um, okay, the week after that?'

'Sure, yeah, that could work. We'll all meet at the Church'. *We are moving to Amsterdam next week. I'm never going back to Valencia or Paris. Be ready for a surprise.*

Now Mark didn't know that John was being transferred to Paris, John didn't know that Mark had moved out of Paris, and also John didn't know that Mark would be moving to Amsterdam for good. All the three facts were pointlessly trapped in a box of surprise and it would impact them badly.

* * *

8:00 PM
La Roja
Valencia

'My usual.'

'Try someone else, sweetheart, why are you always after her?'

'What's your problem? I'm the one paying,' he said sarcastically.

'Smarty pants!' said the leader of the prostitutes at *La Roja* and collected the money. 'Show me your thing,' continued the eunuch and winked at Mark.

'Huh?'

'Your bag,' said the eunuch, pointing at his black bag pack.

'Oh, yeah, right. I totally forgot,' he said, opening his bag, revealing a few clothes and a few medicines.

'Are you going out of town?'

'Yeah, you know, my work takes me to places.'

'Sure it does,' said the horny eunuch and sent him to Veronica's room, saying, 'Give her a nice ride, hottie. Don't stop until she *begs* you to.'

Mark simply smiled at Ronda and entered Veronica's room. The nineteen-year-old woman of his dreams was sitting on the bed with a baby on her lap, resting her head against the wall and dreaming of a future with Mark and the kid in a far-off place.

Mark walked towards her, with a different reason this time, and woke her up.

'Ma-Mark, hel-hello. When did you – ' she said drowsily.

'Hello, sweetie. I just got here,' he said and kissed her on her forehead.

'How was the journey?'

'Now that I've seen you, it was totally worth it,' he said, shifting his attention to Nahiossi.

'Hello buddy, say hello to daddy...hello, h-hello Naahiosee,' he said, and toyed with the child. 'Nahiossi! Wow! I love that name. I just can't seem to shake it off. Brilliant!'

'It was Estela's suggestion.'

'That-that is so nice of her. Um, could you ask her to come in here?'

'I don't know, you need to ask Ronda.'

'Um, okay, yeah, I'll be right back,' said Mark and walked towards the reception. He then met Ronda and said, 'I'm interested in having a cocktail today.'

'I knew that you wouldn't feast on a single cuisine. So who do you want?'

'Um, Estela.'

'Estela coming right up!' said Ronda and laughed. 'You go in and do your thing. I'll send her.'

'Um, I-I kind of also want you to come in there.'

'Me?' said the eunuch and began laughing sheepishly. 'Are you serious?'

'I need you in there. Come with Estela.'

Mark turned away from her and hustled back to Veronica's room, as the eunuch stopped him and gave him two more condoms.

'I won't need those today,' said Mark and re-entered the room. 'Even if I did do it today, why would I need three condoms? One will do the job.'

CHAPTER 93

Kimberly Airport

The automatic exposure control (AE) SLR camera, FD series lens, interchangeable lens, instantaneous fit-and-lock mount system, desiccant box, file base, film holder, film stock, filter, flash, monopod, tripod, reflector, soft box and zone plate were all contained in a carry-on bag. The customs officer at the Kimberly hanger stopped Nathan upon seeing the bag and told him that he needed to send it through the X-ray machine.

'No, Sir. This can't go through the machine. I have a lot of photography equipment which is not conducive to X-ray screening,' protested Nathan. 'You can check with your authorities.'

The U.S. government started the X-ray scanning at airports only in 1974 and it wasn't until 1977 that every passenger flight going to the US made it compulsory. Most of the countries, with the exception of the US of course, adopted the X-ray scanning only in 1988.

'I'll be just a moment,' said the official and walked towards the chamber of the lieutenant.

He reported the situation to the lieutenant, who in turn placed a call and asked for their advice. Five minutes later, he hung up the call with the FAA and walked out to the security block.

Upon seeing the lieutenant and the officer walking towards him, Nathan lost his temper, 'You are being disrespectful towards an American citizen. I'm standing here like a fool for the past ten minutes! Is this how you treat the passengers?'

'I'm sorry for the inconvenience, Sir. We were checking with the FAA and they have acceded to your request.'

'I didn't request. If you insisted on scanning it, I would have walked back and complained about your dull-headedness at the embassy. Who do you think I am? A bloody smuggler? I'm an attorney at the Boston district court. I am the Senior Partner at Nathan and Nathan,' said Nathan and showed his license.

'I apologise for the inconvenience, Sir, may I check your kit?' asked the Lieutenant, ignoring Nathan's unruly accusations and keeping in mind the fact that he could never argue and win with an attorney.

'Be careful,' said Nathan and passed over his photography kit.

The lieutenant used a metal detector to analyse each piece of equipment and looked for visible signs of danger.

A quarter of an hour later the lieutenant returned the contents back to Nathan and again said monotonously, 'Sorry for the inconvenience, Sir.'

'Fuck you!' said Nathan and stormed towards the gate.

'Where are the *babies?*' asked Cortez, looking stupefied.

'In between the walls of the lenses, in the legs of the tripod stand, monopod stand, in the desiccant boxes, the soft box equipment...'

CHAPTER 94

Mark paid a million pesetas to Ronda and *released* Veronica from *La Roja*. He explained to Ronda that Veronica would never be able to earn so much in her life, even if she worked for more hours, and it would be impossible for him to amass a million pesetas in a single payment. He reasoned with Ronda that a million pesetas would be more than enough to secure Veronica's release.

Ronda, without even a pinch of apprehension, looked at Veronica and said, 'It's good to see one of my daughters...You too... I don't know what to say. I've been in this business ever since my parents threw me out and...'

'You need not explain yourself, Ronda. You are a really good person...you-your parents...we'll tell Nahiossi all about you. We'll come back and meet you soon,' said Mark and unzipped his kit. He quickly drew a million pesetas from it and handed it over to Ronda.

Ronda took the money happily and had it all locked away in his cupboard. He came back with a chain and put it around Nahiossi's neck. It was something he had prized all his life and something he had never taken off. He really liked Nahiossi and Veronica, and that was the only way he knew to show his gratitude, other than rejecting the money, which was obviously never an option.

'Take...look after her well. She is...get out now. I don't want her to see her father cry.'

Freedom is the most essential factor in one's life. Some people say that money can't buy freedom and happiness. But Mark had rivetingly proved the contrary.

On the twenty-first of July, the capital of Italy welcomed the couple and Nahiossi. This was the first time Veronica had gotten out of Paris. All her life she was caged and she lacked care and concern.

They extravagantly spent the next ten days in Rome and visited the Colosseum, Pantheon, St Peter's Basilica, Basilica of St John Lateran, Basilica di Santa Maria Maggiore, Sistine Chapel, Trevi Fountain, Spanish Steps, Piazza del Popolo, Monument of Vittorio Emanuele II and Castel Sant'Angelo, before making their final move to Amsterdam.

CHAPTER 95

November 22, 1978

3:00 PM

Dr. Bertin: We couldn't infer much from blood typing because Ms. Bibiana's and Mr. Huritt's blood group are the same, A+. So the child's is unassailably the same. But the serological testing and human leukocyte antigens typing exclude Mr. Huritt from being the father, the power of exclusion being 80%.

Sebastian: So Dr. Bertin, does this mean that Mr. Huritt isn't the father of Achille?

Dr. Bertin: Yes. He is not the father of Achille.

Sebastian: Respected counsel?

Reyes: I've got nothing to say.

Sebastian thanked Dr. Bertin and showed him off. He then continued to present his case-in-chief.

Sebastian: Mr. Bayol, I proved to you that Achille is Sarah's child and not Huritt's. Now I ask Mr. Huritt to continue. *Monsieur et mesdames,* Mr. Huritt.

Huritt: I would like to answer Bayol's latter question, "Why did you ditch her?" Do you have any idea how hard it was for me to let her go? I hate to vent, but it is utterly necessary for me to say this. I didn't ditch her. I sacrificed by letting her go. Do you know why I did that?

Bayol silently nodded his head and Cortez listened intently, his heartbeat increasing.

'You too loved her when we were in college. Didn't you?' asked Huritt, looking straight into Cortez's eyes.

Cortez remained muted.

'Answer me, Cortez. You loved Sarah, didn't you?' asked Huritt, yet again, not waiting for a cue.

Tears filled Cortez's eyes and he just sat there. Dumbstruck.

'Yes. I loved her. I still do,' said Cortez, fighting the apprehension.

Cortez often didn't speak much. He always answered precisely and to the point. He never exaggerated any issue, be it his personal life or professional life. How ironic for a person who aspired to become a teacher!

'That is why, my-my dear friend. That is why I deserted her,' said Huritt, looking at Cortez, 'sacrificed,' he said, looking at Reyes.

Cortez: How did you know that I loved her? I am sure that I never mentioned it to anyone.

Huritt: Not even to Sarah?

Cortez became speechless on hearing Huritt's question. He remained so for a few minutes, recollecting the events from the past.

'I confessed my love to her on the 24th of May last year, that is two days before our semester ended. I was shattered by the fact that I could not see her anymore. I didn't have the courage to tell her that I loved her, for I considered myself inferior to her. She was way out of my league. However I couldn't resist myself on that day. I knew that I definitely could not have moved on with my life. I knew that I would have always regretted my decision for not having asked her out. Nevertheless I was still afraid of her. It is something that can only be felt, not explained by words. The day before I asked her out, I was told by my Chinese roommate, whom I would never forget, that the great Lao Tzu once said, "Being deeply loved by someone gives you strength, while loving someone deeply gives you courage". So I made up my mind and asked her out on the 24th, only to be greeted by her…I was turned down. She laughed at me…'

Sebastian: Did you write to her after you graduated from the university? I mean, after she rejected you.

Cortez: I wrote to her once every week, eagerly and desperately waiting for her reply.

Sebastian: Did she ever respond in your favour?

Cortez: No!

He bowed his head, felling embarrassed.

Reyes: I want to raise an objection here. I presume that you are trying to tell us that Ms. Bibiana told you that your friend, Cortez, asked her out.

Huritt: No.

Reyes: And if you really wanted to "sacrifice", why wait for eleven months and nine days?

Reyes: How else did you get to know?

'I'll get there in a moment. She never mentioned it to me. She ensured that Cortez's letters never reached my hands, at least tried to. I *presume,*' said Huritt, looking at Reyes, 'that the postman had been tipped to see to it that I never came in possession of those letters. However, fortunately for the two of us,' pointing at himself and Cortez, 'and unfortunately to her, I went to the post office to collect an important package somewhere in the month of April this year, and I got hold of your letter before the postman could lay his hands on it. It was then that I realised that my best friend had avoided and deserted me for this simple reason. All the past memories of our friendship came gushing back to me,' said Huritt, wiping the sweat off his brow.

Let the melodrama begin.

The viewers were up for a play. A few in the audience began to yawn and the media personnel were now seated, their cameras simply suspended on the tripod stand.

Huritt: 'Don't you remember those days, Monte? The days when we were so close to each other, just like brothers. The days when we would bully our juniors and were bullied by our seniors, the days we pranked everyone around us, the days we played, studied, ate and roamed around every nook and corner of Paris, the days when we shared every bit of our feelings and emotions. All the joyous moments we spent together, concealed by the bond of friendship and brotherhood. Do you remember saying, "We shall always be the best of friends, Huritt. We shall work together and one fine day, we shall be the richest people on earth"?'

He gave a break for five seconds, allowing the words to sink in.

Huritt: Answer me, Monte.

Cortez: I-I…remember.

Huritt: But you don't mean it, now do you?

Cortez: I always meant it. It is just that I didn't like you growing close to Sarah, day after day. Do you know how painful it is to know that your best friend, the friend to whom you owed all the happiness in life, was sucking out the happiness out of your own life? It freaked me out! My love for her drove me insane and I began hating you! The more she was endeared towards you, the more I hated you.

Huritt: But at least you could have told me that you liked her.

Cortez: I knew that it wouldn't have helped. I knew that you loved her too.

Huritt: I did, but not as desperately as you. I would have moved on.

Yeah, right! thought Sebastian.

Cortez: I always thought that I still had a chance. She would come back to me if I kept writing to her. She would one day understand how deeply I loved her. I kept wandering by your house and tried to contact her when you weren't there. Later, I found out that even after living together for almost a year, you two hadn't married. So I kept trying.

Huritt: And one fine day, I saw you talking to her.

Neat pickup.

Huritt: I then realised that if I'm not the father, maybe you are.

Reyes: I want to interfere here, Mr. Huritt. I would ask the President to permit us to approach the bench.

Lorenzo: Permission granted.

Reyes, Sebastian, Cortez, Bayol, Huritt and juror #3 approached the bench.

'I just wanted to clear one point. Mr. Huritt, did Ms. Bibiana know about your dysfunction?' asked Reyes.

'No, Sir. She didn't. I hadn't told her about it. As her lover, I knew that she didn't want me know that she had an affair with someone else. No woman would, would she?' asked Huritt, looking at Juror #3, who simply nodded her head.

'According to her, Achille was our child. I didn't want to break open the truth and look at her wail. I didn't want to hurt her.'

'Is that all, prosecutor?

'Yes.'

Lorenzo order them to go back and take their respective positions again. The usher announced the same, and the court was brought back to order.

Sebastian: You were saying that you thought that Cortez might be the father of Achille.

Huritt: Yes. I thought that Cortez might be the father. But I couldn't confirm it. I couldn't ask Sarah about it. It would obviously hurt her. I also couldn't ask Cortez, because he wasn't ready to speak to me.

Sebastian: Mr. Cortez has just testified that he hated Huritt. Do you agree with me and my client, respected prosecutor?

Reyes: Yes.

Sebastian: Thank you. Mr. Huritt, please continue.

Huritt: And I thought that if Bayol got to know about this, he would really be angry with Sarah. The repetitive letters and visits made me think, though I must confess that it was very hard for me, it made me think that she must like him. Even if she didn't, I thought that it was the right thing for a child to grow up with his father. As Bayol said, I had a traumatic childhood and I didn't want the same for Achille. By then, Lucy had proposed to marry me. So I thought that marrying Lucy would either upset Sarah and drive her away from me, or she would happily accept it and go away from me. In any case, she would go to Cortez. She wouldn't go alone to Bayol. She was a really stubborn woman.

Sebastian: Bayol, have I proved to you that he didn't just send away your sister unreasonably?

Bayol silently nodded his head.

Huritt: Once Sarah went to Cortez, they would go to Bayol with the baby, and Bayol, considering Cortez's clean background, his profession and his status, would undoubtedly let them marry each other. Achille would then have a proper future with his able and righteous parents. Everyone would be happy.

Sebastian: Except you, Mr. Huritt.

Huritt: Well, I wouldn't deny it. With my dear Sarah, my best friend Cortez, the nice yet hotheaded brother Bayol and Achille, living together and being happy, even I would be happy.

Sebastian: Now have I proved to you that Mr. Huritt valued his friendship for Mr. Cortez, the compassion to give a stable future to Ms. Bibiana, the desire to consider Achille as his own child and to create a way to make him lead a better and a more decent life, and to make you, Mr. Bayol, content and happy?

Bayol was out of words. His eyes moistened.

Sebastian: And does this imply that he isn't a sociopath and that he truly values relationships?

Bayol: I'm sorry, Huritt. I'm sorry.

Sebastian: Do you believe that Huritt would have murdered his love, Sarah? Mr. Bayol, do you honestly believe that he is the murderer of your sister? We are here to find justice. Not to trash those people who loved your sister. The people who truly cared for her. Do you want this man, the man who loved your sister and sacrificed everything for her, to rot in jail and serve his penance for his crime of wanting your sister to be happy?

'I'm sorry, Huritt. I take back whatever I said,' said Bayol and dashed out of the courthouse, crying.

Sebastian: Well, respected court, I would just like to inform you that so far I have dealt with and completely satisfied five witnesses.

With respect to the other five, can we agree that if I satisfy and account for the fingerprints on Ms. Bibiana's cheek, the inundations on Mr. Huritt's face, the cause and reason for the fight and the fact that she loved him until her last breath, the prosecution's case will collapse?

CHAPTER 96

July 26, 1979

9:00 AM
La Poste

'Here you go, John, your new office,' said the Postmaster at *Le Poste* to his new assistant.

'Thank you, Postmaster Sir. It's a really nice place.'

'Oh, this place is great all right. I got the walls painted and the floors carpeted. This is a fine office. A great one…except for the smell. But I'm sure you'll get used to it. Anyway, I'll be right across the hall. In case you need any assistance, just walk right through the door,' said the postmaster and chuckled.

'I'll keep that in mind, Sir. Thank you.'

'Welcome aboard, sailor. Make yourselves comfortable and… and then I'll show you around the post office,' said the postmaster and shut the door behind him.

John looked around his not-so-bad office for a while. He examined the dusty drawers, the patchy ceiling, the damp carpet, the bedraggled portraits, the icky spider webs and the unorganised files slumped on rusty structures. But none of it bothered him. He was accustomed to it. But the one thing he couldn't stand was the stench. *From where is this foul smell originating?* He thought and curiously toured the room. He looked behind the files, behind the photos, behind the curtains, under the desk, inside the cupboards and after fifteen unproductive minutes he finally gave up.

He sat on the squeaky chair and placed a call to Reverend Saunders. John eagerly waited for the line to be established, but Father Saunders didn't answer the call. *He is probably at the school.*

John put the phone down and stretched himself out. He pushed his legs forward and his hands back. He stared at the ceiling again, and saw a rat, running along the top bookshelf.

He quietly sat for a few seconds and then stood up and walked towards the window. He drew open the curtains and pushed the windows out. *This explains it!* He thought, as the phone jingled. John immediately picked up the phone and said, 'Father?'

'Sorry to disturb you, Sir, but do you have a twin by any chance?'

'Who is this?'

CHAPTER 97

November 23, 1978

Huritt: It so happened that two months ago, we accidentally met at the church. She said that she wanted to talk to me and so she asked me to go to the post office on every alternate day. We exchanged letters and she told me that she wasn't happy with Cortez. She said that she didn't want to ruin Lucy's life, but she really wanted to meet me and talk to me. I reasoned with her that I loved Lucy more than I had ever loved anyone. More than I loved her. But she persisted. I at last agreed to meet her on the 14th of August.

Sebastian: Can we accept this premise?

Reyes spoke to Cortez and Bayol and found no reason to not accept what Huritt said. If they objected it, their last and final solid evidence would become invalid. So Reyes accepted it.

Huritt: Once she saw me there, she was really…really ecstatic. She fought with me, asking me why I left her. Why I didn't reply to her mails. Why I was punishing her…so I asked her to go inside the house.

Sebastian: And that is what Mr. Dominique and Mrs. Absolon saw and described as a "fight". I want to call it fight #1.

Now to fight #2.

Huritt: Once I entered, she dragged me to the bedroom and showed me Achille. She said and I quote "Look at our son, Achille. How could you desert him? Don't you love him?" I said and I quote the same "I love him. But we can't be doing this. I am happily married and I love my wife. Even you are engaged to Cortez. It would be better if you could please tell me what you called me here for". She suddenly came on to me and tried to kiss me. She was out of her mind. I'd never seen her like that before. I said I had to leave. But she begged me not to. She didn't let me go. All of a sudden with a fit of rage and outburst of energy, she pounced on me and began strangling me. Her nails scraped my throat, and that's when I slapped her.

Sebastian: Dr. Denis, thus the scattering of shoe prints, the fingerprints on Ms. Bibiana's cheek, the inundations on Mr. Huritt's face, the cause and reason for the fight. Do you think that this is plausible?

Dr. Denis: Well, I can't –

Sebastian: – Can you change your probability to less than 50%?

Dr. Denis: I don't know. This is just another explanation. Another hypothesis. There isn't any proof!

Sebastian: Dr. Denis, what proof do you have to support your account of what happened inside? At least I have one of the two people who were actually present inside and were a part of it all. Logically, Mr. Huritt's account should hold more water.

Reyes: All the evidence is circumstantial…

Sebastian: Dr. Denis, I have presented an account for the fingerprints, the inundation and the cause and reason for the fight! You yourself –

Dr. Denis: How can we just admit what Mr. Huritt said – '

Sebastian: – said on oath that you would –

Dr. Denis: Less than 50%, fine! Less than 50%.

Reyes: You needn't…Dr. Denis. Mr. President.

Sebastian: What has been once said cannot be undone. Dr. Denis agreed to the –

Reyes: – you tricked him! He was misled. He was –

'Order in the court!' shouted Lorenzo and silenced Sebastian and Reyes.

Lorenzo: Dr. Denis, tell me, do you wish to answer the defense's question?

Dr. Denis: Yes, Mr. President.

Lorenzo: Do you think that the probability of Mr. Achak murdering Ms. Bibiana is less than 50%?

Dr. Denis: Yes, I do.

Lorenzo: Thank you, doctor. You may return to the stands now.

Dr. Denis: Thank you, Mr. President.

Sebastian: Now Mr. President, by the law of implications, it is apparent that all the five witnesses accept the fact that there is less than 50% probability for Huritt to have murdered Sarah.

Dr. Denis, Jean and Felipe assented. They had no other option.

Sebastian: Now I have completely satisfied four out of the five remaining witnesses. But Cortez still appears to be apprehensive.

Reyes: Yes, Mr. Sebastian. We still have one more piece of evidence.

Sebastian: Again, if I discredit that evidence, would it mean that Mr. Huritt is "not guilty"?

Reyes: Yes.

Cortez: Yes.

Bayol: Yes.

Sebastian: *Monsieur et Mesdames,* I have no more witnesses. The witnesses to the events mentioned by my client are Sarah, who sadly is not with us today, Achille, who isn't old enough to give testimony, Mr. Cortez, who has accepted everything said by my client, Mr. Bayol, who agrees with Cortez, and Mrs. Fermont, who already gave her testimony. Hence the defense rests.

Lorenzo ordered a brief recess after which the prosecution's rebuttal would begin.

CHAPTER 98

July 26, 1979

9:00 AM
Trellick Tower, Notting Hill
London, England

The President of the Government, The Ministry of Economic Affairs and Competitiveness, Minister of Commerce, Minister of the Finance, Secretary of State, Secretary of the Universal Bureau of Finance, Secretary of Justice, Political Government & Finance, The Ministry for Foreign Affairs and Cooperation, Subordinate to the Ministry, The Ministry of Labor and Immigration, Ministry of Labor and Social Protection, Ministry Health and Justice, Ministry Social Attendance, Ministry of Agriculture, Ministry of Trade Union Action and Organization, Secretary of the European community and a few other local officers of both France and London had signed the documents pertaining to the sale of the French Fermont Familial assets to London-based companies.

Franklin's ten *compadres* were terribly exhausted. They had slogged for nearly a month and ultimately on the twenty-sixth of July, the long awaited moment finally arrived. Huritt, Sebastian,

Adrian, Ethan, Franklin, Arthur, Doriane, Cadice and Serge were assembled at the registrar's office in addition to the various buyers and their contingent from London.

Four hundred years of family legacy was now being transferred to fellow alien administrators. A few resolute workers and concerned citizens protested, but they could achieve nothing. Their voices were dimmed down and their opinions buried.

Eloy, two local witnesses and a notary were sitting by the phone at Huritt's flat in Notting Hill, as they intently waited for the agents who were, as requested by Huritt, bringing in the money. Upon receiving the money in pounds, they would call Paris and ask Huritt to sign the papers.

On completion of the auction on the 15th of July, Sebastian had apparently taken the documents to Canberra, leaving Huritt and Eloy back in Paris, as requested by Lucy who had apparently called Sebastian and put forth her conditions. But then in reality, Sebastian had handed over the documents to Mark in Charles de Gaulle's restroom and had flown down to Australia empty handed. Mark had then taken the document to his garage and forged Lucy's signature on every document. Then, he and Sebastian ran the same errand of swapping once again, giving Sebastian the documents that were duly signed by Lucy. Robert had no reason to doubt the authenticity of the signature for he had no reason to doubt Franklin's judgment. So he simply approved it.

At 9:15 AM London time, two men representing William & Lloyd Construction Conglomerate boarded the lift to the seventh floor of the Trellick Tower.

The Trellick Tower, run by the Social Housing Council of England, was constructed with a separate elevator, linking the service corridor at every third storey, to the access corridors in the main building. The building contained 217 flats and the floors above and below the corridor levels had internal stairs. The Trellick Tower showed fidelity towards crimes, with rapes in lifts and staircases, attacks by drug dealers, molestation and schemes of other such anti-social behaviour stewing up every inch of its structure. Tenants resisted and detested a transfer to this building, but it made Huritt and Sebastian accept it with open arms.

'3 mills,' said one of the two agents and placed the two briefcases on the dining table, while the other drew some papers from the briefcase. The two local witnesses and Eloy signed it, following which the two agents let go of the briefcase.

Eloy took the briefcases and safely tucked them in the cupboard, as the document was notarised. The notary then called for his assistant and asked her to go with the two agents and get the documents photocopied.

Then, 'We have received the money,' said Eloy and handed over the phone to the notary, who confirmed the same.

The usual errand of choosing, requesting, authenticating, officiating, contesting, signing and notarising commenced, and by 12:30 PM Paris time, that is two-and-a-half hours after Eloy had placed his first call, the Fermont group of hotels were sold to the Imperial group of hotels and the Fermont Hospital was sold off to The Cradle.

CHAPTER 99

The court reconvened. Reyes looked tense, Sebastian was confident, the Fermont couple was as passive as always, Bayol and Cortez appeared to be perplexed, the witnesses were fatigued, the audience was tired, the judges were as passive as ever, and the jurors, well, they showed all possible emotions.

Reyes: The defense's case was really interesting. It made me speechless. It was a good piece of fiction. Now I as well as my client, agreed on almost everything the defense counsel said. But keep in mind that we don't know for sure what might have happened in Mr. Cortez's residence on that particular day. Before I present my final evidence, I just want to go through the witnesses for one last time. *Monsieur et mesdames,* may I?

Lorenzo: You may proceed, counsel.

Reyes: Thank you, *Monsieur et mesdames.* Mr. Dominique and Mrs. Absolon saw Huritt at approximately the same time as that mentioned in the post-mortem. Even the defense agrees upon this. Right, Mr. Sebastian?

Sebastian: Right.

Reyes: The defense argued that the witnesses didn't hear the conversation between Mr. Huritt and Ms. Bibiana, and that their testimonies are fallacious. Now we have two scenarios. One, either we have to accept Mr. Huritt's story, or we have to consider the case wherein she was upset with him and that she didn't want him to enter the house. What does the learned defense counsel have to say about this?

Sebastian: Mine seems more probable, considering the past happenings.

Reyes: Story…Mr. Sebastian. Considering the past stories. Well, we have two scenarios now and a probability (once again looking at Sebastian) of 50% each. Are you with me?

Sebastian just nodded.

Reyes: Let us now move to Dr. Denis. In accordance with my version of the case, he said that there was more that 50% probability for Mr. Huritt to have been responsible for Ms. Bibiana's death. And in accordance with defense's version, he said less than 50% probability. Now Dr. Denis, what do you think is the exact probability?

Dr. Denis: Considering the fact that there were no fingerprints on the bottle as well as the glass, and also owing to the fact that their explanations given by the defense were reasonable enough, I think the balance is inclined more in favour of the defense.

Reyes: With all due respects, didn't you say there was maximum probability for Mr. Huritt to have been involved with Ms. Bibiana's death?

Dr. Denis: Yes, I did. But then I hadn't thought about the fingerprints on the bottle and on the glass.

Reyes: So you mean to say that the prosecution's analysis of the case was reasonable enough?

Dr. Denis: Yes.

Reyes: So the "equilibrium" of your examination is distorted just by the absence of the fingerprints on the bottle and on the glass. Is that right?

Dr. Denis: Well, I…

Reyes: As they say, "Doctors lack common sense!"

Sebastian: Objection –

Reyes: The fingerprints on Ms. Bibiana's cheek, the inundations on Mr. Huritt's face and the cause and reason for the fight might be explained by tons of other theories! Mr. Huritt forced his way inside Mr. Cortez's house. Ms. Bibiana resisted. She tried to alert the cops. So he slapped her. Thus the fingerprints on the cheeks. She then fought to free herself by strangling him. Thus the inundations on Mr. Huritt's face. This led to a fight. Thus the distorted shoeprints. Huritt might have then held her at gunpoint or threatened to kill the child or cause trouble to Cortez if she didn't kill herself. Thus there are no fingerprints on the bottle and on the glass.

Sebastian: But what is the reason? Why should Huritt be angered with Ms. Bibiana?

Reyes: Who knows? Maybe they were married in some other country. Maybe she threatened to file a suit or maybe Mrs. Fermont isn't telling the whole truth. Maybe she is under duress! Maybe she is trying to stick by her husband.

Sebastian: I object this accusation, *Monsieur.* He can't point his finger at Mrs. Fermont! Her father…

Reyes: There you go! Father! Yes. Her father was truthful and noble and every-other-adjective-you-find-plausible. Fill in all the available words of praise available in the dictionary! But we don't know about Mrs. Lucy Fermont's credentials. As far as this case goes, she is Huritt's wife and she will do all that is possible to prove her husband's innocence…even if he actually isn't.

Sebastian: But –

Reyes: Well if you opt to go by that analogy, you may have to accept that a son of felons is a felon.

Sebastian was dumbstruck.

Damn it. Fuck!

Reyes: If you produce any other evidence or witness, I shall accept your story. Do you…have any?

Sebastian: I need –

'Oh! I'm sorry, just a moment,' said he and took a sheet from a stack of papers. 'You said, "I have no more witnesses. The witnesses to the events mentioned by my client are Sarah, who sadly is not with us today. Achille, who isn't old enough to give testimony, Mr. Cortez, who has accepted everything said by my client, Mr. Bayol, who agrees with Cortez, and Mrs. Fermont, who already gave her testimony. Hence the defense rests". I repeat the significant part again, "I have no more witnesses". Meaning…you have no more witnesses, counsel.

The court chuckled. Sebastian boiled with rage. Reyes enjoyed the fight.

Reyes: So Dr. Denis, do you accept that the scenario I just stated is equally possible?

Dr. Denis: It's a bit out there, but I'm going to give it a yes.

Reyes: So what is the probability of the occurrence of this scenario?

Dr. Denis, to spare himself from further questioning, said 50%.

'Thank you, doctor. Now *Monsieur et mesdames,* I want to read another statement made by the defense,' he said, again retrieving a sheet of paper. '"By the law of implications, it implies that all the five witnesses accept that fact that…", the witnesses being Cortez, Bayol, Dr. Denis, Jean and Felipe. Now by the same law, the five witnesses share a common 50% probability.

Brilliant! thought Sebastian.

Reyes: In totality, Mr. Dominique, Mrs. Absolon, Inspector Felipe, sub-inspector Joseph, Jean, Steve, Dr. Denis, Cortez and Bayol *feel* that the probability of the accused murdering Ms. Bibiana is fifty percent. No more, no less. Mr. Sebastian, everything else, I mean everything relating to Achille, the college romance triangle, the video recording at the police station and the assertion that Ms. Bibiana loved Mr. Achak till her last breath are all a part of your fascinating storyline. There exists no distinctive or conclusive proof to support your preposterous assumptions.

Sebastian was stunned.

Sebastian: Well, let me jog your memory, Mr. Reyes. Your client agreed with me –

Reyes: He agreed with you. Yes. But his accession had nothing to do with the case at hand. He merely approved your "storyline". He agrees with my case study too. Don't you, Mr. Cortez?

Cortez: Yes. I do.

Lorenzo: Does the defense counsel agree that there is equal probability for both parties?

Sebastian, after a brief thought process, reluctantly replied yes.

Lorenzo: I can't ask the jury to deliberate on this. They can't come to a unanimous conclusion.

Reyes: There is no need for that, *Monsieur et mesdames.* The next evidence that I'm going to present will surely shift the balance in favour of my client.

Lorenzo eagerly asked him to proceed.

'*Monsieur et mesdames,* this is my next evidence,' he said, holding the polythene cover high up in the air. 'This is our most reliable evidence.'

He asked his assistant to distribute recreated copies of the burnt note.

stop bothering me. I don't care
I no longer destroy
ur family Sarah. Y ver I tel
Don't you dar If y
sobey me, you ession
again. I hope that you don't wa
to be responsible th of Cortez and
our child. Burn this letter rightaway.

Reyes: What you hold in your hands are recreated copies of this burnt note. This is a note that Mr. Huritt wrote to Ms. Bibiana a few months ago.

Sebastian: *Monsieur,* I need some time to analyse this. Mr. Huritt wrote many letters to Ms. Bibiana. We need some time to place this.

Lorenzo: You have one hour, Mr. Sebastian. The session will continue at 2:00 PM.

CHAPTER 100

July 20, 1979
La Poste

12:15 AM.

'Good morning, Sir. Um, I was asked to hand over this envelope to you,' said Ricardo and passed the envelope containing Mark's letter to the supervisor.

Mark had posted two letters from Rome. One was the one on which the supervisor had signed and the other one was the one explaining the reason for the delay.

Ricardo,

As ordered, I have kept the evidence at the post office. I lost the key that you gave me. So I had to take a new locker, the key to which is with the department supervisor at La Poste. Show him the other letter that I have enclosed and introduce yourself as my brother. He'll provide you with the key. Goodbye.

Ricardo wondered as to why Mark hadn't called him. But then he reasoned that Mark was always against telephonic conversations. Mark always believed that the letters were safer. Evidently Huritt's plan of murdering Mark seemed impossible.

The supervisor studied the letter for some time and then went to fetch the key. He returned a minute later and asked, 'Does your brother work for the postal department?'

'No, uh-he's a mechanic. Why?'

'It's just that he is... maybe my mistake. Good day, Sir,' said the supervisor and ushered a clerk to escort Ricardo to the locker room.

He looked just like the assistant postmaster. Never mind. It's been a week since you saw him. Plus you saw him for just over a minute. They aren't the same. Maybe I'll ring him up and ask.

12:45 PM

'Ricardo, everything is done on our side. How did yours go?' asked Sebastian, over the call.

'Bad,' replied Ricardo and explained everything about the post and the change in the locker.

'He sure is smart,' said Sebastian. 'Why don't you go down to the garage? Maybe you'll find him there.'

'But the letter he sent had a Roman stamp.'

'This is Mark we are talking about. It could as well be a decoy. Just go there and look for him.'

'It's too risky. It's *his* place and I...I'm actually afraid to go there.'

'Come on, Ricardo. You have to do this for Huritt.'

'Well, I'll think about it. It's just that I haven't done this before and...'

Sebastian had cut the call. Ricardo knew what that meant.

1:00 PM

Ricardo reached *Rue de Conflans* and parked his car on the side opposite Mark's garage. He hesitantly crossed the road and walked inside the garage to check on Mark. The garage was deserted, save a bit of scrap metal. He looked around the garage thoroughly and then walked back to his car. He wore the black mask on his forehead and waited, smoking his cigarette. He was to wait there for the whole day. He was to wait for Mark.

...or someone who *looked* like Mark. At fifteen minutes past one, Mark's identical twin brother, John, crossed the road right in front of Ricardo's car and entered the garage, as Ricardo ducked and hid himself. John studied the deserted workplace and then knocked on the trailer's door.

...But no one answered. He just sat in front of the trailer for some time, and then at thirty minutes past one he left.

Ricardo started his car in a flash, pulled his black mask over his face and hit the accelerator. When John was half way down the street, Ricardo thwacked him with his car, making him ram him face against the asphalt, ten feet away from where he was standing. John fell with a loud thud, as the wheels of the car screeched. Ricardo swiftly shifted into reverse gear and ensured that one of the wheels ran over John's neck.

Father Saunders...Mark...Jesus.

2:00 PM

'We have done it, Brother! We are rich! We are fucking rich!'

'Yes, we sure are, Brother.'

Once he had run over John, Ricardo propped the gear forward and sped away from the scene. No one dared to come near his car or stop him. The reflexes of the stunned people were delayed and by the time the stumped crowd shook off the trepidation and approached the victim, Ricardo was far out of their reach. Since this was a street in the more under-developed part of Paris, there wasn't any hint of police officers in the vicinity. The onlookers examined John and then called the police.

Ricardo hustled through various crossroads and alleys and finally emerged out on *Avenue Robert André Vivien.*

At 12:50 PM, Sebastian, with his number plate changed, had driven Ricardo to the Avenue and parked his car in a certain slot. Ricardo casually got out of the car and then scanned a few parking meters along the path in front of him. The analogue parking meter at the third slot in front of Sebastian's slot showed 90 minutes. Ricardo casually broke into the car that was parked on that spot and climbed into it.

As Ricardo pulled out the stranger's car from the slot, Sebastian pulled out his car from his current slot and parked it in the slot from where Ricardo had just drifted. Then Ricardo drove it to Rue de Conflans and murdered John. The entire errand took 40 minutes. When Ricardo returned, Sebastian pulled out from the slot and let Ricardo park the apparently stolen car. Ricardo again casually exited the car and walked towards Sebastian's car parked at the end of the road. The two then went to Sebastian's office, replaced the number plate and each one of them separately hailed a taxi to the Charles de Gaulle.

Huritt and Sebastian took the flight to London, while Ricardo took the flight to Cape Town.

CHAPTER 101

'Huritt, when did you write this to her? I told you to be careful!'

'I don't know. Maybe a few months ago.'

'A few?'

'Let me think,' he said, and gazed at the sky. A few minutes later, when he was successful in referencing the memory with the timeline of events, he enthusiastically said 'Yes! It's been three months. I sent it exactly a week after you told me about the will.'

'Okay. Well we surely cannot discredit it. He'll have solid evidence to prove the contrary. That would be catastrophic! We can't talk about the disclosure...'

Sebastian silently thought of alternatives. When he was halfway through, he said, 'By the way, why did you people talk in English?'

'I don't know. For the same reason we talk in English.'

'Okay, never mind. It's not important. You stay here. I'll have to go down to the library.'

An hour later, the court reconvened and Sebastian was sitting next to Huritt, pondering over the note. He looked exhausted and disgusted. On the other hand, Reyes looked highly overjoyed and confident.

Everyone rose as Lorenzo and the associate judges walked in and took their positions, just before the jurors swept in.

Lorenzo: Is the prosecution ready to proceed with its evidence?

Reyes: Yes, *Monsieur.*

Lorenzo: Proceed!

Reyes: Thank you, *Monsiuer de la president.* I have asked a few experts who have successfully filled in the gaps. Here's what it looks like.

> stop bothering me. I don't care about my wife. I no longer fear her. I will destroy your family Sarah. You just do whatever I tell you. Don't you dare tell him anything. If you dissobey me, you won't see that possession of yours ever again. I hope that you don't want to be responsible for the death of Cortez and your child. Burn this letter rightaway.

Reyes then called in three experts and made them testify to the correctness of the sentences on the burnt note.

The Jurors looked appalled. The balance began to shift.

Reyes: My client came in possession of this piece of note when Ms. Bibiana threw it into the grate. She was repeatedly throwing letters into the fire and he wanted to know what caused her so much distress, not that he was suspicious. One day, he found this piece of letter in the grate, but hid it from her. Now what does the defense counsel have to say about this note?

Sebastian: We won't deny the fact that Mr. Huritt wrote this letter to Ms. Bibiana. He thoroughly remembers that he wrote this letter to her in the month of July, last year.

Reyes: So, you mean to say that Mr. Huritt is indeed guilty?

Sebastian: But...but can a verdict solely stand on this piece of letter? I mean, Mr. President, there are many other –

Reyes: Mr. Sebastian! It sure can. It sure can stand on this piece of letter. As I said earlier, this note shifts the balance. This note, *Monsieur et mesdames,* is the key evidence to all the misgivings...and the deciding factor of this case.

Sebastian: There has to be something else. I mean, if given some time...

Reyes: No, respected defense counsel. You can't just buy time by arguing unreasonably. The court will function for two more hours and you cannot keep stalling the proceedings.

Sebastian: So this is it? The decider?

Reyes: I'm afraid so.

'Thank you,' said Sebastian, raising his voice gleefully. '*Monsieur et mesdames,* Mr. Huritt keeps a copy of every letter that he writes. Every letter he has written till date. A very good practice... indeed. So during the last hour, I went to his residence and got this,' he added, raising a letter. '*Monsieur et mesdames,* this note, which the prosecutor presented, is the middle portion of this letter. The sides have been burnt and only this,' raising the photocopy which the prosecutor handed over, 'remains of it, and I assure you, the "expert" analysis is copiously farcical!'

Reyes flushed. He felt the sky collapsing in on him. He ghastly started at Sebastian.

Sebastian: Respected prosecutor, could you please ask your experts to analyse the handwriting, grammar and all the other requisites?

Reyes asked them to analyze Huritt's copy of the letter, and after a brief break, they said that the handwriting, grammar, style of writing, lengths of characters in a word, a line, a paragraph and every other pivotal factor was consistent with the burnt note.

> stop bothering me. I don't care **about** **you now.** I no longer **love you. Don't** destroy **yo**ur family Sarah. Y**ou just do whate**ver I tell **you.** Don't you dar**e tell him anything.** If y**ou** **dis**sobey me, you **will face disposse**ession **of** **love once** again. I hope that you don't wa**nt** to be responsible **for the ru**th of Cortez and **y**our child. Burn this letter rightaway.

Sebastian: *Monsieur et mesdames,* let me remind you that this letter, rather this particular paragraph "is the decider". Even the prosecutor agrees with me.

Now I would also like to bring up two more essential points at this stage. One, please observe that Mr. Cortez addresses Mrs. Absolon as Sylvie, and Mrs. Absolon addresses Mr. Cortez as Montego. Notice that they address each other by their first names. Now when Mrs. Absolon spoke about Ms. Bibiana, she didn't address her by her first name. She addressed her by her second name, *Monsieur et mesdames.* Point number two, consider the case of Mr. Dominique. When Mr. Dominique spoke about Ms. Bibiana, he said Sarah. Not Ms. Bibiana, but Sarah. Mr. Cortez testified that Ms. Bibiana seldom went out and was, most of the time, confined to the house and preferred to stay inside rather than going out. It is hence interesting to note that the neighbor, Mrs. Absolon, addresses Ms. Bibiana as Ms. Bibiana…her second name, while Mr. Dominique addresses her by her first name, Sarah. This shows that Mr. Dominique, a medical store dealer, I repeat "A medical store dealer" was well-acquainted with Ms. Bibiana. Not the housewife, but the medical store guy. Dr. Denis confirmed that this drug, Midaxolac, is available at all retail stores. Supporting this finding, Mr. Cortez testified that she was mentally disturbed and was insomniac. The purpose of this drug, *Monsieur et mesdames,* is to cure the same. So I would like to say that Ms. Bibiana easily procured the drug from Mr. Dominique.

Augmenting this, when Mr. Huritt rejected to take her back into his life, she was deeply depressed and hence she decided to commit suicide. Now what happened after that, lies in the balance. But nevertheless the prosecutor has graciously given my "story" a humble fifty percent probability.

Monsieur et mesdames, I kindly request you to find my client, Mr. Huritt Achak, a loyal friend, a faithful husband, a caring guardian, a gifted student of our schools, a patriot of the French Republic, a wise and honorable entrepreneur, and above all, an innocent human being, just like all of you, not guilty. I adjure you to kindly avoid further trouble and mental trauma to my client and his respectable family by acquitting this case. Thank you for so patiently witnessing this trail. Justice alone prevails.

Crucified defeat through deceit.

CHAPTER 103

2:30 PM.

'Hello, Eloy?'

'Huritt, congratulations. We have done it. We have the money with us now. 650 million pounds!'

'That is wonderful. Thank you so much.'

'Where are you right now?'

'We are at Charles de Gaulle. We'll be there by dusk.'

8:45 AM.
Harvard University.
Boston. USA.

At the Charles de Gaulle, Sebastian took the pay phone and called Montego Cortez, Huritt's apparent best friend.

'Cortez?'

'Speaking.'

...

3:30 PM.
Ryk Douglas, SA.

A few minutes after Cortez had bid *adios*, Nathan went to the Femhörnig, New York and called the Ryk Douglas, Northern Cape.

...

4:35 PM.
Femhörnig, London.

'Welcome to Femhörnig,' said the Krista, the lady receptionist, picking up the hotline.

'Good morning, Krista.'

...

4:40 PM.
The Frälsare, London.

Morgan walked to his private elevator in the lobby just outside his room. This elevator stopped at two levels only, his office and the basement.

Epilogue

It was early Sunday morning in New York. Rupert woke up at the first glimpse of the sun and got dressed in a tux, which once belonged to his father, Alfred W. Barker.

Dear son, you can fly
High above, in the skies
Be yourself, don't ever change
Be yourself, achieve your dreams

The song that his mother wrote for him resonated in his head, as he walked down the fifteen flights of stairs. Jimmy, like always, was waiting for Rupert at the door, clutching a bouquet of lilies and waiting on a rented car. 'Time to go home, son,' said the loyal street vendor and took his seat behind the wheel.

Meanwhile at PiCorp, the Wolf got a text from Thomas's number, which read: *Want to your see your dear Rupert alive? Go down to the house on Wilbur Street. Pronto.*

The Wolf, who quite often received threats from hundreds of people, was shaken to his very bones on reading this particular message on his screen. Nobody, including Thomas and Cole, knew about the house on Wilbur Street. It was a shrine for Rupert, and it was a place which none but Rupert and Jimmy visited, once every month.

Wolf was quick to pull back into reality and pick up the phone to call Cole, but another text came in: *Thomas and Angelika are having breakfast in the beautiful lady's bedroom and Cole is taking a stroll at the Central, just so you know.*

The Wolf frantically placed a call to Thomas, as he jumped off his desk and picked up his P229 from the locker that was behind the portrait of his dear wife. Two beeps later, Thomas's phone buzzed, only Angelika, who had previously put her boyfriend's phone on silent under the pretense that she didn't want them to be disturbed, cut the call immediately and replied with the text: *I'm not masking the number. I am truly in possession of Thomas's Zfone. It's time you took me seriously.*

Five minutes into the drive, Rupert opened his mother's diary, which to him was the Bible, and read a select few passages which had shaped him as a detective, as a shepherd of the law and as a human being. *"Justice isn't about choosing between right and wrong, it is about finding the balance. Nothing is truly right or no one is absolutely wrong, it all lies in weighing between the two and finding who disrupted the balance."*

Wolf's phone buzzed again and he saw a video that showed Cole being held at sniper point, which followed with a text: *Rupert is just five minutes away from the house, you better hurry.*

'Jimmy, can I ask you something?' asked Rupert, as they turned towards the west and headed stopped at a signal. 'You have been driving me here for so many years now, right? Aren't you at all curious what that place is and what I'm doing in there?'

'I am,' replied Jimmy, coolly.

'Don't you want to know?'

'I do.'

'Then why don't you ask?'

'Well, you'll say it when you have to say it. I don't want to go nosing into your business. I'd hate it too if you'd ask me where I'd go every Friday night.'

'Point taken,' said Rupert and grew quiet.

'You going to tell me?' probed Jim.

'Maybe next time,' replied Rupert and read the next passage, *"Our histories shape us. Yesterday's happenings feed the unresolved vengeance, guilt and issues that turns a person's mind numb and forces his hands to do things of grave consequence. The law might judge him according to a set of instructions in a rulebook, and as a judge, I am obliged to act within the confines of the law. To such people I can offer my deepest sympathy, nothing more, for I am just another subject under the eyes of the law and bound by the law."*

The Wolf called the PETS and told them to go and check on Cole, Thomas and Rupert, and see to it that they were taken to The Eternal Light, for he had something of grave importance to discuss with them. He then dashed to the elevator and hit the button to the ground floor.

"If you feel that something isn't right, you most certainly are right," read Rupert, as Jimmy took a right turn into a narrow street and brought the car to a halt. 'Time to get off now,' said Jim and opened the door, slightly irritated with Rupert reading the same passages over and over. *"Life isn't about choosing the right path, it is about making the path you choose right."*

As the Wolf climbed inside his Hummer and sped towards the house on Wilbur Street, Angelika deleted all the texts she had sent and put the phone back inside Thomas's bag. 'I'm coming in now, honey,' said Angelika through the bathroom door and turned the knob.

Meanwhile Rupert entered the house and closed the door behind him, when instead of the words of his mother, the words often said by his father screamed in his head. *"Those of us who have chosen a path to help serve true justice and bring about peace must never express our vulnerabilities to the outside world, for there are many to prey and many to end our existence."*

"If we live today, I will end you tomorrow," swore the Wolf to the air around him, as he brought his Hummer to a halt and opened the door to the sound of bullets.

The Tree

Jordan
Butler
Theodore Sebastian
Lawyer
Montego Cortez
Partner / Friend
Sir Bennoit
Daughter
Lucy
Wife 1
Father Saunders
Adopted Children
John
Mark
Veronica
Sarah
Vaughn Fletcher
a.k.a Huritt
Laura
Wife 2
Adopted Son
Biological Son
Biological Daughter
Nahiossi Griffiths
a.k.a Albert
Juliette
Aide
Anastasia
The Fuhrer
Aide
The Wolf
Children
Coleman
Rupert
Thomas
Angelika Presley
Jamie Edwards

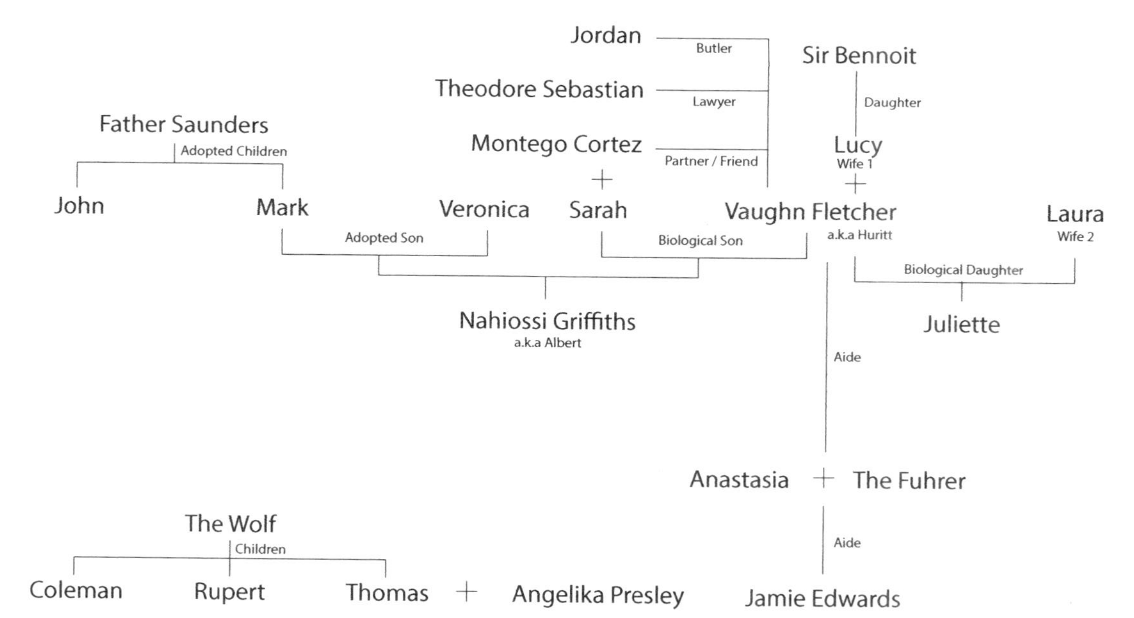

TIMELINE

1974	Huritt, Cortez and Sarah meet at the university
May 24, 1978	Cortez confesses his love to Sarah
June 21, 1978	Lucy and Huritt's wedding
August 14, 1978	Sarah's murder
September 12, 1978 *Chateau de Fermont, Le Septieme* Paris, France	Preparation of Sebastian and Huritt for the case
September 13, 1978 Alexis Hospital. Valencia, Spain. September 14, 1978 Alexis Hospital	Veronica's visits with Denver at the hospital. Tampering of Huritt's medical records

October 17, 1978 Cour d'assises Paris, France October 19, 1978 October 20, 1978 Cour d'assises ... November 22, 1978 November 23, 1978	The case of Huritt v. Cortez
June 19, 1979 5:00 PM – 6:30 PM Sebastian's office, *La rue Joseph-Kessel,* Paris, France	Discussion between Huritt, Sebastian, Oscar, Felix and Ricardo with regards to the Fermont Triathlon
June 20, 1979	Triathlon Discussion on the Soft Law Kidnapping of Lucy
June 21, 1979	Execution of the Will at the Registrar's office
June 24, 1979. CNRS - The Human and Social Sciences Library Paris Descartes	Sebastian's research on soft law
June 25, 1979 4:00 PM The Fermont Hospital	Conversation regarding how to move the money between countries

June 26, 1979 9:30 AM Justice Franklin's residence, Xe arrondissement	Verifying the request for transfer of proceeds from the sale of asserts, which is said to be requested by Lucy
July 20, 1979	Completion of all monetary transactions between the members of Huritt's team Mark and John meet in Barcelona
July 26, 1979 9:00 AM Trellick Tower, Notting Hill London, England The Frälsare London, England Harvard University Boston, the USA	Disposing off the assets of Fermont John moves to Paris and gets killed Morgan, Isak, Cortez are introduced Conversation with Ryk Douglas regarding the diamonds
July 27, 1979 London, England	Diamonds are obtained. Huritt, Sebastian and Eloy are in London, where they meet with an accident
August 1979 – August 1980	Mark and Veronica move to Amsterdam
September 27, 1992 Henry's office, Roulette Construction Site Amsterdam, the Netherlands	Henry and Veronica's meeting Veronica's suicide

September 28, 1992	Henry's death
October 29, 1992 Amsterdam, the Netherlands October 30, 1992 Amsterdam October 31, 1992 Amsterdam ... November 26, 1992 Amsterdam	Mark and Nahiossi go over the life of Veronica, while Nahiossi recovers from the mental shock
February – April 2005	Concerning Wasyl and Kiev
April 1, 2005 Berghof, Germany	Introduction of the *Führer* Anastasia meets with the *Führer* for the first time
April 13, 2005 PiCorp's Office, New York	Discussion on Wasyl, Alex Sedakova, Abu al Khayr, Anastasia and the progress of the investigation
February 10, 2006	Armored truck robbery in New York
February 11, 2006	Proceeding investigation on the robbery
February 23, 2006	Framing-up of Mariano Castillo for the armored truck robbery
March 3, 2006	Discussion on the robbery case and establishing that Castillo was involved with the robbery

April 3, 2006	Meeting at *La vita Eternal*
February 13, 2007	Discussion between Sieger and Vaugh regarding the takeover plan
February 14, 2007	Proposal of Jamie's plan
February 28, 2007	Introduction of PiCorp Delhi and PETS in India (First arrest in the case, 26th December 2005)
March 1, 2007	Initiation of PiCorp's prison break procedures in India
March 2, 2007	Rajiv's breakout during the prison transport
April 9, 2007	Sebastian's murder
September 27, 2007	Cole asks Rupert to take a look at Sebastian's murder case
September 28, 2007	Rupert meets his brothers at Central Park and then later goes to his office with Thomas
October 29, 2007	Murder of Fletcher Nahiossi's escape FBI Investigation at the Fletcher Manor
October 30, 2007	Summoning of F-16 and Delta Force, and negotiations with Nahiossi
November 21, 2007	Discussion at the FBI field office

November 22, 2007	Continuation of discussion
December 20, 2007	Nahiossi's extradition to the United States
December 26, 2007	Nahiossi in court
January 7, 2008	Sentencing Nahiossi to Attica